Praise for *Some of My Best F̶* P9-CEB-108

PENGUIN BOOKS

SOME OF MY BEST FRIENDS ARE BLACK

Tanner Colby is the author of *Belushi: A Biography* and the *New York Times* bestseller *The Chris Farley Show: A Biography in Three Acts*. He is a frequent contributor to *Slate* magazine. He lives in Brooklyn, and yes, that is his actual preschool class photo on the cover.

To access Penguin Readers Guides online, visit our Web site at www.penguin.com.

SOME OF MY BEST FRIENDS ARE BLACK

The Strange Story of
Integration in America

TANNER COLBY

PENGUIN BOOKS

PENGUIN BOOKS
Published by the Penguin Group
Penguin Group (USA) Inc., 375 Hudson Street,
New York, New York 10014, USA

USA | Canada | UK | Ireland | Australia | New Zealand | India | South Africa | China
Penguin Books Ltd, Registered Offices: 80 Strand, London WC2R 0RL, England
For more information about the Penguin Group visit penguin.com

First published in the United States of America by Viking Penguin,
a member of Penguin Group (USA) Inc., 2012
Published in Penguin Books 2013

THE LIBRARY OF CONGRESS HAS CATALOGED THE HARDCOVER EDITION AS FOLLOWS:
Colby, Tanner.
    Some of my best friends are Black : the strange story of integration in America / Tanner Colby.
        p. cm.
    ISBN 978-0-670-02371-4 (hc.)
    ISBN 978-0-14-312363-7 (pbk.)
    1. United States—Race relations.   2. Racism—United States.   3. Whites—Race identity—United States.
4. Whites—United States—Social conditions.   5. African Americans—Race identity.   6. African Americans—Social
conditions—1975-   7. Colby, Tanner—Travel—United States.   8. United States—Description and travel.   I. Title.
    E184.A1C537 2012
    305.896′073—dc23   2011043901

Printed in the United States of America
10 9 8 7 6

Set in Palatino with Verlag
Designed by Carla Bolte

FOR DANIELLE

Contents

Contents

Preface

In May of 2008, I was lucky enough to do something most writers only dream about. I'd written a book, *The Chris Farley Show*, a biography of the *Saturday Night Live* star who died from a drug overdose at the age of thirty-three. It was published to great reviews, hit the *New York Times* bestseller list, and stayed there for four glorious, ego-massaging weeks. Then I was unemployed. I needed another book to write, but my sophomore publishing effort had proved to be as much a curse as a blessing. My previous book had been a biography of John Belushi, the *other* larger-than-life *SNL* star killed by a drug overdose at the age of thirty-three. Everywhere I went people would say, "Huh. Dead, fat comedians? That's what you do?"

I'd pigeonholed myself. I wasn't interested in writing about dead, fat comedians anymore, and there weren't many of them left, besides. But I wasn't an authority on anything else. As far as the market was concerned, it was all I was qualified to do. Even my literary agent and my editor, sympathetic to my plight, advised me that the only kind of book I could sell was something in the ill-fated celebrity genre. I pitched my publisher a number of ideas in a different vein, all of them politely batted down. So like any unemployed person, I started watching a lot of television.

It was the summer of the 2008 presidential election. The twenty-four-hour news cycle was churning at full tilt, and I was glued to the drama. Hillary Clinton was desperately clinging to a primary campaign that was already mathematically over. John McCain was running around the country, rapidly shrinking before our eyes from a war hero "maverick" into some crotchety old dude. And there in between them was pretty much the awesomest guy ever to run for president in my lifetime, Barack Obama. I'll admit it: I was totally in the bag for the Yes We Can crusade. I didn't just drink the Obama Kool-Aid. No, I sucked those flavor crystals right out of the packet. The speeches, the audacity—I bought all of it. My friends and I, we'd gather on Tuesday nights to drink and cheer as the primary results came in. For the first time in my life I gave money, and not a small amount of it, to a political candidate. The night he finally clinched the nomination, my friends and I all let out a collective *"Yes!"* But somewhere in all my excitement over America's first black presidential nominee, I came to a not-small realization: I didn't actually know any black people. I mean, I've met them, have been acquainted with a few in passing, here and there. I know *of* black people, you could say. But none of my friends were black. I'd never had a black teacher, college professor, or workplace mentor. I'd never even been inside a black person's house. I knew it wasn't just me. I started randomly polling friends and associates—most of them enlightened, open-minded, well-traveled, left-leaning white folks like me—asking them how many black friends they had. The answers were pretty pathetic.

"Um, I work with a black guy."

"I had a biracial friend in high school."

"I've got . . . one—wait . . . no, two! I've got two."

"Real black friends? You mean ones that aren't on television?"

By the time election season was done, it was pretty clear to anyone who was paying attention that there were black people supporting Obama and there were white people supporting Obama, but we were doing it the same way black people and white people do just about everything: in different zip codes. Even inside the big arenas, how many of those people cheered their candidate on only to return at the end of the night to separate homes, neighborhoods, and lives? Obama's election was astonishing, unprecedented. But what did it really prove other than that it's easier to vote for a black man than to sit and have a beer with one?

With a black president headed to the White House, every publisher in New York was being flooded with proposals for books about his candidacy and race and politics and the rest of it—all coming from authors, academics, and important people far more impressive than I. So I called my editor and told her I didn't want to write a book about Barack Obama. I wanted to write a book about why I didn't know any black people. I wanted to skip from dead, fat comedians to the history of racial integration in America. There was no reason in the world for her to agree to let me do it. There was certainly no way she'd pay me actual money to do it. But my pitch was pretty simple. Sure, I had no idea what I was doing, but to be a white person writing a book about race, ignorance was the only qualification I would need.

Sold.

....

Once I sat down to work, one of the first things my memory dredged up was a date I'd been on a couple years before. I was seeing this young woman who worked in international humanitarian relief. A perky go-getter type, she had made it her dedicated mission to save all the starving children of Africa. On one of our earlier outings, when she was telling me about all her trips to Sudan, she shared one of the defining moments of her life, the thing that had spurred her in this calling to help save the world: the time she got to meet her hero, Nelson Mandela.

She'd been in college and had gone to South Africa to do research for her senior thesis on the history of Apartheid. Through a random connection she was invited to a smallish, intimate meeting where the former South African president was going to be. She told me she got to shake Mandela's hand, look into his eyes, and tell him how his life and his struggle had inspired her so deeply.

"That's great," I said. "Did you tell him you belong to a restricted country club?"

Because she did. Or her parents did, anyway. She would use the membership when she was home, so same thing. Her brain froze for a few seconds after I'd said it. Then there was some nervous laughter.

The young woman and I are no longer together. But that's not the point of the story. The point is that you don't have to be crushing on Nelson Mandela during brunch at your restricted country club to live your life in a cloud of cognitive dissonance. When you're white in America, life is a restricted country club by default, engineered in such a way that the problems of race rarely intrude on you personally. During the time of Jim Crow, it took a great deal of terrorism, fear, and deliberate, purposeful discrimination to keep the color line in place. What's curious about America today is that you can be white and enjoy much of the same isolation and exclusivity without having to do anything. As long as you're not the guy dumb enough to get caught emailing racist jokes around the office, all you have to do is read about black people in the newspaper. And, really, you don't even have to do that. Where you need a deliberate, purposeful sense of action is to go the other way, to leave the country club and see what's going on out in the world. It also helps when a publisher agrees to pay you to do it.

This book is not a memoir. It's dotted with a few anecdotes of mine here and there, but it's not about me. Nothing has ever happened to me that anyone else would ever care to read about, ever. The only interesting thing about my life is that it's not interesting at all. It's the standard, white, middle-class American Dream—dating from the time when such a thing was taken for granted by standard American white people. My great-grandparents were Louisiana sharecroppers on my mother's side and dirt-poor farmers from Texas on my dad's. Neither of my grandfathers finished high school but both got steady working-class jobs—factory worker and flooring contractor—in the post–World War II economic boom. My mother and father were first in their families to go to college—state schools—becoming a teacher and an architect, respectively. From there, my brother and I were bootstrapped into good neighborhoods, the best schools, private universities, and rewarding careers. If neither of us is rich, it's because we took the opportunities that weren't about the money, which is its own form of luxury. There have been some ups and downs, but it's mostly the story of things working out the way we tell everyone that America is supposed to work out.

My life becomes interesting only when you use it to compare and contrast. My peers and I came of age alongside a singular generation of black Americans: the Children of the Dream. Born in the late sixties and early seventies, they were the inheritors of a world without Jim Crow, vested with the hopes of all that their parents had fought and perhaps died for. Starting with the *Brown v. Board* decision that overturned the principle of separate but equal schooling, the civil rights movement overcame white hostility and resistance to pass landmark legislative victories that outlawed segregation in the voting booth, the workplace, and public accommodations. Starting in 1968 and 1969, busing and other school desegregation plans were implemented to improve access to education. Fair housing laws were enacted to eliminate segregated neighborhoods. Sweeping federal mandates for affirmative action opened the doors for college admissions and job placement. The Children of the Dream were now supposed to get everything I got. Only it didn't exactly happen that way.

From humble beginnings, my parents pole-vaulted into the middle class and started a family in the mid-1970s, right about the same time all the mechanisms of integration were allegedly working full-steam to give black families the same. Though born in Houston, Texas, I can't really claim it as home. We moved around a good bit. From toddlerhood, I grew up mostly in the small town of Lafayette, Louisiana. I went to high school in Birmingham, Alabama, attended college in New Orleans, and have since spent my entire adult life in New York City. All of these places have substantial black populations. Yet my standard middle-class pipeline was then and is now virtually all white. As I sat around marinating in the 2008 election coverage, I figured that fact had to be illustrative of *something*. What, I didn't really know. But to retrace the color line through all the places I've lived, I figured, would have to yield a pretty thorough catalog of the mistakes that were made in trying to take it down. And somewhere in that catalog of mistakes might be the answer to fixing them. That was my hunch, at any rate.

....

There is only one way to fit the subject of race into a single book. You cleave off the part you're going to talk about and leave the rest for someone else. Otherwise you'll never finish. So it's worth starting off with a brief word about what this book is not.

Integration requires agency, some degree of social mobility. Any discussion of it tends toward those, black or white, with enough socioeconomic leverage to have options. So while this book explores life on both sides of the color line, most of it takes place on one side of the class divide. The ills that hobble the mobility of the underclass, and the gulf that separates the haves from the have-nots, is a related but separate set of issues.

The problem addressed here is the fact that the majority of black Americans are not poor, not any longer. In my generation more blacks have graduated from college than at any other time in history, yet the social, cultural, and economic gaps persist. The unemployment rate for black college grads is double that of white college grads. Rich/poor, North/South, red state/blue state, the color line seems to follow us everywhere.

This is also not a book about politics or policy. The macropolitical history of race is well and thoroughly documented, even if we don't actually bother to teach any of it in our schools. The landmark court decisions and government programs that have shaped the way we deal with race have been woven in where necessary for background, but most of the book is just stories about people—the accumulated experiences and reflections of some fascinating individuals who were generous enough to share them with me. Taken together, they make for a personal, ground-level view of history as it happened. They're largely anecdotal, rarely objective, and hardly definitive. Which is the only way it can be, really. But as I found in the dead, fat comedian business, even where objective fact is elusive, if you cobble together enough honesty you usually end up somewhere close to truth.

While the stories of the people I met are all unique, I endeavored to shape them into something universally accessible. To that end, I didn't write about integration in the military or in professional sports or in restricted country clubs—nothing that specific. I wanted to look at the everyday places where people should meet and interact, but don't. Given the limits of word count and time, that boiled down to four major things: schools, neighborhoods, the workplace, and church. Everybody's sat in the school cafeteria. We all live somewhere. Before the second Bush administration, most of us had jobs. And we all belong to something that serves as our church, whether that thing meets on Sunday morning or not.

On the subject of school integration, I started by going back and looking at the history of busing at my high school in Birmingham, Alabama. Digging into the issue of fair housing and white and black neighborhoods, I wound up in a place I've never lived but where the segregated American cityscape came into being: Kansas City, Missouri. For the history of workplace discrimination and affirmative action, I went back to my onetime employer, New York's advertising industry, where I worked as a copywriter starting in the late 1990s. And lastly, to try to understand what is still the most segregated hour in the country, I went all the way back home to southern Louisiana, where small towns dot the countryside and the Roman Catholic Church still today maintains separate black and white parishes—right across the street from each other.

When I say I had no idea what I was doing when I started this endeavor, I'm not exaggerating. But my ignorance, it turns out, really was the single greatest asset I could have packed to take with me: I walked out my front door with nothing but questions and couldn't come home until somebody gave me the answers. Astute readers may have already noted what I only fully came to realize along the way. The strange career of Jim Crow took root and grew out of the same place that I did. It was in Louisiana that a minor statute to mandate separate white and colored railcars overcame a challenge from local activists and went on to be upheld by the Supreme Court in the case of *Plessy v. Ferguson* in 1896, thus establishing the legal precedent for constitutionally sanctioned segregation across the country. And it was just down the road from my high school in Birmingham where Martin Luther King, Jr., and the civil rights movement did the impossible in the spring of 1963, breaking through the color line of the most segregated city in America to expose the violent inhumanity of segregation and ultimately bring about its demise. Quite by accident, retracing the persistence of the color line in my own life took me down that same road in reverse. I went from the streets where Jim Crow was killed back to the swamp where he was born. I started at the end and wound up at the beginning, and it was there that I found what I went looking for.

SOME OF MY BEST FRIENDS ARE BLACK

[PART 1]

LETTER FROM A BIRMINGHAM SUBURB

[1]

Bus Kid

"Turn on the heat, Mom."

"It's on, baby. It's on."

It's way too early. The sun is barely up, it's cold out, and Alicia Thomas is warming up the engine of her big yellow school bus. She cranks the heat for her two young boys, Robert and Walter, who sit a few rows back. Still bundled up in winter coats to stave off the February chill, they're pulling out their schoolbooks to get in some last-minute studying before homeroom.

Up in the front row, I reach over and hand Ms. Alicia—as all the kids call her—the warm cup of coffee I'd promised when she invited me along for the ride. She says thank you with a sweet, sunny Alabama smile, which seems impossibly bright given the hour. We idle a few minutes while she double-checks some gauges. Then she puts the bus in gear, and we're off.

Alicia Thomas drives the bus. Not the regular bus, and not the short bus. She drives the other bus, the bus that brings the black kids. Every weekday morning for nearly four decades, her bus, or a bus quite like it, has followed the same well-worn route: out from the suburbs of Birmingham, Alabama, along Highway 31, up Columbiana Road, down the far side of Shades Mountain, and out into the Oxmoor Valley below. There, in Oxmoor, the bus picks up its quota of federally mandated integration and hauls it back to the leafy, lily white enclave where I went to high school: Vestavia Hills. It's a route Ms. Alicia could probably navigate blindfolded. In the early 1970s, long before she drove the bus, she rode it as a student.

"It used to get so cold," she says with a shiver, remembering her mornings at the stop. "The boys had to light campfires to keep us warm until the bus came."

"You had *campfires*?" I say. "At your bus stop?"

"Oh, yeah," she says. "We were so country."

Less than ten miles from the million-dollar cul-de-sacs of Vestavia Hills, the Oxmoor where Alicia Thomas grew up was little more than a rambling crisscross of back roads on the outskirts of nowhere—not a town at all, really. There were a few ranch-style brick houses for those who could afford them, but clapboard and cinder block shacks were more the norm, some with dirt floors, others with no running water. There wasn't much else to see in the sprawling seven thousand acres of the Oxmoor Valley. It was a scrapyard, a garbage dump for the industrial waste of the U.S. Steel Corporation, which at one time held a monopoly on Birmingham's steel trade.

Back then the Oxmoor kids had to be up at five a.m., Alicia tells me, to walk through fields of chickens and cows, some of them upward of a mile, just to reach the bus stop. In her day, the bus they rode was a rickety, scrap-metal clunker, lurching around the hairpin turns of the city's mountainous terrain. Their bus driver? Some old white guy clutching the wheel, half scared to death by the rowdy children crammed in behind him. "I can just remember riding down those big hills," Alicia recalls. "The brakes going out and the bus *packed* with kids. It was three to a seat with the rest on the floor or standing in the aisle, with no air-conditioning. And here's this one old white guy driving all these black kids? He couldn't handle all those kids."

"What was the guy's name?" I ask.

The question brings her up short. "You know," she says, "in all those years of driving us, I don't think he ever even spoke to us once to tell us his name. We just called him Shaky, 'cause he was always so nervous. *'Shaky, slow down! You gon' kill us!'*"

....

Vestavia Hills sits just south of Birmingham, the largest city in Alabama and, at one time, the largest industrial center in the South. Together with the neighboring towns of Mountain Brook, Homewood, and Hoover, Vestavia forms the nucleus of "Over the Mountain"—the catchall term for Birmingham's suburban sprawl, so named because you go "over" Red Mountain to get there from downtown.

Having lived there, I suppose I can say that whites in Vestavia aren't any more or less racist than the ones in the other suburbs. But when the school system was formed there in 1970, born in the exodus of white flight, the city *did* go to great lengths to put its feelings on display. Vestavia's chosen mascot was the Confederate rebel, "Colonel Reb." An ornery, cartoony-looking fellow, the Colonel resembles a cross between Yosemite Sam and an angry Mark Twain, his hat cocked back and a clenched fist sticking out. The official school banner? The Confederate battle flag. Flown from pickup trucks and waving high in the bleachers, the Stars and Bars was always on proud display. If you stumbled onto a Vestavia football game by accident, you might think you were at a Klan rally with a concession stand.

That's the image Vestavia wanted, and it stuck. To this day, racial incidents land the school on the five o'clock news. There are many in Birmingham's black community who still refuse to set foot in "that racist suburb," because, to them, this isn't just a suburb. As a symbol, Vestavia Hills was nothing more than white flight's parting shot at the civil rights movement, the final insult.

Alicia Thomas first arrived here as a five-year-old kindergartner in 1971. Friends of hers had come the year before, so what she encountered wasn't a complete surprise. There were problems. Name calling, graffiti on bathroom stalls. Huddled around the bus-stop campfire, the stench of smoke would sink into your clothes; once you got to school, you'd sometimes hear "God, what's that smell?" or "Those niggers stink" as you walked down the hall.

For the first several months, Alicia says, she and the black students were all put with a black teacher and had their classes in a corner of the cafeteria, still segregated from the white kids. Even after she was put in regular classes, white teachers didn't always treat her fairly. They assumed she was slow, less capable. "My third-grade teacher was a mean lady," Alicia recalls. "I had to say to her, 'I *can* read. I *can* write.' One day she told me I had to get out of her class and go down to the learning lab. I ignored her and just sat there and read my book. I wanted her to know that I could read."

It was the same when she went out for the volleyball team in middle school. The coaches told her she couldn't join because the bus kids had to leave at three thirty and couldn't be counted on to stay for practice. "So we didn't even try out," she says. "I didn't know they couldn't tell us not to try out for something. And my parents had a car. They could have driven us back after school. But the coaches told us no."

And so went Alicia Thomas's time in Vestavia Hills: kinda separate, not exactly equal. Yet she looks back on it without regret, even when remembering the worst. "I don't feel like I got as much out of the system as the other kids," she explains. "I don't. We didn't have anybody fighting for us. My feelings got hurt. But the little stuff I went through, it's nothing. I'm okay with it. I didn't have anything growing up, and Vestavia gave me something I probably wouldn't have had. I know how much it did for me, and I hope it can do the same for my boys."

Her sons, the two young men diligently doing their schoolwork behind us, are the reason Alicia Thomas is driving the bus today. After graduating from Vestavia, she went to the University of Alabama at Birmingham on scholarship, got married, and settled in the small town of Midfield, just west of downtown. She landed an office job in the personnel department of the Saks Fifth Avenue store out at the Galleria. Then, ten years ago, Saks downsized and Alicia was let go.

While she pondered what to do next, an unlikely job offer floated in from her past: Vestavia Hills needed a new bus driver. Her children were about to start school, and like all parents she wanted them to get into a good one. She'd long ago moved from the busing zone in Oxmoor, and she couldn't afford to move into Vestavia itself. But every employee of the Vestavia school system, from the principal to the lunch lady, can enroll his or her children for free. "I knew Vestavia was the best," Alicia says, "so I decided to drive the bus."

So here we are.

It's the end of the first leg of our bus ride, and we've reached Oxmoor. "That's where we'd wait by the campfire," Alicia says, pointing to the corner of Goss Street as we go by. She calls out a few other landmarks from her childhood here and there, but Oxmoor is no longer the place it once was. In just the past few years, this onetime industrial scrapyard has been consumed by suburban sprawl. The old shacks and shanties are all still there, still inhabited, but they're surrounded by a sea of McMansions, golf courses, and condominiums. On Ostlin Street, one of the frontiers between old and new, these three-story, new-money monstrosities literally tower over tumbledown clapboard shacks right across the way.

When we reach Ostlin, Alicia pulls over to let her boys out; they have to switch to the middle school bus, which will be along in a minute. Then we pick up the high school kids. They climb in one by one, either plugged into their iPods or yammering about this week's big basketball play-off game. We head back to Vestavia and up to the high school—newly renovated and nearly doubled in size since I was here. The kids all pile out to a steady refrain of "Thank you, Ms. Alicia!" and "Study hard now, baby!" And then it's back to the bus yard.

....

Alicia Thomas's tale bookends the strange and strangely American phenomenon known as "busing." After being one of the first to ride the bus, she may be one of the last to drive it. Because of those big, fancy Oxmoor McMansions, Vestavia's forty-year saga of court-ordered integration is coming to an end. On December 13, 2007, the District Court of Northern Alabama vacated the desegregation order against the city of Vestavia Hills, granting the school system "unitary status," the legal jargon used to describe the very simple state of being made whole—no longer dual, no longer separate.

As a slaveholding nation dedicated to the principle that all men are created equal, America built its house on two fundamentally irreconcilable ideas. We've been struggling to reach unitary status ever since. The particular chapter of this struggle that pertains to Vestavia Hills began in 1954 with the Supreme Court's landmark decision of *Brown v. Board of Education*, which nullified the use of segregated facilities for blacks and whites in public education. Separate but equal was inherently *un*equal, and therefore unjust, said the court in its unanimous reversal of *Plessy v. Ferguson*. *Brown*'s sweeping indictment of segregated schools, however, did nothing to eliminate them. For fifteen years, white school districts kept blacks out by evading and stonewalling, forcing the government to devise a solution. And the solution we came up with was this: the school bus. In the same decade that America put a human being on the moon, our nation's finest minds could offer no better fix for four hundred years of slavery and segregation. Just some nervous white guy named Shaky in a busted jalopy lurching down and around the mountain with everyone screaming for him to slow the hell down.

There was a lot of extra weight riding on that bus, too—possibly more than it could bear. With *Brown v. Board*, America had set its eyes on the ultimate prize: social integration, racial equality—unitary status. Many had even dared to dream that this big yellow school bus would take their children to a place where they would be judged not by the color of their skin but by the content of their character. Shaky wasn't just taking these kids to school. He was taking them to the Promised Land. Some of them made it, and some of them didn't.

2

A Place Apart

In 2000, the History Book Committee of the Vestavia Hills Historical Society published the city's authorized biography, *Vestavia Hills, Alabama: A Place Apart*, by Marvin Yeomans Whiting. A handsome, gold-embossed collector's piece, it was issued to commemorate Vestavia's fiftieth anniversary. "Commemorate" is the operative word, as you won't find a whole lot of history going on inside its covers. Not unless you count the history of the men's garden club or the mayor's annual prayer breakfast. The book is a whitewash. During the cataclysmic civil rights campaign of 1963, we learn, Vestavia was opening a brand-new swimming pool and Little League field. School busing is given slightly greater coverage, but only in the context of how difficult it was to endure: the city had "survived" court-ordered integration.

All of this is in keeping with Vestavia's carefully cultivated image. It's a town with "good schools," people say. "A great place to raise a family." There's a Chuck E. Cheese anchoring the strip mall and a Protestant church on every corner and the Little League facilities, it must be said, are really quite nice. When I was growing up here in the eighties, it was like living inside a real estate brochure. The actual real estate brochures, the ones that the Realtors here use, present a heartwarming story about how Vestavia's name comes from a local building modeled after the temple of Vesta, the Roman goddess of hearth and home. Here in Vestavia, they say, "you'll find that spirit of hearth and home" in your own three-bedroom, split-level slice of the American Dream. Like a lot of what you read in brochures, it's complete bullshit.

The real story of Vestavia Hills begins with George Ward, a financier who served as mayor of Birmingham from 1905 to 1909 and as president of the city commission from 1913 to 1917. Birmingham was a steel town. Unique in the agrarian South, it sits up in the Appalachian foothills on some of the richest deposits of iron ore found anywhere in North America. As the city's industry grew after the Civil War, black sharecroppers from across the cotton belt left the land in hopes of finding better jobs in the mines and steel mills. But even if the wages were a touch better than sharecropping, the working conditions were not. Blacks were relegated to the lowliest and most dangerous jobs. As one Northern observer noted, if horses and mules had been subjected to the same treatment as blacks, the Humane Society would have come in and shut everything down. At the dawn of the twentieth century, Birmingham was little more than a polluted mining colony. Ward turned it into a thriving city of industry. He modernized the water system, paved the roads, added hundreds of acres of parkland; he even created a red-light district with legalized prostitution to control the spread of venereal disease.

In 1910, Birmingham annexed several of its surrounding municipalities, tripling its population and bringing the outlying areas—semirural, mostly white, and very Protestant—into a growing metropolis with a large population of blacks and Catholic immigrants. Among Southern Protestant fundamentalists at the time, prejudice against Catholics was often as virulent as that against blacks; the Church of Rome and its foreign-born, papist followers were a scourge, a threat to real American values. When Ward ran for reelection in 1917, his chances hung on the fact that his chief of police was Catholic and, despite growing protests, Ward refused to fire him. A local Baptist minister organized the Protestant opposition under the banner of the True American Society. They ran a smear campaign, calling Ward a leading conspirator of the Catholic menace—never mind that he was an Episcopalian. On the eve of the election, Ward stood by his principles, declaring that he would rather lose his office than terminate a man "merely upon religious grounds."

He lost.

The "True Americans" took hold of Birmingham, consolidating power on the side of those who would seek to crush the civil rights movement four decades later. The extractive policies of U.S. Steel and the stifling politics of Jim Crow began to slow the material progress of the city. As the 1920s began, the moneyed elites began their exodus, quietly slipping out and resettling in what would become the blue-blooded enclave of Mountain Brook. In 1925, George Ward left Birmingham and its politics behind for good, choosing for himself a very different retreat.

The area now occupied by Vestavia Hills has always been "a place apart." It was once so isolated that Native Americans lived there unmolested long after being routed from the rest of the region. Only four miles from downtown Birmingham, it sits high atop Shades Mountain, the north face of which had always been too rocky and steep for large-scale settlement to reach the top. Before the Highway 31 expressway cut through in the early 1950s, the only way up was a winding, switchback road that climbed slowly around the side.

George Ward was what we in the South politely term "an eccentric." During a trip to Rome as a young man, he'd fallen in love with the temple of Vesta. He gave a replica of it to his architect, pointed at the crest of Shades Mountain, and said to build him one. And lo, "Vestavia," a four-story temple/mansion ringed by imposing Doric columns, gilded with Italianate scrollwork, and bedecked with marble statuary. Imagine Graceland crossed with the Parthenon. Ward carved twenty acres out of the mountaintop and cultivated them into gardens of international renown. On Sundays, he opened them to the public free of charge—even, once a year, to people of color.

So, yes, there was a building called Vestavia and it was a home and it probably had a hearth, but that's where any similarity with the real estate brochures ends. Ward threw lavish, fabulous theme parties, bacchanals of wild abandon; one year an airplane showered guests with rose petals from the sky. The former mayor "loved a parade," it is said, and he "was often seen in costume." His nickname while in office was "the fighting bachelor." His only marriage, at the age of fifty-two, lasted little more than eighteen months. For reasons that "remain uncertain," he insisted that the marriage never be made public. His wife never "lived in the Vestavia temple." They never "had any children." When he died he "left everything to his nieces." And the "faithful retainers" on his staff were strapping young black men. Ward nicknamed them Lucullus, Pompey, and Scipio. On special occasions, he liked to dress them up in Roman centurion uniforms.

We're all on the same page here, right?

Vestavia Hills didn't start as a refuge of wholesome, middle-class family values. It was a refuge *from* wholesome, middle-class family values—a place apart from the religious and racial intolerance dividing the city below. That would not last. The Great Depression left Ward penniless. He suffered a debilitating stroke, lingered for years, and died of throat cancer in 1940, his gardens choked with weeds and his temple nearly in ruins.

In 1947, a real estate developer named Charles Byrd bought the abandoned estate and much of the surrounding land. Starter homes began sprouting up—homes proudly advertised as "fully restricted." From now on, the only people of color allowed in Vestavia's gardens would be the ones who were planting them. Officially incorporated on November 8, 1950, the city of Vestavia Hills took the landmark mansion as its namesake, but by that time the rugged wilderness where Native Americans and sexually ambiguous politicians once roamed free had ceased to exist.

And the Vestavia temple itself? In 1958, George Ward's stately pleasure dome was turned into a Baptist church.

....

Other than George Ward, the man probably most responsible for the future success of Vestavia was Supreme Court Chief Justice Earl Warren, who in 1954 handed down the decision of *Brown v. Board*, which sent white people running for the hills.

Less than two months after *Brown* was announced, Indianola, Mississippi, formed what would be the first of many White Citizens' Councils, groups of civic and business leaders who used their power and influence to thwart any attempts to implement the court's decision. In Louisiana, when the archbishop of New Orleans announced that the Catholic

Church would follow the spirit of the court order and integrate its parochial schools, the legislature convened in Baton Rouge to debate whether or not police power could be used to bring the church under state control. In Virginia, Senator Harry Byrd called for a campaign of "massive resistance" against *Brown*. The state enacted a sweeping program of obstructionist legislation, defunding schools that attempted to integrate and providing vouchers and tax credits for white families to enroll in private, all-white "segregation academies." Similar legal challenges across the South would clog up the courts for years.

And that's just the stonewalling that went on during the daytime. Under the cover of darkness, the Ku Klux Klan and other groups waged campaigns of murder and intimidation to keep blacks on their side of the color line. The combined effort of legal obstructionism and extralegal terrorism made for an effective deterrent. By the early 1960s, less than 12 percent of schools in the South had integrated; in the Deep South, the figure was as low as 2 percent. In Virginia, Prince Edward County shuttered its entire public school system for five years rather than integrate. At the rate things were going, one activist estimated, the South was on track to be in compliance with *Brown* in about seven thousand years.

At the time, the white residents of Birmingham enjoyed one of the finest school systems anywhere in the South. Its flagship high schools— Woodlawn, Ramsay, Phillips, West End—were grand and imposing, built by a city with great pride in its public works. No black student had ever set foot in any of them. The black children of Birmingham attended schools that were considerably less well endowed, but not all of them fit the newsreel stereotype of the dilapidated, one-room Jim Crow schoolhouse. Parker High, originally founded in 1900 as The Negro School, had an enrollment of more than 3,700, making it the largest black high school in the world. Parker was a cornerstone of the black community. It supported the professional class with hundreds of teaching positions. It educated the future lawyers and activists who would lead the local civil rights efforts, and its vocational programs were an important pipeline to get work in the steel industry. And as the threat of desegregation loomed, Birmingham, like other Southern cities, began making sizable investments in its black schools; if separate were made to appear equal, maybe this whole *Brown* thing would go away. The all-new, all-black Hayes High would open in 1960 on a seventeen-acre campus complete with gymnasium, auditorium, library, labs for home economics and industrial arts, and so on.

Birmingham was determined to keep Jim Crow alive no matter the cost. Martin Luther King, Jr., called it the most segregated city in America. Others referred to it as "America's Johannesburg," after the capital of Apartheid-riven South Africa. Its most colorful nickname was simply "Bombingham," a tag that stuck once dynamiting black neighborhoods had eclipsed the steel industry as the city's principal claim to notoriety. In April of 1963, King and the Southern Christian Leadership Conference (SCLC) descended on Birmingham to lead marches and protests against the city's draconian Jim Crow laws. It would be the most high-profile effort yet from the young preacher who had risen out of 1955's Montgomery Bus Boycott to become the leading figure of the civil rights movement. The centerpiece of the Birmingham campaign was a march on the city's downtown department stores. Though launched with high hopes, it quickly stalled. King found himself in jail, and movement organizers were running short on money. Most local black citizens, employed by the steel industry in one way or another, couldn't march for fear of losing their livelihoods.

The mantle of protest fell to their children. On May 2, the black youth of Birmingham took to the streets in what would become known as the Children's Crusade. Thousands of boys and girls poured out of downtown's Sixteenth Street Baptist Church and into the streets, singing triumphantly. Then, on television, the world watched in horror as the Birmingham police turned fire hoses and dogs on the defenseless children and hauled them away to jail. The Children's Crusade exposed the violent, dehumanizing reality of segregation. Jim Crow's days were now numbered. But that victory came with a heavy cost. The blowback was violent and swift. The Ku Klux Klan escalated its campaign of terror, detonating bombs all over black neighborhoods. One went off at Martin Luther King's vacant motel room. Another, most infamously, was planted at the Sixteenth Street Church some months later, killing four little girls.

That fall, federal intervention finally made desegregation inevitable for the Birmingham city schools. In a society built entirely around the social value of whiteness, that reality was simply unimaginable. And so, having built a thriving city of industry with comfortable neighborhoods and good schools, instead of sharing it, the white people of Birmingham chose to abandon it wholesale. On September 5, the day two black children were first admitted to West End High, white students left their classrooms and gathered on the football field. A rally to call for more massive resistance turned into a two-hour funeral instead. At the climax, the crowd sat silent while one boy played a somber, down-tempo "Dixie" on his trumpet. Like a requiem, it was said. And with that, they hit the road. Somewhere over the mountain, they would build a new world, one even brighter and whiter than before, in Vestavia Hills.

....

In the long run, the backlash to the civil rights movment would do its greatest damage not in assault, but in retreat. Few places offer a clearer picture of this than the place that used to be Vestavia before Vestavia was Vestavia. Prior to white flight, Woodlawn was the Vestavia Hills of its day. It was the nice, quiet family community—inside the city but just outside of downtown, right on the streetcar line that would take you wherever you needed to go.

Woodlawn High was one of the jewels of the Birmingham school system. Today, the posts on its alumni website are chock-full of "Where Are They Now?" updates and Kodachrome memories. Here's Martha and Bobby from the class of '55! There's Peggy and Jenny Lou from the '64 Sigma Tau Beach Beauties! Check out the whole '65 reunion doing the electric slide at the Marriott! Everyone's happy and spiffy and all-American. And everyone's white. Then you come to the early seventies and . . . there's nothing. No more reunions, no more Beach Beauties. It's like the whole place just vanished.

In the meantime, Vestavia blossomed. Its property values soared. Its Baptist churches were fruitful and multiplied. After 1963, families were flooding out of Woodlawn and heading Over the Mountain in a hurry. They were seeking refuge from—as Marvin Yeomans Whiting neatly threads it—"the troubles that were breaking upon the metropolitan area." When the 1970 census was tallied, Birmingham's population had fallen nearly 12 percent in just a decade. The population of Vestavia Hills, meanwhile, had ballooned to 8,311, up more than thirteenfold from its 1950 incorporation. That same year, the total number of black residents in Vestavia was three. Not three percent, three.

Next door, in old-money Mountain Brook, things were booming as well, but the city leaders there had been very prescient in organizing their secession. They'd founded their own schools in 1959, and the only "policy" instituted to keep blacks out was old-fashioned, unspoken social custom: blacks *did not go* to Mountain Brook. Having broken no laws, its schools were subject to no lawsuits. Vestavia, on the other hand, was born on the run. Every year, more and more children were deserting the Birmingham school system and crowding into the surrounding Jefferson County system. Which was *packed*. White kids stacked to the rafters. Berry, the county school serving the families of Vestavia, hadn't been built for this kind of traffic. By the late sixties, its parking lot was jammed with trailers serving as makeshift classrooms. Student-teacher ratios ran in excess of forty to one, and no matter how many teachers were hired in the spring there were never enough come fall. For *this* whites had abandoned their nice, comfortable campus in Woodlawn. The county system, for all its drawbacks, had managed to remain segregated. It wouldn't for very much longer.

U. W. Clemon grew up all too familiar with Jefferson County's segregated schools; his was the archetypal wood-framed building with no indoor plumbing. The son of former sharecroppers who'd come to Birmingham seeking work in the steel trade, Clemon was born in 1943 in nearby Fairfield, a company town built by U.S. Steel to house its laborers. Thirty-seven years after that, in 1980, he would be nominated by President Jimmy Carter to serve as the first black federal judge in Alabama history. In between, in 1969, he was the lawyer who brought the school bus to Vestavia Hills.

At the height of the civil rights movement, Clemon was a student at Birmingham's historically black Miles College, where he took part in the 1963 demonstrations, joining the group that desegregated the downtown public library. He graduated from Miles as valedictorian of the class of

1965, and then, under the peculiar logic of Jim Crow, the state helped pay for him to go to Columbia Law School in New York; that way, none of the all-white in-state programs would have to accept him. Three years later, armed with an Ivy League diploma and a fellowship from the NAACP Legal Defense Fund, Clemon returned to Birmingham and started kicking its ass in court.

One of Clemon's first tasks was to file suit against Jefferson County for maintaining its segregated school system in flagrant violation of *Brown*. That case, *Stout v. Jefferson County*, was eventually consolidated with several similar motions from school districts across several other Southern states under the umbrella of *Singleton v. Jackson*. In December of 1969, the fifteen judges of the U.S. Fifth Circuit Court of Appeals sat en banc at the New Orleans Federal Courthouse in the heart of the French Quarter to hear the arguments in *Singleton*. Clemon was barely a year out of law school and only twenty-six years old. Opposing him, the various school districts had assembled a dream team of attorneys drawn from the preeminent white-shoe law firms of the South. "I don't recall being particularly nervous," Clemon tells me. "I had what, in hindsight, appears to be overconfidence. We had the wind at our backs."

The legal momentum that U. W. Clemon rode to the New Orleans Federal Courthouse had been painfully slow in gathering, and it would evaporate almost immediately. But for a very brief window the champions of racial integration had all the leverage they could wish for. During the time of massive resistance, white school districts had been hiding behind bad-faith solutions known as "freedom of choice" plans. Under these, black families were allowed to apply on an individual basis for enrollment in majority-white schools, and those schools were, in theory, obliged to accept them. In practice, however, black families who exercised that freedom usually woke up with a burning cross on their lawn. Few bothered. In 1965, President Lyndon Johnson finally brought the weight of the federal government to bear through Title VI of the Civil Rights Act, which denied federal funds to any government agency engaged in discrimination. The White House enacted blanket reforms requiring school districts to file desegregation plans with the Department of Health, Education, and Welfare (HEW) or else face severe budget cuts. Under the stringent HEW guidelines, schools were now required to provide "statistical proof" of "significant progress."

One year later, America saw the release of the 1966 Coleman Report, the result of an exhaustive government survey to determine a) just what disparities remained between black and white educational opportunities, and b) what to do about it. The Coleman Report showed that minority students who attended majority-white schools fared much better academically—not simply because of access to better textbooks and resources, but also because of the exposure to middle-class peer groups, which raised educational expectations. The report gave a major boost to the proponents of integration.

In May of 1968, the Supreme Court finally called foul on "freedom of choice" remedies in the case of *Green v. New Kent County*. Echoing HEW, the justices held that for a desegregation plan to be considered constitutional, it had to produce actual black students, in real desks. Writing the court's unanimous opinion, Justice William Brennan called on the country to eliminate the last vestiges of state-sponsored segregation "root and branch." Despite this sweeping directive, most districts still didn't budge. November of 1968 had brought the election of America's thirty-seventh president, Richard Milhous Nixon, who took the White House by playing to whites' fears of integration, campaigning on a promise to roll back Washington's enforcement of HEW's desegregation policies. Once in office, he did. After another year of stonewalling by Southern schools, the Supreme Court was compelled to take up the matter once more in the case of *Alexander v. Holmes*. On October 30, 1969, the court issued another unanimous decision, saying the exact same thing it had just said eighteen months before, only this time telling white people to get on with it already.

When U. W. Clemon arrived at the Fifth Circuit Court of Appeals in New Orleans, his only task was to ask that the court apply the precedent of *Alexander* to the *Singleton* case. "Basically," Clemon says, "all we had to do was stand up and give them the facts about how many blacks were enrolled in formerly all-white schools in each of the districts. And of course the number was zero.

"One of the defense lawyers was telling the judges that they 'needed a little more time,' that this had come up on them 'all of a sudden'—fifteen years after *Brown* was decided. But there was a judge from Tuscaloosa, Walter P. Gewen. He looked at the lawyer and said, 'Sir, the Supreme Court told us that we have to desegregate these schools now, and if you don't know what *now* means, just look at your watch.'"

In Vestavia, people were looking at their watches very intently. As soon as Jefferson County came under the government's desegregation order, they started pulling their kids out of Berry. In less than five months, the city raised, campaigned for, and passed a tax issue to break its schools off from the county's, attempting an end run around the law. It didn't work. So transparent was Vestavia's motive that, in less than ninety days, Clemon had appealed and a judge had slapped the new school system with the very same desegregation order it had tried to escape.

"The county was quick to point out," Clemon adds, "that Vestavia was saddled with blacks *because* it acted precipitously."

....

On July 23, 1970, the U.S. District Court of Northern Alabama ordered Vestavia "to have 25 percent faculty integration by September 1971" and to take responsibility for "those who live outside the city limits between Wenonah and Oxmoor Road." Soon, a five-year-old Alicia Thomas would be out by her campfire in the predawn chill, waiting for Shaky's rickety death trap to come rumbling out of the darkness.

The school bus became a lightning rod almost immediately, a thing on which white America could unleash its inchoate frustration and anger. In Boston, court-ordered busing sent mobs of Irish and Italian protesters into the streets. In Detroit, armed with dynamite, members of the Michigan Ku Klux Klan broke into a city bus barn and blew several school buses into the night sky. School busing was easy to hate. It was big-government social engineering of the worst kind. It was a "socialist plot" foisted on "real Americans" by "East Coast liberals." But the history of Vestavia Hills is useful for highlighting an important truth: big-government liberals didn't create school busing. Southern conservatives did. They willed it into existence with fifteen years of massive resistance.

In 1965, when HEW first issued federal guidelines for school desegregation, busing wasn't even mentioned. Preserving neighborhood schools to the greatest extent possible was the overriding consideration, HEW said. To that end, the two initial tactics the government used were pairing and zoning. Pairing was done by taking the black and white schools in closest proximity and merging them. With zoning, school districts were simply redrawn to encompass mixed populations. As a desegregation tool, busing was first used on a large scale in Charlotte, North Carolina, which adopted the tactic as an experiment in reshuffling the student population of its district.

Prior to that, busing had been used primarily as a means to *stop* integration. In small Southern towns, blacks and whites lived in relative proximity, often in checkerboard patterns. School boards hauled black and white kids all over the map on circuitous routes across gerrymandered districts in an attempt to keep them separate; many of the earliest desegregation plans often simplified the route kids took to school and redrew "neighborhood" boundaries in ways that made sense. Southern conservatives had used busing and redistricting for years. It was only when those tools were deployed against them that shipping kids across town suddenly became unfair and un-American. "It's not the distance. It's the niggers," Clemon and his colleagues liked to point out.

The constitutionality of busing was eventually upheld by the Supreme Court in 1971's *Swann v. Charlotte-Mecklenburg*, but the court's unanimous opinion was also very candid about the program's flaws, calling it "administratively awkward, inconvenient, and even bizarre." Even the supporters of busing thought it was a pretty cockeyed way to go. But whites had resisted and resisted and pushed the law to its breaking point, leaving little choice but to man up a fleet of big yellow diversity wagons to go and track everyone down. Thanks to its twenty-year temper tantrum, white America wound up saddling itself with *far* more black students and *far* more government intrusion than if it had just given blacks the only thing they'd asked for in the first place: freedom of choice.

Massive resistance made it so that integration had to be legally coerced, and that in turn has left us with an eternally vexing question: legally, what is integration? Once you start suing people, how do you know when you're done? The only available metric was the one put forth by HEW: statistical proof of significant progress. Or: "How many blacks ya got?" Once the precedent of *Brown* actually went into effect, the lofty but vague notion of "integration" by necessity evolved into the more quantifiable goal of "racial balance." Whites had been so disingenuous for so long, the only way to make sure they weren't cheating was to add up all the black students in the classrooms and use them as a measuring stick.

What had begun as a crusade for equal rights and educational opportunity had given birth to a big racial accounting system, one with mandates and timetables and "quotas." And despite its noble intentions, that system very quickly began to reveal its shortcomings. All the Supreme Court said was that Vestavia had to put the Oxmoor kids in the building. Earl Warren wasn't checking to see if Alicia Thomas made the volleyball team.

....

Up in Washington, on HEW's spreadsheet, the racial accountants could see that Alicia Thomas was right where she was supposed to be. But when the bus dropped her and the other Oxmoor kids off every morning, they were alone in a place apart that was straining with every muscle to pretend that they weren't actually there at all.

These days, every February during Black History Month cable news viewers get treated to a steady diet of grainy black-and-white newsreel footage from the 1960s: Klansmen setting crosses alight, urban youth being nightsticked and teargassed. Acts of terrorism against blacks, both vigilante and state sponsored, were all too common, but a more well-rounded version of history would also show what the vast majority of white Americans were doing at the time. They were at home, raising good Boy Scouts, watching *Bonanza*, and thinking this Negro thing wasn't much to get worked up about. And that's if they were thinking about it at all. Denial was so pervasive, and local media so censored, that the historic events of Birmingham probably had a greater immediate impact on newspaper readers in Japan than on many of the whites living in the middle of it.

Sue Lovoy grew up smack-dab in the middle of it, in Selma, Alabama.

She was in high school when the epic Selma to Montgomery March took place in 1965. That march would be the apex of the civil rights crusade, culminating in the passage of the Voting Rights Act. Eight thousand demonstrators mustered at the Edmund Pettus Bridge and marched some fifty miles to Montgomery, but for Sue and her friends it was just another day to hang out at the malt shop. She didn't march across the bridge or even go down to see the spectacle. "I was totally detached from it," she says. "It had nothing to do with me."

But she couldn't remain detached for much longer. Six years later, the forces unleashed at Selma would bring her and the children of Oxmoor face-to-face in a classroom at Vestavia Hills High. After graduating from Birmingham-Southern College, Sue Lovoy was hired to teach American history at Vestavia in the fall of 1971. Twenty years later, she'd be my American history teacher, too.

During my first visit back to her classroom, she showed me a fairly disturbing artifact of the "history" she was given to teach when she arrived. It's a copy of *Alabama*, third edition, by Charles Grayson Summersell, the state history textbook adopted by Vestavia when the school was formed. Even though it was published in 1965, it makes no mention of Rosa Parks, no mention of Martin Luther King, Jr., not one word on the firebombing of the Freedom Riders in Anniston. Nothing. What it does say, in its sole gloss on the entire civil rights movement, is this:

> In June, 1963, Governor [George] Wallace made good on his promise to stand "in the schoolhouse door," by taking his *now-celebrated* position at the entrance to Foster Auditorium on the University of Alabama campus when two Negroes, Vivian Malone and James A. Hood, sought to enroll. (Italics mine.)

Alabama remained a staple of the school's curriculum well into the late 1970s.

Vestavia had fallen all over itself trying to get out from under the desegregation order imposed on the county; however, shortly after the Oxmoor plan was announced, the court ruled that the city's white kids would not be bused out into black neighborhoods, which was really white parents' greater fear. Once that decision was made, the opposition to busing in Vestavia vanished, almost overnight. There was no more avoiding it, but it was also no longer something they had to bother themselves with. It was now an accounting matter between the school and the government. The everyday folks could go back to reading fairy tales about George Wallace. So they did.

William Clark was the district superintendent at the time. He says he received only one formal grievance over the integration issue. A white father barged into his office saying it was unfair that whites had to drive their children to school while the government gave black kids a free ride. White families should get as much as the blacks got, he said. Clark sent the man home. Beyond that, he insists, "I saw no racial animosity, didn't get any complaints, and we had no trouble." Even as Vestavia's own children were being hurled into one of the biggest social experiments in American history, the prevailing attitude of the community, still, was that this wasn't really about them. Typical of Alabama: once the busing situation was settled, Clark said, "my biggest problem was football."

While Vestavia's parents fretted over whether Colonel Reb and his angry mustache would make the conference finals, the families in Oxmoor were grappling with an actual problem: fear. Legally, the Oxmoor children now had no choice but to attend Vestavia, and Vestavia would be hauled back to court if they didn't. But many families didn't want their children hauled off to "that racist suburb." Given a choice between Vestavia Hills and dropping out, some kids were dropping out. So as year two of the busing plan was about to begin, Sue Lovoy's first task as a teacher was to load up with several other faculty members and drive into deepest, blackest Oxmoor for a very unusual parent-teacher conference. "There was a tremendous fear factor," she recalls. "They were afraid for their lives. We all rode over there, and I had to explain to them that I didn't care what color their children were; I was there to educate, and I was going to educate whoever walked in my door. But we really did have to go and convince them that we were not trying to corral their kids so we could bring 'em over here and kill 'em."

Eventually, most of the children came, and back at school Ms. Lovoy found herself responsible for two of them. Both girls, and both seniors.

One did poorly. She retreated from the unfriendly, unfamiliar environment around her. She fumbled through, barely got out, and went right back to Oxmoor, having gained little from the experience, academically or personally. The other girl did the opposite. If the school's intimidating atmosphere bothered her, she never let on. She arrived in class every day with confidence and a keen sense of humor, and she was a good student. "She and I had an interesting relationship," Lovoy says of the second girl. "We always used to pick at each other, tell jokes, have fun. The one thing I'll always remember is the morning I was standing there with my cup of coffee before class. She scooted up right behind me and she leaned in and said, 'Don't you know drinkin' that stuff'll make you black?'

"I *hooted*—I laughed so hard. And I determined then that if she could say that to me, and if she felt comfortable saying that to me, that meant she was going to be okay."

Thanks to U. W. Clemon, the doors to Vestavia Hills had been forced open. Soon the next generation of black children would be free to come in, and some of them would do better than okay.

....

3

Oreo

....

In a racial accounting system that leans heavy on the letter of the law, the law is only as good as it's written. The affirmative action clause mandating that Vestavia hire black teachers, for example, said the school had to meet a 25 percent minority faculty quota. It never said Vestavia had to *maintain* a 25 percent minority faculty quota. At the start of the 1971 school year, the system had hired thirty-six black teachers. With retirement and attrition, by the late 1980s only a handful remained. By the late 1990s, at the high school, there was only one left.

Jerona Williams was born in 1950 in the hamlet of Elloree, South Carolina. Her father, Raymond J. Anderson, was a bricklayer and a committed civil rights activist. Even in the early 1950s, he was openly registering voters and circulating petitions to integrate the schools, drawing a lot of the wrong kind of attention. One night when Jerona was seven years old, the Ku Klux Klan came over to send them a warning.

"They put it up right in front of our house," Jerona says. "They'd come in their white robes and put up the cross, saturate it with gasoline, and burn it. They were talking through a megaphone—they'd call out your names. I remember my daddy coming in and waking me up and lifting me out of bed. He carried me and he took me to the front door and he opened it. I looked out and the cross was burning and the men were standing there in their hoods. And my daddy held me in his arms and he said, 'I wanted you to see this so that you know you never have to be afraid, because your daddy will always be here to protect you.'"

Then he closed the door, put her back to bed, and returned to his business, undeterred. When Jerona was fourteen, Anderson applied for her to attend the town's all-white high school under the district's freedom of choice plan. She would soon be the first black student in the history of that school, but her father found himself blacklisted for his efforts. Unable to get work anywhere in South Carolina, he drove back and forth to North Carolina every week to lay brick at Fort Bragg for the federal government, the only employer who would have him. When Jerona finished high school, she enrolled at the historically black South Carolina State College to become a teacher. Still driving to Fort Bragg year after year, her father worked to keep her there—literally worked himself to death, dying of a heart attack when his daughter was only twenty; he wouldn't see her graduate from college.

At South Carolina State, Jerona met and dated Tyrone Williams, a young man from Birmingham, also the first in his family to go to college. As graduation neared, she says, "Tyrone went home for spring break and brought me back three applications for teaching jobs. He said, 'I got you Homewood, Jefferson County, and this new system, Vestavia Hills.' Vestavia called while I was still a student, because they were under court order to find black teachers. If it weren't for that, I wouldn't be here."

Jerona started teaching algebra at Vestavia in the fall of 1972. Tyrone, who would eventually be a school principal, went to work in the Birmingham city system. Together they bought a home on the north side in Forestdale and had four children: Tycely, Tyrenda, Tyra, and finally a son, Tyrone, Jr. For several years, despite being able to do so, the Williamses chose not to enroll their own kids at Vestavia. "The principal called me in," Jerona says, "and asked me why I wasn't bringing my kids to the school. Vestavia wanted them because they had to make the count. I told him I wanted my kids to be grounded, to be rooted. I wanted them to know black culture and know what's what before they came over."

When her oldest daughter was ready to start middle school, Jerona decided it was time.

....

When I say I don't know any black people, that's not *exactly* true. I used to know one. I just haven't spoken to her in seventeen years. Tycely Williams and I met in eighth grade at Vestavia's Pizitz Middle School in the fall of 1988. I was the skinny new kid with braces, recently arrived after my parents moved my brother and me from Lafayette, Louisiana. Freshman year, Tycely and I joined the debate team together. Your typical debate nerd was prone to spend his Friday nights playing Axis and Allies or smoking clove cigarettes while moping around to The Cure. But Tycely was one of the most popular kids in school. Member of the homecoming court, student government chaplain, Class Favorite, Best All Around, Ms. Vestavia finalist—you name it. After we graduated in 1993, we lost track of each other the way people used to do before Facebook. The only thing I'd heard of her since then came from a mutual classmate who'd picked up some random news through the alumni grapevine. "I think she's friends with Oprah or something," he said.

Tycely is not friends with Oprah, but she does run her own nonprofit management consulting business in Washington, D.C., which is where I tracked her down in the summer of 2008. If I was going to write a book about why I don't know any black people, it only made sense that she would be the first person I'd call. I drove down from New York, we had lunch, caught up, and began what has become, for both of us, a very illuminating high school reunion.

During our time, the Vestavia school system as a whole was 4.4 percent black, but the high school itself was closer to 3 percent—only 38 out of 1,238 students. Almost all of them were from Oxmoor. In our graduating class, Tycely and one other student were admitted because they were teachers' kids, and only one black student, Chad Jones, actually lived inside the Vestavia city limits. Chad was the superstar athlete, our double state champ in basketball and soccer. His mother, a single parent, had moved to Birmingham from Tupelo, Mississippi, when he was twelve. She worked nights at the local phone utility as they struggled to keep both feet inside the school district, moving from unit to unit in the handful of apartment complexes located on Highway 31. ("I think we lived in all of them," he says today.) Being the superstar athlete, Chad enjoyed his own set of rules when it came to crossing the color line. Tycely didn't have that advantage. She had only one chance to fit in, and that was by being the Black Girl with a Really Great Attitude.

"Even on my first day of school," Tycely says, "I promised myself that I would be nice to everyone, because there was a fear that people would not be nice to me because of my race. But all of my experiences proved otherwise. I never had to be anything other than who I was. I think I was able to make as many friends as I did because I had a level of sensitivity that most teenagers don't have, and I had that because I was black. There were skaters and jocks, and this group wouldn't talk to that group—I never fell victim to those classifications, because I was so cognizant of being classified myself. I tried to learn everybody's names, be friendly to everyone. I think if I hadn't been black, I wouldn't have been as popular as I was. I would have just done whatever the majority was doing."

Much like the self-assured girl in Sue Lovoy's first class, Tycely crossed the color line so fast it never had a chance to hold her back. In a world without black people, it was her advantage to define what black was; we didn't know. And if black meant Tycely, then black was pretty great. By the time we got to high school, Tycely says, she'd crossed so many lines and had so many friends that she'd neutralized whatever racial animus might have come her way. When pressed to dredge up all the racist things that had happened to her in Vestavia, she didn't have much to offer. Racking her brain, she could really only come up with one, and then not even something directed specifically at her. "After a football game," she recalls, "a bunch of Vestavia kids were hanging out, and of course I'm the only black kid. But we were playing Homewood, and Homewood had a lot of black guys on their team. And as they were walking back to their bus, this Vestavia kid said, 'You know, I hate those niggers.'

"Then one of the cheerleaders was like, 'Oh my God, how could you say that in front of Tycely?' Not 'How could you say that?' but 'How could you say it *in front of Tycely?*'"

To which the young man shrugged and offered the standard Southern defense, "What? She's not like them."

"I dismissed it," she says of the incident. "I just felt sorry for people. It wasn't their fault they were ignorant. I had a lot of kids say to me that I was the only black person they'd ever spoken to besides their maid. I'd invite friends over to visit, and they'd be *shocked* that I lived in a normal, regular house. They'd say, 'My parents were really nervous for me to come over here.' It wasn't their fault their parents were so fearful and afraid—of what, I don't know. Going to Vestavia is supposed to be all about getting this great education, but it's not *really* about getting an education, because if your parents were concerned about giving you an education, they would educate you about the fact that there are black people who can read and write."

When *Brown v. Board* ruled that segregated educational facilities were harmful, the court's decision focused almost exclusively on the psychological damage segregation caused to black children, the feelings of inferiority they developed by being stigmatized as second-class citizens and lesser human beings. Whites were assumed to be the healthy, well-educated norm. And because we were the norm, rarely did anyone stop to ask, "How is segregation screwing up the white kids?"

The answer, it turns out, is quite a lot.

Vestavia was seriously serious about education. Less than twenty years after bolting from the overcrowded classrooms of the county, our high school had risen to become, arguably, the best public school in the state. In 1991, the U.S. Department of Education officially designated us a Blue Ribbon School; some people came from Washington and gave us a flag.

But Tycely's right: if education were really the goal, how good could our education have been if we weren't actually educated about this integration thing in which *we* were supposedly the key players? Our history textbooks had improved since the days of Charles Grayson Summersell, but barely. The entire civil rights movement had grown to a good three, three and a half pages—now with Martin Luther King and everything. Black History Month might get you a grainy, warbly filmstrip about Jackie Robinson, but then it was back to the three branches of government.

High school curricula suck everywhere, of course, not just in Alabama. But what was uniquely perverse for us was the community's collective, blue-ribbon ability to ignore the elephant in the classroom. The Oxmoor busing program was still in full swing. We were a living experiment intended to repair centuries of racial animosity, yet this was never discussed. Ever. I polled dozens of my former classmates, and no one can remember any official acknowledgment of or discussion about the Oxmoor kids' situation: who they were, why they were being bused in, where they were being bused from, or even what busing was. Vestavia's botched retreat from U. W. Clemon's desegregation suit *was the only reason our school existed.* Yet as far as we were taught, God created Vestavia in six days and went golfing on the seventh.

Between 1970 and 1980, Birmingham tipped from majority white to majority black. So did most every major metropolis across the country; they became donut cities, rings of white suburbs surrounding a black urban core. My classmates and I were born in 1974 or 1975, right at the midpoint, just as that wave was beginning to crest and break on the suburban shore. We were the Children of White Flight, spirited away and raised in captivity. "Y'all were kept in a box," Jerona Williams says. We were. When the school hosted a foreign exchange program my junior year, it was with a group of kids from Denmark—the only place on earth actually whiter than Vestavia Hills.

As we began to go off to college in the 1990s, Rodney King was viciously beaten and O. J. Simpson did or did not kill a white lady and suddenly race was everywhere. President Clinton was all over TV calling for a National Conversation About It. Words like "multicultural" and "diversity" started creeping into the lexicon. But in the eighties, back when we were growing up, it seemed as if this whole black/white thing was way down on the to-do list, somewhere below "Fix Levees in New Orleans."

Black America's only real intrusion into our consciousness came through popular culture: professional sports, bootleg hip-hop cassettes our friends were passing around, and *Cosby.* With a five-year run as the number one–rated sitcom in the country, *The Cosby Show* normalized blackness for white America. The Huxtables went through the same ups and downs as everybody else. Theo missed curfew! Vanessa's got boy problems! The message to kids like me couldn't have been clearer. Black People: They're Just Like Us.

And in the end, that's how we related to Tycely. She was the Huxtable kid, our wacky sitcom neighbor, the black girl who'd whirl into class, toss off a few sassy catchphrases, and then exit with the applause sign going. On debate trips, we'd crack jokes about her having to sit at the back of the bus, and she'd snap back some line about Black Power or fighting the man. Then we'd all laugh and go to the food court. It was a game, a way to defuse the tension we all knew was there underneath the surface. And Tycely went right along, quite deliberately. "It was a coping mechanism," she says, "always making the issue of race something that people could laugh about. It made people comfortable because they knew I would never be confrontational."

It worked. And in truth, it was her only option. For Tycely, it was sink or swim with the white kids. With the Oxmoor kids, she would have drowned. From day one, she says, "they hated me."

....

The philosophical thrust behind school desegregation, over and above access to better classrooms, was predicated on the fact that children's peer relationships exert the single biggest influence over their academic performance. Students compete and strive for achievement, social status, etc., because they see their friends doing the same. Therefore, black children were entitled to, and needed to, socialize with peer groups in which they would be exposed to the cultural norms of the majority of society. Which was a great idea, except that the Oxmoor kids and the Vestavia kids were not peers.

It's hard to have a relationship with someone you never actually see. Vestavia, like many other schools, tracked its students into tiered learning programs: advanced, general, and remedial. Tracking, or "ability grouping," is a commonly known practice today. What is less well known is that tracking took off in the wake of, and largely as a response to, forced desegregation. The state of South Carolina, for example, started pushing for implementation of the practice in 1964. In school districts across the South and around the country, tracking programs cordoned off black students, shunting them into lower-level classes by default, much like Alicia Thomas's teacher assumed she belonged in the remedial reading lab.

In the 2007 settlement of Vestavia's desegregation suit, the court found no evidence that the school had ever tracked students as a deliberate mechanism of segregation, but the de facto result was no different. At the high end, Vestavia's honors program was a bustling hive for the over-achieving spawn of social-climbing, learning-obsessed helicopter par-ents. The Oxmoor kids, on the other hand, were coming from a place where living conditions hadn't much changed since Alicia Thomas was a girl. Some Oxmoor students were still living in clapboard houses and cinderblock shacks. It was a place stuck in the Great Depression, only this was in the early 1990s, less than two miles from the mall.

The racial achievement gap was stark. From 1989 to 1993, out of a cumulative 246 inductees to the National Honor Society (minimum 3.53 GPA required), only two black students were tapped to join, neither of whom were from Oxmoor. Nor were any graduating black seniors named for any of the year-end departmental honors. In four years on the advanced and college-prep track, I never had a single class with a black student other than Tycely, and Tycely never had a single class with an-other black student.

A quick spin through the clubs and activities in my senior yearbook shows life beyond the classroom to be no different. In sports, you had two black students on the varsity basketball team, and one each in foot-ball, wrestling, track, and soccer. But all the cheerleaders were white. Girls' volleyball, white. Tennis team, dance team, gymnastics—white, white, white. And athletics was the high-water mark. Theater was white. French club, white. Spanish club, white. Yearbook, school newspa-per, math team, scholar's bowl—white, white, Asian, white. There was one black freshman on stage crew, a few others here and there. But that's about it. For God's sake, there was only one black student in the Multicul-tural Awareness Club. (Actually, there were also four black guys who joined Vestavia's Future Homemakers of America. But I have to assume that this was a joke. An awesome, hilarious joke.)

The Oxmoor kids may have been at Vestavia, but they were not *of* Vestavia. When black children attended their traditionally black schools, like Parker High, extracurricular involvement and academic achieve-ment were not things they automatically opted out of. Education was highly esteemed. Schoolteachers were generally among the most respected members of the black community. *Brown v. Board* led the way in civil rights precisely because black leaders felt that access to better schools would arm the next generation with the knowledge and skills to create a more open and free society. But when theory met reality, being forced into hostile, unfriendly classrooms didn't always serve to lift up black students.

"Integration was devastating for that first generation of black children," Jerona Williams says. "In black schools, they'd had teachers that cared. Now white teachers had no idea what they were dealing with, and the black kids were just passing through, unattached. No nurturing. James Cameron, another black teacher, and I used to have to take those bus kids to the bathroom and talk to them about hygiene, things that you'd think would have been dealt with at home. But the conditions in Oxmoor were unbelievable. James kept baby wipes and deodorant in his classroom, and would make them go to the bathroom and use them in the morning."

It was often a harrowing ordeal. Some who went through it, like Alicia Thomas, choose to look back and see the glass half full: it was difficult, but she got something in return. Other black students came away feeling differently. Because white schools had rejected them, they rejected white schools—rejected everything white. Advanced classes were white. Standard English was white. The debate team was white. Oppositional personality, psychologists call it, striking a preemptive defiant pose. Someone won't let you join their club? You didn't want to be in that club, anyway. The Oxmoor kids rejected our club. And the fact that Tycely was allowed to join just meant something was wrong with Tycely.

If children conform to the standards set by their peers, in the seventies and eighties the peer pressure for black children to keep with their own was intense. Before desegregation, "acting white" was a phrase no one had ever heard with regard to school involvement or academics. Yet in the wake of busing, it rose to become one of the most hurtful insults one black student could level at another. Talking white, dressing white, being enthusiastic about anything "white" was forsaking one's own. For the thirty-eight black students at Vestavia, there was the black cafeteria table and there were the other cafeteria tables, and it was one or the other. There was no going back and forth.

Unfortunately, to sit at the black cafeteria table was to cut yourself off from 99 percent of what the best public school in the state had to offer. For someone in Tycely's position, crossing the color line wasn't a choice. If she wanted to be a part of all those activities you're supposed to have on your college résumé, she had to be the sellout, the wannabe, the Oreo—black on the outside, white on the inside—and suffer the consequences. "The black kids were horrible to me," she explains. "The only saving grace was that Vestavia was still so internally segregated that I never had to be in class with them. Otherwise it would have been a nightmare. They treated me like, 'You're trying to be something that you're not.' Or, 'She wants to be white,' they'd say. But I felt like I wanted to be in activities where I had the most in common with the people. Being on the debate team and student government, doing community service—that's how I saw myself, and so those are the things I wanted to do. But why does that have to mean I don't want to be black? I do want to be black. I *am* black. I can't *not* be black."

But Tycely wasn't black enough, or wasn't black in the right way. The Oxmoor students' hatred of her was obvious. What surprised me was to learn how much they resented Chad Jones, too. I knew Chad in passing, but as we were a debate nerd and a jock, respectively, our paths didn't cross much. With his lanky, laid-back demeanor and long Mississippi Delta drawl, Chad was about as authentically black as you could get. I'd always thought he moved freely across the color line in a way that Tycely couldn't. And yet . . .

"The Oxmoor crew didn't like me *at all*," Chad says. "In the morning, before school started, everybody would be in their little sections—they used to be upstairs—and the guys would yell things as I walked into school, call me names. I was discriminated against more by people of my own color than I ever was by white people. My mom was a single mom, worked from two to ten, so if I had practice, one of the Vestavia families would always come and get me. A lot of families did that; some treated me like I was their own. Probably because I was an athlete, but however you get it, you get it, you know? I can't actually pinpoint an incident where a white person ever called me a nigger. I'm sure it *happened*, but I can't say it was any one time. The black kids were harsher. They would say stuff to my face."

Black students from other schools did, too. Chad was the only black player in town with Colonel Reb on his jersey. When he took the court in the state basketball tournament against majority-black teams, shouts of "Uncle Tom" rang out from the opposing bleachers. It didn't help when Chad and the Rebels walked out with the championship trophy. "They didn't like that shit," he says.

It wasn't until senior year, when Chad had a small flirtation with one of the Oxmoor girls, that they began to accept him even a little. "There was a girl with that crew I liked a little bit," he says. "That made me get closer. It was kind of a blessing because I had dodged them for so long. I really wanted to become friends with some of them because I missed that—hell, I was black! I wanted it. I was with white kids all the time. Maybe they thought I thought I was too good for them? Here I am, over here with the white kids and I'm still successful? That kind of hurt them, and we could never connect. So I was blessed in a sense that I got a chance to know them senior year, but the only time we hung out was before school. We never went to the movies or anything. It was mostly about the girl."

Of course, these politics played out on a frequency most of the white kids weren't aware of, or didn't really get. The only time I remember the problem coming into plain view was at the annual student auction, which worked like a charity bachelor auction. Every year the underclassmen would get to bid on seniors and "buy" them for a day to haze them and what not. It was all good-natured fun, and it raised a lot of money for worthy causes—none of which makes up for the fact that the school called it "Slave Day."

So Tycely was up on the auction block for Slave Day (I know, I know), and the Oxmoor kids had pooled all their money to buy her. Lord knows what kind of hazing they had in mind, but they bid her up *high*. They were determined, and angry. This seemed like their chance to get even. For what, I didn't get at the time. I just remember how terrified Tycely looked standing alone there in the middle of the gym. Finally, the white kids stepped up on Slave Day and bought the Oreo to save her from the black kids.

....

During our senior year, Tycely took her experiences from Vestavia and wove them into a speech for oratory events at our debate tournaments. Her "Oreo" speech took home first prize at every competition she entered. Then she used it as her college admissions essay. She got in everywhere she applied, taking a scholarship to Wake Forest in North Carolina. In 1997, the next Williams sister, Tyrenda, graduated from Vestavia and was named America's Junior Miss, the first black woman to win that title in the forty-year history of the pageant. After graduate studies at NYU, she started her own fashion consulting company in New York. Tyra Williams graduated in 2004 and four years later would return to teach under Sue Lovoy in the history department, making her the first black graduate of Vestavia ever to go back and teach there. The youngest Williams, Tyrone, Jr., graduated just last year and is a freshman at the University of Alabama.

Affirmative action put Tycely's mother on Vestavia's teaching staff, and the fight against housing discrimination allowed Chad's mother to live there. But Tycely and Chad succeeded in an all-white school because they were raised to succeed in an all-white school. They were given the emotional armor required. The children and grandchildren of Raymond J. Anderson learned early on that a football game that looks like a Klan rally is just a lot of posturing. It's not so intimidating once you've stared down the real thing on your own front lawn. Chad Jones, too, credits his mother and grandmother for giving him the confidence and self-esteem to get through like he did. Chad left Vestavia with an athletic scholarship to Ole Miss, and now lives in neighboring Hoover with his wife and their four boys. For the past three years he's been running a restaurant owned by his mother, who started her own business after leaving the late shift at the phone company. In the classes that came behind ours, more children of working- and middle-class strivers would find similar success. The children from Oxmoor, with rare exception, did not.

When the 1966 Coleman Report emphasized the need for integration, it had done so with lots of big, flashing neon caveats, warnings that were brushed aside in the mad dash to create racial balance in every class-room available. One such caveat was that when going into a hostile environment like an all-white school, the single greatest indicator of a black student's success was the socioeconomic and cultural background of his or her home. For black children without strong parental support, the social whiplash of integration might cause them to "fall farther behind the white majority" both in academic learning and in the development of social skills necessary to navigate modern society. If not done properly, integration might only make things worse. And in Vestavia, nothing was done to see that integration was done properly. It was just done to be done with.

Vestavia's class of 1993 graduated, almost to the day, on the thirtieth anniversary of the Children's Crusade. In that triumphant moment, the black youth of Birmingham had seized the cause of freedom with enthusiasm and joy. Now, black or white, the children of Birmingham weren't doing much of anything about anything. If the Children of White Flight were being raised in captivity, then school busing was like being forced to mate in captivity; they just put us in a room and expected us to do something we'd never been socialized to do. It doesn't work with pandas, either. And this was at a time when desegregation programs were functioning *at their best*, according to advocates. In 1988, the year I started eighth grade in Vestavia, 43.5 percent of all black students in the South were attending majority-white schools, the highest level of racial balance our public schools have ever achieved. These were the good times, the numbers tell us. The salad days.

Perhaps I could give you an Oxmoor student's opinion on that, but the truth is I couldn't find any of them, not from my class at least. They weren't at the ten-year reunion, nor in any of the online alumni groups. In interviewing my classmates, a lot of people would stumble and trip up just trying to remember some of the bus kids' names. A woman in Oxmoor gave me a possible work number for one of the boys in my class, and Chad Jones passed along an email address for a guy he's occasionally in touch with. I left a couple of messages, sent a few emails. Nothing back. For a while I was panicked that the story would be incomplete without them, but then I realized that that in itself says it all. I don't need to talk to the bus kids. If I just leave them out, if I give no voice to their thoughts or their memories, that is the most accurate illustration I can give you of the impact they had on our lives. As for the impact that we had on theirs, let's just say that we didn't exactly go out of our way to spark a renaissance of racial healing in Vestavia Hills. Had the circumstances been reversed, I probably would have stayed at my own cafeteria table, too.

[4]

What Can Brown *Do* for You?

When U. W. Clemon was fighting to desegregate Vestavia Hills High School, he was also fighting a very different battle with his senior law partner, Oscar Adams. Adams, who had brought the suit that desegregated Birmingham's schools in 1963, was a graduate of Parker High, the largest black high school in the world. "Oscar had the feeling that Parker should be preserved as a black high school," Clemon says, "but I felt that Parker should be dismantled and the students sent to what was then Phillips High School. I felt very strongly that the black institutions could never be made equal with the white institutions, particularly while the whites were still in control of the system. There was a rather intense debate, and Oscar prevailed."

Parker stayed open, stayed black, and remains so today. The debate it provoked between Clemon and Adams is very much alive, too. It's an argument that's been around, in one form or another, since the days of slavery. Should blacks fight for inclusive equality with whites, or take white racism as a given and bolster their strength through ethnic solidarity? To sit at the black cafeteria table or not to sit at the black cafeteria table? Or perhaps to do both. In the early years of Jim Crow, this ideological clash manifested itself between the era's two most prominent black intellectuals, W. E. B. Du Bois, who argued for civil equality and helped found the NAACP, and Booker T. Washington, who advocated racial uplift through self-reliance.

On the issue of public education, the majority of freed slaves in the South tended toward Washington's point of view. They were especially wary of placing their children in schools run by former Confederates. Colored teachers, they felt, were best equipped to take care of their own; white politicians and philanthropists need only give them equal access to the resources they'd been so long denied. Alongside the black church, the black school became the center of the community. In smaller towns, the church and the school, the preacher and the teacher were often one and the same. New Orleans, Louisiana, was the only major city in the South where blacks fought to establish and maintain an integrated public school system under Reconstruction. Elsewhere, black communities often sought to control their own destiny in the classroom. Many black schools, like Parker, excelled. Most famously, Dunbar High School in Washington, D.C., often outperformed neighboring white schools in standardized testing.

Black America's emotional attachment to its own institutions was and remains tenacious. Those organizations were the glue that held the community together in times of great distress. Life grew around them. Black fraternities and sororities, originally founded as a social refuge for the few blacks at white colleges in the North, took root at Washington's Howard University, "the black Harvard." From there, chapters spread across the historically black colleges of the South, forming extensive social networks and forging traditions that have been handed down generation to generation. Out of the new black professional class came blacks-only trade organizations. Denied entry to the American Bar Association, black lawyers formed the National Bar Association. Ditto the National Medical Association and a host of other unions and professional guilds. The elite black bourgeoisie formed its own exclusive social clubs, the Boule for men and the Links for women. There was also Jack and Jill, an after-school activity group for black children from the "right" families. There were black summer camps, black chapters of secret societies like the Elks and the Masons, and, of course, granddaddy to them all: the black church.

The fight to eradicate the legal sanctions of Jim Crow had been, for all its difficulty, relatively straightforward. It had a moral clarity, a defined goal. But what to do with the world that Jim Crow had wrought? We'd built two separate Americas, and now we had them. They existed. One might not have been equal, but it was not without its own intrinsic value. Where desegregation was a matter of right and wrong, integration was a question of cost and benefit, measuring gains against losses. Forty years ago, the debate over Parker High yielded no easy answers, and it's only grown more complicated since.

....

Given black America's attachment to its own institutions, the campaign for civil rights did not begin as a demand for "integration" per se. It began as an effort to secure equal protection under the law. It was about the right to sit at the lunch counter and be served, not about the right to sit at the lunch counter and have a root beer with Susie and Biff.

The word "integration" itself wasn't even used in conjunction with the movement before 1940, when the NAACP called for "the integration of the armed forces," a demand that President Truman satisfied eight years later by executive order. Bolstered by that success and by the legal victory of *Brown v. Board* in 1954, the NAACP moved to the public fore of the movement. Under the intellectual leadership of Thurgood Marshall, the legal architect of *Brown*'s assault on segregated schools, the organization adopted a stridently prointegrationist posture. Given the disparities of wealth and power in the United States, separate could never be equal, or even remotely sufficient to meet black individuals' needs. The black community's attachment to its own institutions was foolish sentimentalism, integrationists felt; it was clinging to the past for fear of an unknown future. For the good of the race, NAACP leaders said, it was time to let go of the "little kingdoms" that had sustained them in exile. If Parker was a casualty of progress, so be it.

But the NAACP did not speak for all of black America. Not remotely. The organization's critics accused it of elitist, myopic thinking. Only the very smallest percentage of the black professional class was even in a position to integrate with white cultural and social institutions. (The National Association for the Advancement of *Certain* People, some called it.)

What about the laboring black masses and the poor, those who depended on the social cohesion and support provided by black institutions? How would dismantling Parker help them, particularly in the near term?

A second critique of the integrationist platform emerged as the *Brown v. Board* decision moved from idea to execution. Brown held that "separate educational facilities are inherently unequal." This sounded noble, but what did it mean? Did blacks have to integrate if they didn't want to? What about the very best of the black schools that were as good or better than some white schools? What did *Brown* mean for schools that were by-products of residential segregation? Nobody actually knew. *Brown* established a rather simplistic moral and legal standard that said, "Segregation bad, integration good"—a standard that would prove inadequate to address the true complexity of the problem.

Jim Crow had sunk deep in the physical and psychological bedrock of the country. An intricate, interlocking web of social networks and cultural norms had been built on top of it. Closing Parker High would destroy a century's worth of community ties and traditions. Meanwhile, the society that integrationists expected to enter, the one in Vestavia Hills, was built to function quite well without them. Black nationalists insisted that white America was eternally racist, would never offer blacks the benefits of a healthy, mutually cooperative society—the very one they risked destroying at Parker. Integration was a fool's bargain. It was lose-lose.

Black teachers, in particular, feared what integrated schools would do to their jobs. In 1953, on the eve of *Brown v. Board*, a survey of black teachers in South Carolina found that three-quarters wanted to continue working under a segregated system. Two years later in Montgomery, Alabama, black support for Martin Luther King's public transit boycott was near unanimous, yet at the same time local teachers repudiated his call for a legal challenge against the segregated public schools. Montgomery's blacks had no love for the back of the bus; control over their own classrooms was a different matter.

By the early 1960s, however, the momentum of the civil rights movement had shifted decisively in favor of integration, thanks in no small part to King. He put the matter on a moral and spiritual plane. Segregation, he preached, wasn't merely wrong because whites victimized blacks. At the deeper level, it was psychologically debilitating to everyone in society, black and white. It abrogated "the solidarity of the human family," twisted man's perceptions of himself and his brothers. Whether blacks were seen as degenerate beasts or whites were reviled as blue-eyed devils, both sentiments were rooted in segregation's fundamental evil: reducing people to objects rather than recognizing them as fellow human beings.

The cure, King said, was integration. Only sustained, cooperative interpersonal living could undo the damage wrought by four hundred years of slavery and Jim Crow. "Integration seems almost inevitably desirable and practical," he said, "because basically we are all one. . . . The universe is so structured that things do not quite work out rightly if men are not diligent in their concern for others. The self cannot be self without other selves. I cannot reach fulfillment without thou. Social psychologists tell us that we cannot truly be persons unless we interact with other persons. All life is interrelated. All men are caught in an inescapable network of mutuality, tied in a single garment of destiny." Stirred by King's lofty sentiments, many blacks, and plenty of whites, rallied behind him. They allowed themselves to believe, to hope, that this better world was possible. There was only one problem: it wasn't. Not in the 1960s, anyway.

With HEW's authority finally backed up by the Supreme Court's "Do it now" ultimatum, blacks had won enough leverage in the courts to mandate that white schools open their doors, but the execution of that would be handled by the same racist whites who'd opposed it all along. In the final analysis, busing wasn't really implemented to give black students access to better schools. It was implemented so that white schools could avoid lawsuits. The fate of black children was an ancillary concern, if it was a concern at all.

In 1964, only 2.3 percent of black students in the South attended majority-white schools. By 1972, that figure was 36.4 percent. A stunning turnabout, it seemed to vindicate those who believed integration possible. But it came at a steep cost. Nearly every Parker High was liquidated in the bargain. Wherever white and black high schools were compelled to merge or consolidate, the white school was presumed to be better, almost without exception. The neighboring black school was either closed or converted into an elementary or middle school. In North Carolina, the number of historically black high schools fell from 226 to 13.

Some black high schools managed to stay open. They were integrated by busing white students in, but that only brought indignities of a different sort. Before whites would attend a black school, they would, in the parlance of the times, "de-niggerize" it. The schools were fumigated, all the toilet seats changed out. They were given new mascots, new school colors. The Frederick Douglass poster came down, George Washington and his cherry tree went up. Trophy cases filled with the souvenirs of blacks' academic and athletic achievements were emptied and tossed. "One hundred years of history went into the trash," lamented one black principal in Oklahoma.

Any stain of blackness was scrubbed clean—even the names. Black kids had no say in being trundled off to Jefferson Davis Elementary, but no white kid in Alabama was going to be enrolled at anything named after Booker T. Washington. A 1970 report found that out of 321 former black schools "integrated" in the South, 188 had their names changed, usually from something symbolic of community pride to something plain and generic, like Central or East Side. The black school, as a historical cultural institution, was practically made extinct.

With their own schools shuttered, black students were uprooted from familiar environments and distributed as necessary; they would provide the statistical proof of significant progress. Having lived their whole lives with the same kids in the same neighborhood, black children found themselves divvied up and bused off in opposite directions. They lost their clubs, their teams, their student groups. "At the age of fourteen, it was like someone took a knife and cut off everyone you ever knew," said one young black student from Texas. And because of white flight and defections to private schools, the number of white students in these systems was plummeting with each passing year. So to meet the needs of racial balance, black students had to be shuffled around every fall, seemingly at random. At the most extreme, a black student might attend four different schools in four years.

The fears of black teachers proved justified as well. In an integrated system, their credentials mattered little to white administrators; those who weren't fired outright were generally demoted or marginalized. In nine states across the South, the number of black principals fell from 1,424 to 225. The National Education Association estimates that by 1970 more than 5,000 black teachers and administrators had lost their jobs. In Louisiana, one black principal was transferred to a white elementary school and restricted to teaching one fourth-grade class per day, after which he was made to perform all of the school's janitorial duties.

Whatever black America thought the civil rights revolution was going to bring, this wasn't it. And when King's path to the Promised Land left black America seemingly stranded in the wilderness, lofty sentiments lost out. Survival instincts took over. After decades of protesting to get in, now many were clamoring to get out. In 1968, black families in Hyde County, North Carolina, protested the closing of two historically black schools by pulling their children out of the system for an entire year, echoing the same method of massive resistance used by whites in years before. In April of 1969, students and parents from Atlanta's Hamilton High marched on the Dekalb County Courthouse to protest the loss of their school. But the all-white school board would not reverse its decision. Hamilton was shut down, its students split up and bused off as a means of desegregating four different white schools. Resentful alumni would later lament that Hamilton wasn't just closed, "it was drawn and quartered."

Any integration that treated black principals as janitors was an integration blacks wanted no part of. They'd taken care of themselves before, and they'd do it again. In 1972, a Gallup poll found that nearly 90 percent of whites were against school busing—but nearly 50 percent of blacks were against it, too. That same year, an NAACP field secretary working in Natchitoches, Louisiana, reported with some despair that, in surveying the parish's black community, "you won't find twelve people in favor of integrated schools." And three years after that, in 1975, James Coleman, author of the influential 1966 report that fast-tracked school desegregation to begin with, conducted a second study of what the intervening decade had produced. He didn't come back with good news. "Programs of desegregation have acted to further separate blacks and whites rather than bring them together," he concluded. "Busing does not work."

....

For decades now, everyone from the media to the federal government has been relying on this metric of racial balance to tell us if racism in America is getting better or worse. It doesn't work, because racial balance can never illustrate how much of the problem is white people being racist and how much of the problem is black people having lots of good reasons for not wanting to hang out and play Scrabble with us. White resistance and black reticence are hopelessly entwined with each other, endlessly variable from situation to situation. No spreadsheet has yet been invented that can tell us where one leaves off and the other picks up.

This much became obvious when I started looking at the racial balance in Vestavia Hills. The math didn't add up. In the late 1980s, housing discrimination in suburban neighborhoods remained a serious problem. Home prices inflated by property taxes also made for a steep barrier to entry. But at that point Birmingham had had its first black mayor, Richard Arrington, running a powerful black political machine, the Jefferson County Coalition, for at least a decade. The city's black middle class was substantial and growing. And yet in my graduating class at what was arguably the best public school in the state, only two black families had children who were fully, socially integrated into the student body: Tycely Williams and Chad Jones. And only one student—one, out of thousands—actually lived inside the district. That was Chad, the son of a single mom who worked the late shift. I know Vestavia's racist, but it's not *that* racist. Which begs the question: in a city with a large black population and a substantial black middle class, if a single black mother working the late shift could move into Vestavia, stay in Vestavia, and see her son graduate as one of the most popular students at Vestavia . . . where was everybody else?

"Most black people in Birmingham wanted to be around other black people," Tycely Williams says. "They wanted to live around black people, worship with black people, go to stores that were owned by black people."

After all the struggle to eliminate Jim Crow in the most segregated

city in America, the black middle class, those with the means and opportunity to cross the color line, elected not to. They wanted the *right* to
cross it. They wanted legal equality, access to public resources, and socioeconomic progress, but by and large very few crossed over in the
meaningful sense of choosing to live, work, and play on the other side.
And with good reason. White people didn't exactly roll out the welcome mat. And other than the good schools, life in Vestavia didn't seem
to offer much besides angry neighbors and a Chuck E. Cheese. Staying in
Birmingham's black community, on the other hand, offered family, community, pride of ownership.

"Sixth Avenue Baptist Church was the crown jewel in the black religious community," Tycely explains. "All of the Who's Who in the black
community went to Sixth Avenue. You had large social networks that
people had built around the sororities, fraternities, and alumni groups of
the historically black universities: Tuskegee, Alabama A&M, Alabama
State. Those kinds of clubs and affinity groups connected people socially.
Aside from that, maybe the biggest factor on the political front was the
Jefferson County Coalition. There were a lot of professional folks who
were members of that. And that association did a lot of things; it wasn't
just politics. They had their hands in everything. If you owned a black
business and you were trying to get money out of city hall, you were trying to get in with that group."

The affinity for these black institutions didn't die just because the
doors to Vestavia were opened. On the contrary, because Vestavia was
seen as so hostile and so unwelcoming, middle-class blacks turned their
backs on it—pointedly refused to have anything to do with it. For education, they turned to the best options the city had to offer, schools with
solid academics but a strong enough black presence to be culturally comfortable. There was the Catholic school downtown, John Carroll, which
was about 20 percent black. And then there was Ramsay, Birmingham's
public magnet school. At about 75 percent black, Ramsay still drew the
best white students that hadn't left and also skimmed the top black students from across the city.

"Ramsay was the cream of the crop as far as middle-class black people
were concerned," Tycely says. "They preferred it because it was not a

school that was open to *all* black people. It was a magnet. It was the 'safe' school, and there was still some level of exclusiveness. You had to go through testing or know someone who knew someone on the school board to get in there. Their academics were said to be comparable to the suburbs. That's debatable, but that was the perception."

Debatable or not, academics were hardly the point. If Tycely's parents had been concerned only with her grades, Ramsay would have been more than fine. But Jerona and Tyrone Williams believed that book smarts alone wouldn't take their children very far. They needed to be acculturated in the social mores of the country that they lived in—and Tycely didn't just live in black America. She lived in America. Not only did the Williamses send her to Vestavia, they also didn't let her join all-black social groups like Jack and Jill. With the exception of church, which would be the hub of Tycely's social life outside of school, her parents threw her into the deep end of the pool with the white kids and told her she had to learn how to swim.

"When you're forced to live in both worlds as a black person," Tycely says, "it makes you very much aware of things. You've been through the revolving door. You see where the power really lies and how the world really works. And the real world requires a cultural education that black middle-class society alone can't give you. To her credit, my mother always told us, 'You *have* to have a broader exposure. You *have* to be comfortable in different settings.'

"But a lot of my black friends were like, 'Why do you go to *Vestavia*? Why can't you do Jack and Jill?' It was this perception thing where black people felt, 'You think you're better than us.' It was never really spoken, but you could just tell from tone, from looks, from questions. But my mother's hesitation with all of these blacks-only affinity groups wasn't that she felt they were subpar or that they weren't teaching good values, but it was the indirect lesson that was taught: that blacks stay with blacks and whites stay with whites. She was just not an advocate of that."

But many of Birmingham's black parents did advocate that, as was their prerogative. They'd fought for the freedom to choose, after all. Unfortunately, staying on the black side of town has its drawbacks—most of the money and the jobs are over on the white side, for starters. With the city's commercial and residential tax base flown to the suburbs, and with the city governed more by racial politics than by sound policy, Birmingham sank like a rock.

The school system went down with it. Ramsay and a couple of the other magnet programs still post not-horrible results, but because those schools are skimming off the best of what's left, most of the city schools have followed the same downward spiral as Woodlawn. Once as cozy and stable as Vestavia Hills, Woodlawn today betrays (almost) no trace of its white past. The Sigma Tau Beach Beauties are long gone. The academics are appalling, and the dropout rate is staggering. A bank of security monitors dominates the front office, keeping a closed-captioned eye on the violent assaults that seem to break out at random. Legend has it that by the 1990s the bathrooms at Woodlawn were so terrible that teachers would go across the street to McDonald's to use the ones over there. The school has since been renovated. Not that you can tell.

And so, like many troubled metropolitan areas, Birmingham now has black flight. Black families are deserting the district faster than whites did in the 1960s, transferring to county schools, moving to black suburbs on the north side, and, finally, migrating Over the Mountain. And *that* is where the story of federally mandated integration in the suburbs of the most segregated city in America takes a very interesting turn. About ten years ago, a sizable contingent of Birmingham's black flight exodus chose a peculiar destination as their new home. They moved to Oxmoor.

"It's such a prominent community now," U. W. Clemon says of the former industrial scrapyard. "Some developers went in and built houses in that area for blacks and sold them on the very winning point that, thanks to the special zone created by the government desegregation plan, if you buy a house there your kids can go to school in Vestavia Hills."

....

The 1970 desegregation order for Vestavia Hills said only that the school was responsible for "those who live outside the city limits between Wenonah and Oxmoor Road." The court never stipulated *who* or *what* could be inside that footprint.

For decades, suburban sprawl rolled out *around* the Oxmoor Valley, encircling it, built to maximum capacity on all sides. The valley itself remained empty, a vacant parcel of Appalachian bottomland seven times the size of New York's Central Park, smack in the middle of the largest metropolitan area in the state of Alabama. If the people of Oxmoor remained marooned in the past, it's probably because virtually every one of the seven thousand acres around them was owned by U.S. Steel, which for years was just sitting on it.

In 1988, U.S. Steel and the city of Birmingham embarked on a bold "public-private partnership." Birmingham annexed the land into the city. Taxpayers provided the capital for infrastructure improvements like roads and sewerage, thus upping the value of the land many times. Then U.S. Steel started selling. Parcel by parcel. Golf resorts, shopping centers, office parks. And, of course, high-end residential. One particularly canny developer looked at the area "between Wenonah and Oxmoor Road" and saw that it offered black home buyers something they couldn't get anywhere else: access to Vestavia schools without paying Vestavia property taxes—and without the hassle of actually living with white people in Vestavia.

So that developer bought up land in the busing zone and started building. He went in right across the street from the old Depression-era shanties and built big $300,000 and $400,000 homes. Then he went out to the street and put up a big sign that read: VESTAVIA HILLS SCHOOL DISTRICT. People couldn't buy them fast enough. This new and improved Oxmoor was exactly what many in the black middle class had dreamed of: nice homes with good schools, yet situated in a space that was still culturally theirs. It offered what nonintegrationists had always said was black America's due: equal access to public services without the loss of their own community. It seemed too good to be true, and it was.

"They built way too many houses," Clemon explains.

By the early 2000s, rows of spec homes were popping up inside the Oxmoor busing zone. Word began circulating of plans for a large-scale apartment complex. All of this meant dozens of new students entering the school system with no increase in tax revenue to pay for the increased demand on services. It had been one thing for Vestavia to shoulder those costs for the low-income families of Oxmoor. It was quite another to do so for people buying houses at or above the price of homes inside the district. Vestavia called foul.* "And they were right," Clemon says. "I completely agreed with the people in Vestavia."

The courts agreed, too. On December 13, 2007, the federal desegregation order against the city was rescinded. In the terms of the settlement, every child currently enrolled—and the siblings of every child currently enrolled—can attend Vestavia schools until he or she graduates. And any child currently living in Oxmoor but not yet old enough to enroll is eligible for a tuition slot to Vestavia, which comes in at about what the equivalent property taxes would be.

"It was an excellent settlement," Clemon says, "and more than fair to all the parties involved."

Not surprisingly, many in Oxmoor don't see it the same way. The current residents may be grandfathered in, but no new home buyers will be; without access to Vestavia schools, the resale value of these high-end houses just went in the toilet. The original Oxmoor families lost out, too. Their houses had been an underground railroad for relatives to go Over the Mountain. Grandmothers took in grandkids, aunts took in nieces and nephews; they could all claim legal residence and catch a ride on the bus. That's over now, and those families had nothing to do with the over-zealous development that botched everything up.

After my bus ride with Alicia Thomas, I drive out and spend a Friday afternoon in Oxmoor and manage to talk to a couple of parents. One father who lives in one of the newer developments tells me that they should have fought harder against the settlement. "We're finally starting to make a little money," he says, "and they want to knock us back down."

In old Oxmoor—by which I mean just across the street—a family is out on the lawn, burning their trash in a pit, the smoke wafting over to the McMansions across the way. One mother of a Vestavia boy gives me an earful. "I didn't like it," she says. "I think it's wrong. Why block a kid from an education? Regardless if they live in a mansion or whatever? All my life, all my nephews and nieces went to Vestavia. My son's been in the

....

*At the time the lawsuit was settled, the median sale price of a home in Vestavia Hills was around $270,000, plus the higher annual property taxes.

school system ever since he was in preschool. They can't touch him. But if I decide to take my granddaughter, and wanted her to go to Vestavia, she can't go because of the *bull*shit. They just don't want these blacks over there."

Given Vestavia's reputation as "that racist suburb," it's easy to see why she'd say that. Given my own memories of Vestavia, before I did any research I would have thought she was right. But the reality is that the Oxmoor busing plan should have ended the year that I moved there, in 1988, when Birmingham annexed Oxmoor out of Jefferson County. As desegregation law stood at that time, once Oxmoor was a part of the Birmingham system, Vestavia could have vacated the busing order the very next day and walked away clean. And yet, for the next eighteen years, Vestavia continued to bus black students from Oxmoor despite having no compelling legal obligation to do so. During the settlement negotiations in 2007, one of Vestavia's opening bids was a very simple idea: annex the original 1970 busing footprint out of Birmingham city and into the school district, leaving Oxmoor exactly as it is: a majority-black enclave with access to top-shelf public schools. The logistics of it were such that it never went anywhere, but it was noted by the judge as a good-faith offer. And when the school board presented its case to the court, Norman Chachkin, the director of the NAACP Legal Defense Fund, submitted a brief to the court in favor of Vestavia's position, not Oxmoor's.

"Vestavia Hills has paid its dues," says U. W. Clemon. He more than anyone would know.

In the grand scheme, the arc of the moral universe would seem to bend the other way. Vestavia's home owners have profited insanely from investing in land whose price was artificially inflated by keeping black people out. So it should be no great crime that a few black families enjoy a little tax savings every April. But this isn't a binary equation anymore. More than a few black families live and pay property taxes in Vestavia now. Letting people exploit the Oxmoor loophole puts an unfair burden on those home owners, too, not just whites. Alicia Thomas gets up at five o'clock every morning and drives the bus in order to get her kids in the system; she's not getting a tax break on a $400,000 house, either. And besides, the whole point of school busing was to end segregation. The way the Oxmoor footprint was being abused, it had mutated into an economic incentive to make residential segregation even worse.

When I first learned that my old school had terminated its busing plan, I came down and started digging into my Southern roots fully convinced I'd find that the Confederate-flag-waving Rebels were the bad guys. They weren't. Not this time. What I found, instead, was a story that sits uncomfortably outside the bounds of the things we're supposed to say when we talk about race. I found that federally mandated integration in the racist suburb of the most segregated city in America did not come to an end because white people were trying to keep black people out. It ended because black people weren't willing to move in.

[5]

Go Rebels?

James Robinson met his wife Debra at Shades Valley High School, one of the Jefferson County schools desegregated under U. W. Clemon's *Singleton v. Jackson* case. In the arbitrary shuffling of black students around the district, they found each other after being transferred in from different neighborhoods on opposite sides of town—a school-busing love story.

James went on to graduate from Alabama's Tuskegee Institute, the famous industrial education school founded by Booker T. Washington. Today he's national accounts manager at Alagasco, Alabama's largest natural gas utility. After they were married, the Robinsons bought a home in Jefferson County and sent their eldest son, Mauri, to Shades Valley as well. He graduated in 2004 and was accepted at Morehouse, the all-male, historically black college in Atlanta. That same year, the couple's younger twins, Myles and Malcolm, were getting ready to enter sixth grade. The county middle school for which they were zoned was mired in construction delays and administrative problems, so the family decided to move. "My wife and I chose Vestavia," Robinson says, "for the school system."

The Vestavia Parent is a singular species, easily identified by an all-consuming obsession with his or her child's academic advancement. James Robinson was recommended to me as someone I should speak with about being a black Vestavia Parent, a role requiring a unique level of dedication and vigilance. Robinson is fluent in all the latest school board actions and city council zoning issues, the kind of stuff you only read about in the really boring sections of the newspaper. He quotes extensively from books on parenting and education, mainly specific to the challenges faced by black men—books he's read to correct the problems he sees in his own generation. "In the community where I grew up," he says, "males had very little responsibility in the household. The expectation for us was lowered." But in raising his own sons, he says, "the bar is extremely high, and there are no excuses."

At Shades Valley, Mauri Robinson was starting quarterback, captain of the basketball team, and an honor student. No less is expected of Myles and Malcolm, which was part of the decision to bring them to Vestavia. Robinson says he had little concern about the twins' academic transition, but crossing the social and racial divide was not a decision his family made easily. "We were apprehensive," he says. "I grew up playing athletics against Vestavia Hills, and in my day it was seen as a prejudiced school. Whether it was true or not, that was our perception."

Playing for Shades Valley a generation later, Mauri Robinson's perception was exactly the same. "As a matter of fact," his father says, "when we decided to move, Mauri literally said to us, 'How in the world could you send my brothers to that oppressive school?'" Before leaving for Morehouse, Mauri took his younger brothers aside and gave them a stern, brotherly warning about the world they would encounter in Vestavia Hills. "Without my wife and I knowing," James says, "he sat them down and told them that they would have to stick together because they were going into an environment that was unfair and oppressive. He told them, 'I don't know why our parents are doing this, but this is what you're dealing with, and here's what you've got to do to survive.'"

"And?" I ask.

"And to his surprise—quite honestly, to my surprise—what we encountered was totally different. Far from this community that would be prejudiced and not treat us fairly, we were received with open arms."

....

Vestavia, it would seem, has changed. On the surface it's pretty much the same, just more suburbany and sprawly. The Chuck E. Cheese is still there, but now there's a Starbucks with a drive-through. The high school itself has a whole new wing of classrooms, six new tennis courts, a new parking lot, a new soccer field, and a huge new lobby bolted on the front.

There's a brand-new gym, too, which is where I'm headed. It's the area finals in Boys 6A Basketball, and Vestavia's in the hunt for the state trophy this year. Tonight, we have to get past our old nemesis: Mountain Brook. I get my ticket, my Coke and popcorn, and head in. Rebel pride is on full display. There's crotchety ol' Colonel Reb, painted two stories tall down by the scoreboard. I'd actually forgotten that the Colonel doesn't wear Confederate gray. He's in a three-piece suit colored red, white, and blue—the Rebel as Patriot.

Up in the bleachers on the Vestavia side, the first thing I notice is all the black people still huddled off in their own cluster in the corner. Then I realize: it's the parents. Down in the student section, all the kids, black and white, are sitting with one another, laughing, fist-bumping, and generally having a blast.

The last time Vestavia took home the state basketball title was 1992, my junior year, when Chad Jones was the only black player on the team. George Hatchett was the coach then and still is now. Our win in '92, Hatchett tells me, brought in a flood of dubious fan mail. "Way to win one for white people!" folks said. Today, the team has five black players out of fifteen; the JV team, where Myles Robinson plays, is even more integrated. "We're more racially diverse on our athletic teams than we've ever been," Hatchett says, "and they're all really good kids." It's a night-and-day difference from when he first started coaching and had to take the golf team up to practice at the Vestavia Hills Country Club. "No blue jeans, no blacks. That's what they told me," he says.

"No blue jeans, no blacks" isn't an official policy for Mountain Brook, but it might as well be. In 1992, the entire Mountain Brook school system had three black students. As of 2009, it had ten. That's out of 4,367 total. I don't see any of them here. I'm told that Mountain Brook has actually tried to recruit black students for its athletic teams, but it can't get them; it's too white. James Robinson, in comparing school systems, rejected Mountain Brook out of hand. "It was not an option, culturally," he says.

It's a bit of a brain-twisting reversal, but the cheerleaders shouting "Go Rebels!" in the gym tonight are not rooting for the Old South; they're rooting for the New. One set of bleachers is integrated; the other is not. One team is integrated; the other is not. And in the 2009 area finals for Alabama Boys 6A Basketball, New South kicked a little ass. State tourney, here we come.

....

The next morning I find myself sitting in the principal's office for the first time since fourth grade. Cas McWaters is a dyed-in-the-wool Vestavian. He was here when the first Oxmoor bus rolled in thirty-nine years ago. Twenty years ago, he was my chemistry teacher. He later made the move into school administration, then left Vestavia to become principal at Tarrant, a low-income, majority-black high school on the north side. After a two-year stint there, he came back to Vestavia as principal in 2005.

Upon his return, the issue of race was right there waiting for him. Since the day the school opened, every four or five years a black family has filed a grievance with the school to have the Confederate flag banned. Every four or five years they're told no. One such grievance landed on McWaters's desk during his first week on the job. Quite possibly, he feels, as a test from the black community to see where he stood. He weighed all the arguments, and then, reversing thirty-five years of school policy, he banned the flag. "Here's my question," McWaters says of the decision. "Is it healthy for the school environment? My opinion is that it's not. It gives us a black eye in a large portion of the population. It could provoke an incident." The Stars and Bars is no longer allowed on campus during school hours, it's expressly forbidden in the dress code, and it's been purged from the school crest, replaced with the state flag of Alabama.

The one place the flag is most popular, however, is the one place he can't do anything about it: the football stadium. "I can't control what's at a football game," he says. "It's a public event, paid tickets, open to anybody. I can't mandate what is or isn't in there." Since McWaters couldn't ban the flag in the stadium, he did the next best thing. He banned poles, for safety. "It's certainly not safe for anybody to be carrying around a big stick," he says with a wry smile. So even if people bring their rebel flags to the game—and they do—they have nothing with which to wave them.

Cas McWaters is no latte-sipping liberal, either. He's a conservative Southern Baptist Republican with a gravy-thick Alabama accent. So to what, I ask, does he attribute the progressiveness of his attitudes? "Just having black friends here in Vestavia, I suppose." He shrugs. "Gettin' to know them as people. If you'd asked me ten years ago how many black friends I had—meaning friends, not acquaintances—I would have probably said one. Now . . . six? Close friends, people that eat over at my house, go to Sunday school together. And I probably ain't got but fourteen, fifteen close friends to begin with."

What I get from McWaters is the last thing I ever thought I'd find in Vestavia Hills: total candor about race. The Oxmoor lawsuit, campus incidents—McWaters puts it all out on the table. He wants it out on the table, I find. He's even called the editor of the school newspaper to sit in on our interview and write an article about it. "VESTAVIA GRAD TACKLES THE SUBJECT OF RACE RELATIONS." It ran on the front page above the fold. They took my picture and everything.

Honestly, I'm a bit thrown. I thought I'd come down here, tiptoe around the administration, get some off-the-record stuff from my old teachers, and generally sit and listen to a lot of "I'm not a racist, but . . ." Instead I've got a permanent hall pass, carte blanche to poke around.

"Can I take over some classes for group discussions?" I ask the principal.

"Why not?"

"Can I ride the bus out to Oxmoor?"

"Okay."

"Can I hand out a survey to dozens of teenagers asking them questions about the most volatile and incendiary subject in our nation's history?"

"Sure, let us Xerox it for you."

For fun, I also ask McWaters about *A Place Apart* and its euphemistic tap dance around the origins of Vestavia Hills High. He just laughs. "Anybody tells you that this school didn't break off to try and stay all white is lyin' through their teeth."

....

This "new" Vestavia caught James Robinson by surprise, too. After moving into their new house, he and his wife went on vacation, leaving the twins with their older brother. By the time the parents got back, the boys were already involved in the community. School hadn't even begun, and Myles had been drafted to a Little League football team. When the coaches realized that Mauri, the star quarterback of Shades Valley, was now living in Vestavia, they invited him to help coach the kids on their passing game. So before heading off to college, Mauri spent the summer coaching Little League, somewhat bewildered by everyone's neighborliness.

"When Debra and I returned from an Alaskan cruise right before the school year started," Robinson says, "we were amazed at what had transpired. Mauri was helping coach the quarterbacks on Myles's youth football team, and Myles had developed this huge network of friends. When classes start, Malcolm gets elected to student government. All of their teachers are attentive and receptive. I can't speak for anyone else's kids, but our twins adapted very well. The reception exceeded our expectations. It was totally different from what we could have ever imagined."

In personality, Myles and Malcolm Robinson could not be more dissimilar. "Had I not been in the delivery room," their father jokes, "I would not believe that they are twins." Myles plays basketball, Malcolm plays concert piano. Myles hangs with the jocks, Malcolm is president of the German Honor Society. Not being into sports—a one-way ticket to popularity—Malcolm found it a little tougher to adapt. "Myles had an easier time getting along," Malcolm explains. "I had to make my own friends, which was harder for me. At our old school my brother and I had all the same friends. When we moved here, we got different ones."

Far from having to stick together to survive, Myles and Malcolm both say they barely see each other during the school day. They have completely independent activities, interests, and peer groups. Twenty years ago, Tycely Williams had to make an either/or choice—in or out, black or white, Oxmoor or Oreo. Today, Myles's and Malcolm's choices aren't solely dictated by their race. There's still a color line, to be sure. There's still a black cafeteria table and a cluster of black kids in the hallway before school. But navigating that terrain has become far less treacherous.

If the twins have one thing in common, it's that they're both honor students. Not the only black ones, either. The academic glass ceiling at Vestavia has not only been cracked, but shattered. In the class of 2008, William Desmond qualified as a National Merit semifinalist, took home the departmental honors in social studies, *and* was voted Most Intellectual by his classmates. Not only is William Desmond black, he's from Oxmoor. One of the newer, middle-income families, but still. If you'd told me six weeks earlier that a bus kid from Oxmoor had been voted Most Intellectual by the students at Vestavia Hills High School, I would have swallowed my tongue.

James Robinson credits his own boys' academic achievements and high self-esteem to their involvement in an early childhood education program in Birmingham known as Wee Care Academy, which focuses on the historic academic achievements of the black community throughout history. "The background that our kids got there was one that said, 'You are as good as anyone else. You can achieve what anyone else can achieve, black, white, yellow, brown.' So coming into this environment, it wasn't intimidating. I had a little apprehension about whether they could compete academically, but *they* never did. Because of the foundation at Wee Care, they've never bought into that stereotype that being on the honor roll is 'acting white.' If being intelligent is acting white, does that mean being ignorant is acting black? I don't buy that. That's foolishness."

Foolish or not, the problem of "acting white" still persists. It's an accusation Myles Robinson says he still gets from some black students routinely. "There's a long history of not achieving for black men," Myles says, "and so when they see somebody doing something that's not like them, they turn their back to it. They say, 'You dress white. You act white. You talk white.'"

But both Myles and his brother seem to easily shrug it off. "They make straight As," their father says proudly. "As of first semester of sophomore year, they each have a cumulative GPA of 4.3."

....

As my days in Vestavia move forward, it's easy enough to get a read on how black students and parents feel about the racial landscape here—I just ask them. Being in the minority, they're acutely aware of what's going on. I quickly learn, however, that putting direct questions about race to white suburban teenagers is a useless endeavor. Painful, too. A sample quote:

I have a couple black friends, but, like, I know a *lot* of people in the school? I kind of feel like . . . like, not politically—I don't know how you'd say it—but having, like, right now, especially in this school, if you have a black person on a team, it's like . . . bonus points? It's like, look here, government or whatever, yeah, we have racial integration, because—you know what I'm sayin'?

And that was an honor student. Seeing as the direct approach isn't going to get me very far, I decide to poll a wide sample, let them give their answers blind, and then look at the results in the aggregate. Three teachers in Sue Lovoy's history department offer up time in their classes to hand out my two-page highly unscientific survey on the subject of race. All told, the sample pool covers 274 kids: 227 white, 33 black, and 14 other.

First question is a two-parter, asking the white kids how many black friends they have, meaning acquaintances, and how many *real* black friends they have, like the kind of friend you'd call late at night (or text or whatever) to talk about boys. The results:

NUMBER OF BLACK ACQUAINTANCES		NUMBER OF BLACK FRIENDS	
ZERO	2%	ZERO	49%
ONE	8%	ONE	24%
TWO	10%	TWO	13%
THREE	9%	THREE	6%
FOUR	10%	FOUR	3%
FIVE OR MORE	61%	FIVE OR MORE	5%

In my class, there weren't but six possible black friends to choose from total. Today, more than 60 percent of the white kids are at least chummy with five or more, and half of them have at least one close black friend. A turn through the 2008 yearbook backs up what the kids are saying. In the candids section, you can actually see black kids and white kids together in the same photograph. That's new. Same with clubs and activities. Certain groups tend to be more integrated than others, I'm told. So if you're in band or choir, you'll have a diverse set of friends. If you're on the swim team, not so much. Like Myles and Malcolm, black students at Vestavia are increasingly defining themselves by what they do, rather than by their skin color.

"The strongest, most respected choir students are three black students," Cas McWaters tells me. "Twenty years ago, I don't remember a single black student in choir. Now you've got a lot of camaraderie. I don't believe busing alone was ever going to do that. Back then? In the South? I don't know what alternative we had, but I'm not so sure that the school can implement anything, any program, that says, 'We can fix this.' I believe you have to change the culture of your school."

The culture in Vestavia has changed, considerably. And most of that has come in just the last five or six years. The early 2000s, I'm told, weren't substantially different from the late 1980s. Since then, things have improved radically, almost overnight. Vestavia's culture changed because white administrators and black parents finally decided to change it. Banning the Confederate flag was a signal to black families that here, at least, was a principal willing to meet them halfway. Those families, like the Robinsons, set aside their reservations and moved into the community; their presence has made it such that their needs can no longer be ignored in the way they were during the years they spent grousing about Vestavia's racism from the outside. And while this sea change in the school's culture has taken place, the only change in the federal desegregation mandate was that it was eliminated. No longer beholden to the letter of the law, Vestavia is nonetheless making good on its spirit.

The faculty, McWaters believes, has played a major role in this as well. "As our teacher population aged out with retirement," he says, "we've gotten teachers from other schools that weren't all white and all rich. So they've brought different experiences. We had a young man from a single-parent family down in Oxmoor; he was in football and choir. When his mother died, the choir director became his legal guardian.

People of Vestavia went and put together enough money to get him through college. He's at West Alabama now, graduating on time. The choir director is the legal guardian responsible for that situation. And that's how you change the culture: through experiences."

Among the faculty, the most immediately visible change is Tyra Williams, the youngest daughter of Vestavia's Williams dynasty; she's just started this fall, teaching in Sue Lovoy's history department. By the late 1990s, her mother, Jerona, was the last black classroom teacher working in the core academic curriculum. Together with her daughter, that makes two. And Mom has it easy: she teaches fractions. Once you get past the Three-Fifths Compromise, there's not a whole lot of racial tension over fractions. Tyra's juggling American History: 1865 to the Present. She gets to take these kids through Reconstruction, Jim Crow, and all the rest of it. A daunting task.

The institutional racism at Vestavia may be gone, but there's still plenty of the garden-variety kind. As happened everywhere, Barack Obama's presidential campaign brought a lot of it to the surface. Racist jokes and emails circulated. The day after the election, chants of "Obama-nation, Assassination" could be heard up and down the halls. And shortly before the inauguration, Tyra had to stop class and explain to a white girl that our new black president is not, in fact, the Antichrist. "Nuh-uh, Ms. Williams," the girl insisted. *"It's in the Bible."*

It can get personal, too. When Tyra had just started teaching, someone snuck into her classroom between periods and wrote the N-word on her chalkboard. (They didn't write "nigger"; they wrote "the N-word.") She didn't see it until she was up in front of her next class, mid-lecture. "It was a test," she says, "because how do you respond when thirty kids are watching you? I just erased it and kept going like I didn't see anything. After class I went into the bathroom and I cried and cried. I could not believe that happened to me. My mom told me, 'You can't wear your feelings on your sleeve. You can't be all emotional.' She's tough as steel. I'm working my way to that point."

So, just *how* racist is life in Vestavia Hills? One black student described it as "so ignorant it's unexplainable." Another simply sighed: "I could go on for days." Out of all the surveys, I counted nine that one could objectively categorize as "racist" in the true meaning of the word. Some students took the short-answer section and went off into the margins, filling them with angry diatribes. One white kid wrote, "Why do they smell? Why don't they take showers? Why are they so lazy? Why are you even writing this book? Honestly, you're white. Be proud of that. <u>Very</u>." This same student also checked the box for "Racism is no longer a major problem in America."

But that was only nine kids, out of over two hundred. In forty years, Jerona Williams has seen more of this than anyone. She pegs that kind of element as "not even 10 percent" of the students. "The rest of them are genuine," she says. "Vestavia has changed almost 180 degrees."

Whatever the quantifiable level of racism may or may not be, the more important question is how black students choose to deal with it. Out of those polled, only one black student checked the box that said, "Racism at Vestavia stands in the way of my advancement here." The rest said it was something they chose to ignore; they have better things to do. Of that same group, 76 percent wish Vestavia had more racial diversity, but only 24 percent say they would rather be at a majority-black school, even if the quality of education remained the same. And only 33 percent say they prefer to sit at the black cafeteria table; the rest enjoy sitting wherever with whomever.

"It's come a long way," Sue Lovoy says. "I'm proud of the distance we've traveled in these years. In the early days you would see all the black kids sitting together in one group in a class, and the white kids would sit as far away from them as possible. But now black students in my class don't feel the need to sit together. And you're not going to grow if you only surround yourself with people just like you. You'll never understand anybody else."

What Vestavia's children are, for the most part, is confused. Talk to half the kids here and they will tell you, with *absolute* sincerity, that the rebel flag stands for "school spirit." On the survey, I asked all the white kids to write down one thing they didn't understand about black people. "I don't understand why there is so much violence associated with black culture," one wrote. "Why do they talk one way in front of the teachers and another way around each other?" asked another. And then there's my personal favorite: "Why do black people drink Hawaiian Punch?"

They're all legitimate questions. Even the last one. Most of these kids would be teachable if America were ready to teach them, which it's not. I asked Sue Lovoy, "How much of the post–civil rights history on race has worked its way into the accepted high school curriculum?"

"None," she replied.

"Will it ever be included?"

"Probably not. Those of us who lived through it can bring our own experiences to the discussion, but as far as the standard curriculum, all you've got is Rosa Parks on the bus and how Martin Luther King was such a good father to his kids—and that's all they want told."

As head of the history department, Ms. Lovoy has had to seek out other means of diversifying the classroom experience. Hiring Tyra Williams was one. "I went after her," Lovoy says, "and I had to convince her. She wanted to work in an underprivileged school where she felt she could make a difference, but I told her, 'You can make a difference *here*. These kids need you, too.' And she's tearin' it up, really challenging these students to think about what they're going to encounter once they leave the bubble."

The biggest improvement Vestavia could make in educating its kids about race would be to have more black teachers do the educating, sharing their knowledge and experience. But that's easier said than done. As part of the Oxmoor settlement, Vestavia traded its hiring quota for a pledge to increase its minority recruitment effort. A major part of that effort is Pauline Parker. Parker is an exceptional-education specialist at the high school, one of the few black faculty whose last name isn't Williams. She also works overtime as the school's faculty recruiter. Several times a year, Vestavia sends her to job fairs and seminars across the South. "They're trying to show people that African Americans do teach in this school," Parker says. "But because of what is said about Vestavia Hills out in the black community, people don't want to deal with it. Black people do not want to come and work here. The responses I get from other African-American professionals are mostly along the lines of, 'I'm surprised they let you do this.' Or, 'I'm shocked. How many of you *are* there?'"

Under Principal McWaters, Vestavia has been actively recruiting minorities for several years. "And they don't come," Parker says.

If James Robinson had paid attention to his deepest apprehensions, he might not have come, either. But after a tentative arrival, he appears to be all in. He's not only a proud Vestavia parent, but has also joined the board of Leadership Vestavia Hills, a citizen coalition dedicated to improving the schools and the community. When we spoke, he told me of a day a couple years ago at one of Myles's middle school basketball games. During the game, a white student donned a rebel flag like a cape and ran up and down the sidelines, like some Confederate superhero. Offended, Robinson went up to the school the next day to meet with the principal about the incident. But when his boys found out what he'd done, they questioned him. "Both of my kids said to me, 'If you're making an issue out if it because of us, don't. This isn't an issue for us.' Myles told me, 'Dad, when we're tailgating out in the parking lot before the football games, those are the *nicest* people.'

"And I was like, Whoa, I need to rethink this. Who is this about? Is this about me, or is this about my children?"

"Do you think their attitude is just self-confidence," I ask, "or is it from losing some part of their identity?"

"I don't believe they have lost their African-American identity," he says. "That's well cemented. I think what they've lost is they've shed the baggage of their father, and in my opinion that's a good thing.

"I have made it clear that wherever they choose to go to college, they will go. I'll work night and day, two or three jobs, whatever it takes. If Harvard is your dream, there is no reason why you can't go. Period. End of discussion. Here's what I know: the average ACT score of a graduating senior at Vestavia Hills in 2008 was 24.3. This past February, Malcolm made a 25, Myles made a 22, and they're sophomores. Chances are they will qualify to go anywhere they want. Why should my racial baggage hold them back? That's the lesson I've learned living in Vestavia Hills."

On my last day in town, school lets out early. It's the state semifinals in Boys 6A Basketball, and the kids are all flooding out to their cars and heading downtown to the Birmingham-Jefferson civic center. Dressed head to toe in school spirit, they pack the stands, yelling and stomping the floor. The other schools and the other teams are all black; Vestavia, again, has the only integrated bench, the only integrated student section. When we win the semis, the kids go nuts. Two days from now, Vestavia will go all the way, capturing the state trophy for the first time since 1992. New South wins. Go Rebels.

In the wake of the 1963 civil rights campaign, Martin Luther King sat down and wrote *Why We Can't Wait*, a personal remembrance of the monumental events that transpired here. "I like to believe that Birmingham will one day become a model in Southern race relations," he wrote. "I like to believe that the negative extremes of Birmingham's past will resolve into the positive and utopian extreme of her future; that the sins of a dark yesterday will be redeemed in the achievements of a bright tomorrow. I have this hope because, once on a summer day, a dream came true."

Came true for some. As wonderful as life in the New South may seem, there is still the matter of those left behind. There is still the matter of Woodlawn. Vestavia may not be the bad guy anymore, but the *fact* of Vestavia—the gross racial and socioeconomic divide its existence created between city and suburb—remains very much the problem. In Birmingham, the dropout rate is over 20 percent. In Vestavia, 99 percent are walking out with diplomas. While 80 percent of the city's schoolchildren hover at or below the poverty line, not one student in the entire Mountain Brook system is poor enough to qualify for an assisted lunch. As city schools go without working bathrooms, Homewood has just built a brand-new, green-certified middle school. I walked through it. It's like going to eighth grade in the future.

Whites have deserted the city schools for good. In the 2008–2009 school year, out of 27,440 students enrolled in Birmingham city schools, only 263 were white, less than 1 percent. Out of 1,157 students, Woodlawn has ten white kids. Ramsay, the once vaunted magnet program, has only five. The schools in identifiably black suburbs, meanwhile, aren't doing much better: they're less than 3.5 percent white. The greatest diversity, as it happens, is found Over the Mountain. Taken together, Hoover, Homewood, Vestavia, and Mountain Brook have an average enrollment that's 14.9 percent black. If you take out Mountain Brook, it goes up to 17.8 percent. That's light-years ahead of where things were just twenty years ago, but the marvelous new diversity in the suburbs is also an indication of just how low the city schools have fallen, and how desperate black families are to escape. Between 1993 and 2008 the black student population of the Birmingham city schools fell from 37,950 to 26,465, a 30 percent drop. "They'll sell their souls to get out," Sue Lovoy says.

Birmingham's schools are crumbling from within, and the consequences of that are falling squarely on the suburban school districts who spent the past four decades thinking they could run away from it. Kids in the city get passed through the system learning next to nothing; they're oftentimes four or five grade levels behind. If their parents manage to relocate Over the Mountain, the time, energy, and resources it takes to remediate those students turn into a considerable drain on Vestavia's blue-ribbon resources.

Then there are the discipline problems. Violent offenders. Kids wearing ankle bracelets. They get expelled from the city and, after a turn in reform school, head to the 'burbs. "We've had an influx of kids who cannot go back to Birmingham city because they've been in trouble with the law and expelled permanently," Lovoy says. "So we're dealing with them, some successfully and some not."

Call it the White Flight Boomerang Effect: *because* Vestavia legally segregated itself from the city and county, it has no choice but to give a fresh start to the worst troublemakers they decide to cast off. "It behooves all school systems that all school systems do well," Cas McWaters says. "The surrounding systems need Birmingham to succeed. They realize that now. Because this is a topsy-turvy mess we're in."

Secession doesn't work. You'd think the fine people of Alabama would have figured that out the first time. But no.

Forty years ago, the Sigma Tau Beach Beauties of Woodlawn lit out of Birmingham like the place was on fire, seeking refuge in Vestavia Hills.

White folks took the tax base, the property values, their collective social and intellectual capital. They all but ripped out the plumbing. But there's at least one thing they left behind. During desegregation, historically black schools may have been stripped of their names and their mascots, but white schools weren't. At Woodlawn, even as the student body got blacker and blacker, out on the athletic field they were and still are known as the Woodlawn Colonels. By which I mean Colonel Reb. By which I mean Woodlawn has the *exact* same Colonel Reb mascot we have at Vestavia. Only he's black. He's got the same cocked hat, the same angry mustache. Someone's just painted him in blackface to match the building's new occupants. His red, white, and blue three-piece suit has changed colors, too. It's now a bright yellow—well, one hesitates to say pimp suit, but what other kind of three-piece suit is bright yellow?

Vestavia can't run away from Woodlawn, because Vestavia is Woodlawn and Woodlawn is Vestavia. Different schools, different districts, yet bound by a DNA they'll always share. They're brothers, these rebels. Twins. One white and one black, one favored and one forgotten. The District Court of Northern Alabama may have granted unitary status to one of them, but the rift between the two, between city and suburb, doesn't look to be reconciled anytime soon.

$$\left[\text{PART 2}\right]$$

PLANNING FOR PERMANENCE

[1]

There Goes the Neighborhood

In the spring of 1968, Father Norman Rotert was appointed to serve as pastor at St. Therese of the Little Flower, a Catholic parish and parochial school in the Blue Hills neighborhood of Kansas City, Missouri. Once upon a time, before Rotert arrived, Blue Hills had been Kansas City's Woodlawn. One of several Woodlawns, actually.

On Kansas City's wide-open grid, well-to-do whites lived on the west side. Working- and middle-class families lived mostly in little bungalow neighborhoods to the east, like Blue Hills and Troostwood and Linwood, the kinds of places where families used to pass their evenings on the front porch and the neighbors would stop by to say hello. This was Walt Disney's America. Literally. Walt Disney grew up in a gabled-roof cottage at 3028 Bellefontaine Avenue. Just a streetcar ride away, at Forty-sixth and Paseo, was Electric Park, a playland of games and activities with fireworks that went off every night and an electric train that the young Walt would ride. Disney opened his first animation studio here, too, where he kept a pet mouse whose name was not Mickey but Mortimer.

Though far from wealthy, whites on the east side had done well. The local Democratic political machine, run by "Boss Tom" Pendergast, had been instrumental in winning Missouri for Franklin Roosevelt in the 1932 presidential election, and government patronage from FDR's New

Deal insulated Kansas City from the worst effects of the Depression. When the industrial mobilization of World War II got under way, the city snagged its fair share of those contracts, too. Good jobs with good wages were plentiful, creating a solid tax base for public schools.

Kansas City was home to a vibrant black community, too, also on the east side but well to the north. Like New York's Harlem and Chicago's South Side, Kansas City's Eighteenth and Vine District was a hub of black American culture. Music legends like Count Basie and Charlie Parker got their starts here in the 1930s, playing all-night jam sessions and cutting contests at bars like the Hey Hey Club, transforming jazz from New Orleans' Dixieland sound into Kansas City's own signature style. Eighteenth and Vine had generated its own bustling black economy as well, served by black-owned livery cabs, black-owned clothing stores, and the *Kansas City Call*, one of the most widely read black newspapers in the country. Sitting at the heart of the neighborhood was Lincoln High, considered one of the finest black schools in the Midwest.

Ordained in 1957, Norman Rotert had ministered in Kansas City's black community for most of his career, starting at Annunciation parish close to Eighteenth and Vine. He belonged to a new generation of white clergy, committed to reversing Christianity's ignoble past of sanctioning slavery and Jim Crow; he'd marched with Martin Luther King in Selma in 1965. But when Rotert arrived at St. Therese in 1968, he found himself wrestling with a racial problem that was immune to protest marches and prayer. "FOR SALE signs were everywhere," he says. "Like tulips at Easter time."

Blue Hills was going black.

....

For years, white home owners on Kansas City's east side had been in a panic—not simply because blacks were moving south into their neighborhoods at an alarming rate, but because no one understood how or why it was happening. "The priest who preceded me had no grasp on what he was dealing with," Rotert explains. "There was no legitimate real estate company operative anywhere in the area. There were no mortgage loans available, no insurance available, and these people were working the neighborhood for everything it was worth."

"These people" were men like Bob Wood. Wood was a hustler. Through the fifties, sixties, and seventies, all over the country, men like him pioneered an art known as blockbusting. Blockbusters were predatory real estate speculators. They'd buy a house in a white neighborhood, rent it to a black family, wait a few weeks, and then start calling the neighbors. "The coloreds are moving in. Don't you think you should sell? I can get you a good deal—before it's too late." The scare tactics these men used could get quite creative. Some would go into the ghetto and pay a few bucks to the biggest, scariest, right-off-the-chain-gang-looking fellow they could find. Then they'd bring him along, knocking door-to-door, politely informing white residents that "this gentleman is looking in the area." The FOR SALE signs would start to go up.

Once the signs were up, that neighborhood was "in transition." All the licensed real estate brokers would close up shop; their code of ethics prevented them from selling "white" houses to blacks. Once the licensed agents left, the neighborhood's housing market turned into an unregulated free-for-all. The blockbusters would descend. As soon as one black family moved in, all the surrounding white residents found themselves perpetually harassed. Widows and the elderly—on fixed incomes, their entire net worth tied up in their house—were targeted first. Six, seven phone calls a night. More and more yard signs would crop up. Within months, sometimes days, the whole block would go black.

In any selling frenzy, prices plummet. Fear makes a motivated seller. A neighborhood might have an average home price of $10,000, but once the old widow is strong-armed into selling for $5,000, that sets the market value for the rest of the block—the myth of black neighbors lowering property values becomes a self-fulfilling prophecy. But blacks didn't drive property values down; real estate agents did. In truth, the first blacks to pioneer a neighborhood were so desperate to leave the ghetto they'd sign a $15,000 mortgage for that $10,000 house; the arrival of blacks drove prices up. Supply and demand. The first whites to sell could make a bundle and get out. The last whites to sell might be lucky to get $2,500.

Blockbusters also knew that blacks had little access to mortgage capital. So those brokers would offer to finance the purchase themselves for an outsized down payment and an unreasonable monthly note. Trapped in tenements most of their lives, having never dealt with complex mortgage instruments, black families would take the deal. Falling behind on the note almost immediately, they'd find themselves foreclosed on in a matter of months. The deed would then revert back to the broker, who'd turn around and sell it again. An enterprising blockbuster might turn the same house over two, three, maybe four times in the space of a year.

Blockbusting hit the northern frontier of Blue Hills, Forty-seventh Street, early in 1968, just as Father Rotert arrived at St. Therese. He watched as the neighborhood crumbled from within. "These brokers would list a house for a white family," he says, "and then wouldn't even try to sell it. Then the home owners would get scared, go out to Johnson County, and buy something. Now they had two mortgages to carry, so the broker would offer them a pittance for their old house—he'd just steal it from them. Then he'd jack up the price and sell it to blacks. That was going on all over the place."

Like others to the north had done, Rotert tried to hold the line. He thought he could help make an orderly transition to a stable, integrated neighborhood. He failed. His priestly authority held no sway over men like Bob Wood, with whom he had frequent run-ins. "Wood made no pretense that he wasn't doing what he was doing," Rotert recalls, "and he was doing it well. His attitude was 'Try and stop me.'"

The pastor often begged Wood to do just that. Stop. For the sake of the community. "But he'd just laugh at me. He thought I was a fool."

....

The fate of any residential neighborhood is bound to the fate of its schools. Before *Brown v. Board*, Kansas City ran a strictly segregated school system, based on racial attendance zones. Starting in 1955, in order to "comply" with *Brown*, the city announced that school enrollment would now be based on neighborhood attendance zones—neighborhoods that just happened to be all white or all black. For decades, the residential color line on the east side had held unchallenged at Twenty-seventh Street, kept in place by fear. But the all-black tenements and schools of Eighteenth and Vine were packed beyond capacity. Emboldened by the rising consciousness of civil rights, black families began to move out.

Keeping the schools white now meant keeping the neighborhoods white, and the well-to-do whites on the west side were going to make damn sure that their side stayed whitest the longest. City officials drew a boundary right down the middle of the city along its longest north-south thoroughfare, Troost Avenue. Let the east side go black, it was decided. We'll hold the line here. Still today, nearly every zip code, every census tract, every voting ward—and, for a long time, every school district—all split right along Troost.

Most every city in America has a Troost. In Chicago, it's the fourteen-lane Dan Ryan Expressway that divides the South Side from the Bungalow Belt. In Detroit, it's Eight Mile Road, a jurisdictional barrier excluding city residents from county services. In Birmingham, it's a mountain you have to go over. Kansas City's Troost Avenue is unique in that it's not an elevated thruway or set of railroad tracks—it's merely a street, like any other, running down the center of the city's flat, open grid. Yet everyone who lives here knows. East of Troost is black; west of Troost is white. A local newscaster once dubbed it "the Berlin Wall of Kansas City." The name stuck.

Before 1955, no real estate listing in the city had ever used the designations "East of Troost" or "West of Troost." Now they all did. Under the city's new neighborhood attendance policy, the vertical axis of Troost remained fixed, but as blacks began to come south on the east side, the school board would resort to gerrymandering the northern boundaries of the schools on the color line; year to year, the attendance zones twisted and contorted themselves around the expanding black residential areas in order to keep schools white. Once the black migration had reached a critical mass and the school district could no longer pivot around it, the city would reverse itself and regerrymander the neighborhood boundaries the other way, shifting the attendance zone to go majority black. In the name of preserving "neighborhood schools" and "neighborhood stability," the school board was tearing the east side neighborhoods apart one after another.

Once a neighborhood school was zoned to go black, the neighborhood it served had essentially been thrown to the blockbusting wolves; Bob Wood knew the whites in that district would be the most vulnerable to threats. One of the first schools to flip was Walt Disney's own Benton Grammar School. Just a year after *Brown*, it was suddenly reborn as D. A. Holmes Elementary—named after a local black preacher—and thrown out as a sacrifice by whites fleeing the broken color line at Twenty-seventh Street. Then Thirty-first Street fell. Then Thirty-second. By 1960, block-busting had flipped nearly every street clear down to Thirty-ninth. As school districts were gerrymandered this way and that, black residential tracts cascaded down the east side, always moving in unnatural squares and rectangles. In 1954, the two main high schools serving east of Troost, Central and Paseo, had both been 100 percent white. By 1962, Central was already 99 percent black; by 1968, Paseo was 88 percent black and rising. That same year, west of Troost, the well-protected Southwest High was still 99.5 percent white.

Catholic schools on the east side were inundated by the blockbusting turnover as well. Some had tried to set a limit on the number of incoming black students, as an incentive to get whites to stay. It hadn't worked. "It just turned off the African-American community," Rotert says, "and then the church lost those schools anyway. I decided we were not going to do that here." In the spring of 1969, Rotert announced that there would be no cap on black enrollment at St. Therese in the fall. "Some of the parishioners were angry that I did that, but I said, 'Look, we are not going to destroy this parish. We're going to welcome these people into our school and our community.' I hoped that people would stay, but by then I knew it was over. The following year, the school went from 80 percent white to 98 percent black. Just like that."

....

You can't destroy a Woodlawn without first creating a Vestavia Hills. White flight requires a place to flee, and the road to Vestavia Hills, it turns out, starts in Kansas City, Missouri. If you're like me, and have ever lived in a house in America, Kansas City probably plays an important role in your story, too. And so, after leaving Birmingham, I've come to find myself in the heart of the Midwest on a gray February afternoon driving up a desolate and deserted Troost Avenue.

As racial divides go, Troost may be a purely mental construct, but the real-world effect it has is astonishing. If you go four blocks east of Troost, you can buy a three-bedroom bungalow for about $45,000. Four blocks west of Troost, that same house will run you upward of $130,000. If you live west of Troost, your car insurance payments might be, say, $80 a month, depending on make and model. That same car registered any-where east of Troost will run you upward of $130 a month. Because black people steal cars, evidently. I guess black people rob delivery guys, too, because you can't get a decent pizza delivered over there to save your life. All the good pizza places are west of Troost, and they won't deliver east of Troost. They'll go across the state line, into Kansas, but not over the Berlin Wall. Average annual income, average level of educa-tion, average life expectancy—nearly every statistical measure you can name, they all break right down the line, and the good news always tilts west.

Driving north on Troost, you see little but empty storefronts, one after another. Abandoned homes, burned out and boarded up. Vacant parking lots and junked cars, grown over with weeds. Block after block. There are a few operating businesses here and there. An auto parts supplier, a wig shop, a dollar store next to a self-storage unit. A few people are out and about, all of them black. Mostly it's just empty. Once a thriving com-mercial artery, Troost turned into the front line of a long and bitter turf war, after which both armies retreated and turned their backs on it. Ply-wood and busted glass and crumbling concrete lie in every direction. It's been this way for decades.

Out your passenger window as you head north are all the Woodlawns—the formerly white, blockbusted neighborhoods that have since fallen into the sinkhole of urban blight. Some pockets, like the Santa Fe area, are stable, safe, middle-class communities. But most white people wouldn't know the difference, even if they've lived in Kansas City their whole lives. It's all just east of Troost. It's the Murder Factory—that's the popular nickname of the 64130 zip code sitting in the middle of the east side. With just 6 percent of the city's population, 64130 produces 20 per-cent of the city's incarcerated killers. Blue Hills is in the Murder Factory.

Just adjacent to the Murder Factory is the plot where Electric Park, the inspiration for Disneyland, used to be. It burned down in 1925; today it's low-income housing. As you keep going past Thirty-first Street, just one

block east of Troost, you pass Walt Disney's old Laugh-O-Gram animation studio, now an empty husk left exposed to the elements. Somewhere
east of that is Disney's elementary school. After going black, by the 1980s
it had been shuttered, too. Turn right off Troost at Armour Boulevard,
and that takes you four blocks east to the Paseo. The Paseo was once the
gilded heart of nineteenth-century Kansas City. Most of its mansions are
long gone. Park Avenue–style apartment buildings, once imposing and
grand, now sit either boarded up or packed with tenants on government
Section 8 vouchers.

Take Paseo all the way up and you come to the center of Eighteenth
and Vine. Today it's a shell of its former self. The city has tried to make it
into a historic district and tourist destination; there's a new jazz museum
and a Negro Leagues baseball museum. But with the exception of Arthur
Bryant's Barbecue—the kind of old-line institution where politicians go
to have their picture put up on the wall with a big plate of ribs—there's
not a whole lot going on. It's not a living place. When Robert Altman
made his 1996 film *Kansas City*, he restored Eighteenth and Vine to its
Depression-era heyday with a hefty dose of movie magic, painting fake
storefronts on plywood in the windows of abandoned buildings up and
down the street. Fourteen years later, the fake storefronts are still here:
old Negro taxi stands, dance clubs, soul-food joints. Lifeless replicas of a
long-gone era, cracked and peeling in the winter chill.

Pull a U-turn and head back west of Troost, and you find a very different scene. The skyscrapers of downtown are just three minutes away.
Twenty years ago, even the white man's business district was a ghost
town, almost totally abandoned. Now everything is shiny and new, completely gentrified and reborn. In the past decade, massive government
reinvestment in downtown has created the glittering Sprint Center
sports arena and the KC Power and Light District, an open-air shopping
mall of restaurants, bars, and movie theaters right in the middle of the
city. The once blighted warehouse district just south of the downtown
loop is now the trendy Crossroads neighborhood, chock-full of wine bars
and artists' lofts and other things that require exposed brick. A bit farther south, you'll pass the World War I memorial and the Nelson-Atkins
Art Museum and come to Ward Parkway, which runs crosswise along

Brush Creek before turning south to cut a magnificent, tree-canopied corridor through Kansas City's Country Club District.

Sitting less than two miles from the urban blight of Troost, the Country Club District is one of the most beautiful cityscapes ever built by man. The city's rigid north-south grid yields to curving, winding boulevards and cul-de-sacs that run with the gently rolling topography. The homes are stately and grand. Impressive, but rarely ostentatious, every house sits perfectly situated with regard to the trees and lawns that surround it. The Country Club Plaza is home to all the nice restaurants and high-end retailers. Pembroke Hill, the finest college prep school in the city, is nestled at the heart of the area. It's just a quick stroll from Jacob Loose Park, the jewel of the city's public park system.

And we haven't even gotten to the good part.

Just across the Kansas state line is the toniest of the Country Club District's many subdivisions: Mission Hills. The most sought-after zip code in town. Home to the Kansas City Country Club, one of the nation's finest and most exclusive. Mission Hills is where houses become mansions, where driveways have gates and sometimes bridges and moats. It's suburbia's molten core. There's even fresh, piping-hot pizza delivered right to your door anytime you want. You just pick up the phone and call. And nearly all of this—pretty much everything that exists from here looking south and sprawling west into Kansas—sprang fully formed from the brain of a single man, real estate magnate J. C. Nichols.

In the twentieth century, Kansas City produced two uniquely American geniuses who would both forever alter the physical and cultural landscape of the country. One of these men built a magic kingdom, a fantasy world that offered nonstop, wholesome family fun and a complete escape from reality. The other one moved to Hollywood and opened a theme park.

"Have You Seen the Country Club District?"

During the first half of the twentieth century, Jesse Clyde Nichols was the most influential real estate developer in the United States. One could make the argument that he still holds that title today, despite being dead for sixty years. Neither J. C. Nichols nor Walt Disney was an inventor. Disney didn't invent "fun." He built a company that took amusement and made it into a product. Then he packaged it, commodified it, and sold it. J. C. Nichols did the same thing for the ground beneath our feet.

At the end of the industrial revolution, America's cities were ugly. Factories and meatpacking plants belched coal fumes into the sky. Residential districts grew haphazardly around them. There was little beauty and less order. Cities had not yet fully grasped the idea of zoning—setting aside green space for parks, cordoning off industrial enterprise from residential quarters and dictating, in turn, how those residences should be built. Wealthier home owners had their Fifth Avenues and their Paseos, but even those had no zoning laws to protect them. Build your three-story mansion, and there was nothing to stop a feedlot for hogs from going in across the way. In the nineteenth century, neighborhoods rose and collapsed at random, destroying accumulated property values in the process.

For residential property, that began to change with Llewellyn Park, the country's first high-end suburban development, founded in West Orange, New Jersey, in 1853. Four years later came Lake Forest outside Chicago, the first neighborhood ever built around a golf course. Similar developments followed in Baltimore, Boston, and Philadelphia. For the well-heeled, these places became oases from urban life, protected by the use of restrictive covenants—stipulations embedded in the property deeds that designated minimum lot size and number of bedrooms, and also forbade unwelcome intrusions.

In Kansas City, Missouri, J. C. Nichols would radically expand and revolutionize people's ideas of what restrictive covenants could do. In his neighborhoods, he used them to specify the placement of every tree and the curve in every sidewalk. He learned how to make a city do what he wanted it to. Nichols also pioneered and innovated the use of "public-private partnerships." Once upon a time, municipal governments had the crazy idea to plan their city grids themselves, as was done in New York and Philadelphia. Nichols led the way in making deals with city and county officials in which taxpayers would pay to build out an area's infrastructure, but they would do it according to his needs, which then allowed him to plan subdivisions to attract the wealthiest residents, whose property taxes would then flow back into the government's coffers. In his spare time, Nichols invented the shopping mall. In 1922, he opened the Plaza, America's first-ever retail center designed specifically for the automobile. When Nichols built it, he was ridiculed. Who would ever drive out to the middle of nowhere? In a car? To shop?

But Nichols's most important contribution to the way we live wasn't something he invented himself. He just perfected it. And the thing he perfected was the all-white neighborhood, hardwired with restrictive covenants that dictated not only the size and shape of the house but the color of the people who could live inside. This idea, the racialization of space, would take root deep in the nation's consciousness, for both whites and blacks alike, becoming so entrenched that all the moral might of the civil rights crusade was powerless to dislodge it. In the South, Jim Crow was just the law. In Kansas City, J. C. Nichols turned it into a product. Then he packaged it, commodified it, and sold it. Whiteness was no longer just an inflated social status. Now it was worth cash money.

∙∙∙∙∙∙∙∙∙∙∙

J. C. Nichols was born in 1880 to a prosperous family of merchants in the small farm town of Olathe, Kansas, but he wouldn't be content to stay there long. Just across the border in Missouri, Kansas City was booming.

Founded as a frontier trading post dead in the center of the continental United States, Kansas City had grown to become the starting point of the Oregon, Santa Fe, and California trails. When the industrial revolution came, factories and stockyards drew people to the city by the thousands, black and white. They all needed somewhere to live.

At the outset of the Civil War, Kansas City's black population had consisted of just 166 slaves and 24 free people of color. By 1900, it had reached 17,567, roughly 11 percent of the total, which itself had more than quintupled since the war. Blacks were coming west in part to seek opportunity, but also to escape the insidious rise of Jim Crow in the old Confederacy; the legal system of segregation that J. C. Nichols would soon privatize was just then taking shape in the Deep South.

When threatened by the civil rights movement in the 1950s and 1960s, whites often spoke of segregation in fevered, delusional terms, as if it had been ordained by God, like it had been man's natural state since the dawn of time. It hadn't. Measured from *Plessy v. Ferguson* in 1896 to *Brown v. Board* in 1954, the lifespan of constitutionally sanctioned segregation was only fifty-eight years—exactly the same length as the professional recording career of Frank Sinatra. During Reconstruction, blacks and whites in the South had often coexisted freely in restaurants, railcars, and other public accommodations. Even after Reconstruction ended with the Hayes-Tilden Compromise in 1877, an entire decade would pass before the first Jim Crow statute showed up on the books in a Southern state.

This is not to say that Southern race relations were *good*, but they were not yet predicated on the absolute necessity of racial separatism. In his seminal civil rights text, *The Strange Career of Jim Crow*, historian C. Vann Woodward noted the experience of one T. McCants Stewart, a black man from Boston traveling through South Carolina in 1885. Stewart reported from the Palmetto State that he could "go into saloons . . . and drink a glass of soda and be more politely waited upon than in some parts of New England." The whites of the South, he felt, "are really less afraid to [have] contact with colored people than the whites of the North."

Indeed, as Jim Crow laws began cropping up for debate in Southern statehouses, they were often derided as unnecessary—even absurd. In 1898, the year South Carolina passed its first Jim Crow statute, the conservative Charleston *News and Courier* ran a scathingly satirical essay on the sheer ridiculousness of it all. "If there must be Jim Crow cars on the railroads," it said, "there should be Jim Crow cars on the street railways. Also on all passenger boats . . . and waiting saloons at all stations . . . and Jim Crow eating houses . . . and Jim Crow sections of the jury box . . . and a Jim Crow Bible for colored witnesses to kiss. . . ." And so on. Within a few years, nearly everything the editorial had predicted *as a joke* had actually come to pass.

The turnabout was driven by fear. The ideology of white supremacy used to justify slavery had been rooted in the notion that blacks were somehow less than human, childlike in their feeblemindedness. They were destined to be kept—even happy to be kept—in a state of bondage. The working relationship between master and slave was one of physical proximity, not separateness. By the 1880s and 1890s, however, the economic dislocations of the industrial revolution and global trade had triggered a recurring cascade of market panic and financial insecurity. Across the South, a populist People's Party rose up in an effort to galvanize the working class—black and white, reaching across the color line—to rise up against the robber baron industrialists and landowning aristocrats who exploited their labor. The ruling class in the South had no interest in dealing with a third party that united working-class blacks and whites in a solid voting majority. Fortunately for them, any popular uprising built on racial cooperation was a fragile one, quickly divided and easily conquered.

The white supremacist ideology that had underpinned slavery was still baked into the country's mentality. No longer held in check by the civil rights protections of Reconstruction, those feelings of racial superiority were easily stoked. As populists tried to tie the economic ascendance of blacks and whites together into common cause, the ruling establishment painted the economic ascendance of blacks as a threat to decent white society. Birmingham, Alabama, being the most segregated city in America, was a textbook example of Jim Crow at work. In the 1890s, Alabama's big planters and industrialists drummed up fears of the Negro menace to get whites behind a poll tax to disenfranchise blacks. Whites supported it, and 98 percent of Alabama's voting-age blacks were stricken from the rolls. But those same restrictions left thirty-five percent of eligible white voters disenfranchised, too; numerically speaking, more whites lost the right to vote than blacks. When union leaders from the Congress of Industrial Organizations (CIO) came South to organize blacks and whites in the steel mills for better working conditions, U.S. Steel put thugs from the Ku Klux Klan on its payroll to terrorize anyone who engaged in union activities. The company also founded its own League to Maintain White Supremacy, which educated workers on the dangers of race mixing and tarred the CIO as "the nigger union." Driven by racial animus, the white steelworkers of Birmingham spurned the one organization actively lobbying for their own interests, siding instead with the very company that was exploiting them.

But for those keen to present blacks as a threat, the stereotype of blacks as feebleminded children was of little use—children pose no threat. Racism required an overhaul. Blacks needed to be dangerous, disease ridden, violent. These images were pumped into the public consciousness through the work of newspaper propagandists and political demagogues. Scientists got behind the notion, too, propagating biological and psychological theories to explain the black man's animal nature and his criminal appetites. Leading this charge, same as it had with slavery, was the church. For four hundred years, Christian priests and pastors had exhorted whites to reach down and lift up our little brown brothers for whom Christ also died, to hug them closer to God's bosom. Now those same clergy pivoted 180 degrees. They started peddling a segregationist theology—God had ordained the separation of the races to keep them pure. A Nashville clergyman, Buckner H. Payne, sold a translation of the Bible in which the devil in the Garden of Eden wasn't actually a serpent but a Negro man-beast. Race mixing wasn't just a sin;

it was the original sin. And the "serpent" that Eve found so tempting was . . . well, you can guess what it was. Forbidden fruit, indeed.

Even though Jim Crow did not come north and west as a fully articulated legal framework, the mentality behind it proved highly adaptable to cooler climes. At the turn of the century, many of Kansas City's blacks lived in enclaves like the Vine Street corridor, Belvedere Hollow, Church Hill, and in one of the worst slums any city has ever seen: Hell's Half Acre. But these weren't "ghettos." Before 1900, no city in America had a black ghetto or even what you'd call a majority-black neighborhood. America had plenty of slums, but it didn't have ghettos—there's a difference. A slum is a place with deplorable living conditions. A ghetto, technically defined, is a slum where certain people are compelled to live by law or by extralegal threat (e.g., the Jewish ghettos of Warsaw or the Bantustans of South Africa).

In Kansas City, working-class blacks lived not in ghettos but in apartments and row houses alongside Irish, German, and Italian laborers. A small percentage of black professionals and skilled laborers lived in modest single-family homes among whites of the same socioeconomic class. In 1900, the typical black resident of Kansas City lived in an area that was less than 14 percent black. At such a small percentage of the population, they were of little worry to white Kansas City. Indeed, they were so geographically dispersed, there was no one place you could point to if you wanted to highlight the dangers of "the black side of town."

The evolution of Eighteenth and Vine as an ethnic enclave was organic, at first. As more blacks came west, they naturally sought company with people they knew. Families reached back and sent home train tickets to bring relatives out. Cousins followed cousins. The established helped the newcomers find jobs, find the right church, meet a nice girl. A strong, tight-knit community began to form, bound together by relationships forged in the Sunday pews and in the after hours. Community brought purpose. Black civic leaders grew more assertive in calls for civil rights and equality. Black workers began going on strike to demand better pay and better working conditions. In 1904, the livery drivers' union went on strike, led by a majority-black coalition. Black meatpackers did the same. But in becoming a more visible presence, in making demands for economic rights and civic equality, blacks could also be more easily scapegoated as a threat, same as they had been in Alabama.

Before 1900, Kansas City's black newspapers contained not one report of purposeful discrimination aimed at keeping blacks out of a residential area. By 1907, white real estate brokers would only sell or rent to blacks inside the Vine Street corridor. In 1911, on the still-white fringe of Vine Street, a house was dynamited when a black family tried to move in, the city's first recorded incident of violence being used to protect a "white" neighborhood. Only one suspect was arrested and sentenced for the crime—a black man charged with trying to scare off whites so blacks could take over. More bombings followed.

As the Great Migration gathered steam in 1910, former sharecroppers came pouring out of the plantation South, seeking the economic rewards of the industrial North and Midwest. Hemmed in on all sides, Eighteenth and Vine grew denser. Jerry-built "apartments" were tacked onto tenement homes in back alleys. Families were crowded into crudely subdivided basements. One survey conducted in 1912 found that 20 percent of the houses in Eighteenth and Vine lacked any water supply at all, 50 percent had no sink, and bathtubs averaged one per every twenty-two residents. Infection rates ran twice the city average for pneumonia, tuberculosis, and other communicable diseases. By 1920, the population of Eighteenth and Vine had nearly doubled in size. At the same time, it had gone from 25 percent black to 75 percent black. Kansas City had its first ghetto.

The driving force that shaped this ghetto was the local Democratic Party. In the city and county elections of 1908, the Democrats had little to run on. Republicans dominated Missouri politics at the time, and the economy was humming along, giving them a strong advantage. But Republicans were also the Party of Lincoln, with a loyal and growing black constituency. If these "dangerous" blacks were seen as a threat to public safety, with the Republicans responsible for helping blacks usurp whites, the Democrats might orchestrate a return to power.

In 1905, a black male guard at a women's penitentiary, hired under Republican city rule, had allegedly beaten a white female inmate. This guard would be the Democrats' political cudgel, their Willie Horton. The left-leaning *Kansas City Post* trumpeted every report of black murder or theft, illustrating its pages with bug-eyed black monkeys riding Republican elephants and truncheon-wielding black gorillas beating white women. Republicans had infested Kansas City's government with "Negro brutes." A vote for the GOP would make Kansas City "the stronghold of Negro equality in the whole United States." In November of 1908, the Democrats swept every available seat in the county.*

This new Democratic political machine, run by "Boss Tom" Pendergast, would control Kansas City for the next thirty years. To keep that position, the party would have to appease whites' now hysterical concerns over the Negro threat to public safety—a threat, of course, that didn't actually exist. All the organized crime and vice in Kansas City was controlled by . . . well, by the Democratic Party, which was in bed with the mafia. So in order to "reduce crime," Boss Tom moved all the white-owned brothels and gambling houses into the heart of Eighteenth and Vine. There he gave the vice trade free license to operate so long as the racketeering, whoring, violence, and murder were kept away from anybody who mattered.

Blacks didn't matter. They could vote, but they didn't own. In 1910, only 800 of the city's 23,566 blacks owned property of any kind. What they did own amounted to 0.0112 percent of the total property in Kansas City. Blacks had no leverage, no control over their own turf. By the end of the 1920s, there would be more than fifty cabarets within a six-block radius of Eighteenth and Vine. Illegal liquor flowed at jazz joints twenty-four hours a day. Prostitutes worked the sidewalks in front of Lincoln High, even during school hours. To whites on the outside looking in, the quality of life in the ghetto seemed irrefutable proof of the Negro character. The Negro's degeneracy had created the ghetto, and not the other way around. In the moral geography of Kansas City, a black neighbor-

....

*Ironically, before the election-year fearmongering began, local black leaders had been thinking of throwing their support to the Democrats. Decades of loyalty to the Party of Lincoln had yielded them only a token amount of civic patronage, no real economic progress, and a lot of empty promises; many blacks were starting to get frustrated that their political voice was beholden to a single party that took them for granted. (Some of this may sound familiar.)

hood was now a bad neighborhood—and that presented a remarkable and exciting business opportunity.

....

"HAVE YOU SEEN THE COUNTRY CLUB DISTRICT? 1,000 ACRES RESTRICTED FOR THOSE WHO WANT PROTECTION."

Thus blared the headline of an advertisement heralding the launch of J. C. Nichols's brand-new suburban development—christened in 1908, the same year Kansas City's Democratic machine rode the Negro menace to political victory.

Just six years before, Nichols had graduated Phi Beta Kappa from the University of Kansas. Then it was off to grad school at Harvard. Returning to Kansas City, he undertook a few modestly successful ventures and used the profits to buy up a vast tract of seemingly worthless land in the middle of nowhere along the Kansas-Missouri border: an old garbage dump, an abandoned racing track, a brickyard, several tracts of farmland. Then he started building.

J. C. Nichols didn't sell houses. He sold "suburbia." He sold a way of thinking about residential living that in turn created the demand for houses in neighborhoods that he owned. According to Nichols, the right protections and restrictions could create an island of certainty and stability in an uncertain, unstable world. Escape "the commonplace of the city street" for "the refinement of the suburban estate," his Sunday newspaper ads declared.

Having sold this beautiful empty space cordoned off from the tumult of daily life, Nichols then had to give it life. People needed something to do. For the ladies, he started lawn beautification contests and competitive flower shows. To feed the male ego, there was golf and the prestige of membership in the right club. For the kids, Nichols organized annual "Community Field Days" with three-legged races and model-boat regattas. He didn't invent these sorts of activities. What he did, in the words of one biographer, was to synthesize them. He scheduled them accordingly with the seasons, and gave them the imprimatur of time-honored tradition. He created a culture for a place that had no culture of its own. Nichols even had a name for it. He called it "community work." Community work fell squarely under the purview of his company's public relations department. It wasn't really culture at all. It was just advertising.

Underneath all that, the bedrock of suburbia's appeal, as Nichols framed it, was the idea that a certain kind of physical space was inherently more virtuous than another. The right kind of leafy green cul-de-sac—and the right kind of neighbors—were essential to raising children with proper Christian and American values. A man's choice of home said something about his moral character. Is your family a Mission Hills kind of family? What kind of man lets his children live on *that* side of town? In billboards and newspaper ads, Nichols drove his message home again and again:

> *Wouldn't you and yours take pride in a home built in the Country Club District . . . where your children will get the benefit of an exclusive environment and the most desirable associations?*

> *Children's lives are affected by the atmosphere in which they are reared. Give them the advantages of out-of-doors living, pure fresh air, desirable associations and beautiful surroundings.*

Desirable associations. Subtle. But when translated into legal terminology on Nichols's property deeds, the meaning of the phrase is perfectly clear: "None of said land may be conveyed to, used, owned, or occupied by negroes as owners or tenants."

This was the racial covenant, and it would be Nichols's most lasting contribution to America.* The flaw in racial covenants, as they had been used before Nichols, was that they were applied only to the deed of the individual lot for sale. You could have a whole block of individually restricted houses. If one person decided to sell to a black family and get out, there was little his neighbors could do, legally, to stop that from hap-

....

*It is not known who first came up with the idea to include an owner's race in a property's zoning requirements, nor can anyone pinpoint where the first such clause was actually written into a contract. The first verifiable use of explicit racial restrictions against blacks has been traced back to 1908, in Baltimore's Roland Park and in Kansas City's Country Club District.

pening.* Then, in 1909, J. C. Nichols broke ground on Sunset Hill and Country Side, the first of his developments laid out on land unencumbered by earlier deed restrictions. Here, he attached the racial covenant not to the deed for the lot, but to the plat for the entire subdivision. Thus it became harder for one person to break.

Property restrictions at the time were also typically written to expire after a decade or two; as much as stability was sought, most developers allowed that property owners' needs might change. Nichols disagreed. His faith in his own vision for Kansas City was such that he wanted it to be in place for his grandchildren's grandchildren. "Planning for Permanence" was his company's lofty motto, and he meant it. Starting in 1911, with Country Club Ridge, Nichols began writing his restrictive covenants to last twenty-five years with the option to renew. Two years later, when Nichols opened his crown jewel, Mission Hills, he went one better. He wrote all his property restrictions to be self-renewing every twenty-five years unless a group of owners controlling the most street-facing footage† opted to change those restrictions five years prior to the auto-renewal date. It was the first use of self-perpetuating racial covenants anywhere in the country, a fact often touted by Nichols himself. "Self-perpetuating restrictions," boasted his new Sunday ads, "conceived by the developers of the Country Club District, solve the problem of shifting and declining residential sections, a menace to every city, including our own."

Nichols's greatest innovation would come in 1922 with the subdivision of Armour Hills. Up to that point, home owners in each successive Country Club District development had formed voluntary neighborhood associations for general upkeep. In Armour Hills, Nichols made membership in the neighborhood association a contractual obligation incumbent with the land purchase. He then assigned that association and its members full legal liability, alongside the Nichols Company, for maintaining and enforcing the property restrictions, racial and otherwise, for

....

*The older, working-class houses east of Troost were built with these kinds of limited property restrictions, part of the reason they were more vulnerable to blockbusting.

†Meaning a minority of voters with large lots could quash a majority of voters with smaller lots.

the entire community. Now the home, the home owner, the land, and the land developer were all legally bound together as one entity, protected by an impermeable contractual seal against any undesirable element that might seek to intrude. One by one, Nichols went back to the neighborhood groups for his other developments and proposed a similar arrangement. Each of the neighborhoods voted to adopt it. And, by this point, Nichols's success had spurred on lots of local competitors. Developers were buying land adjacent to his and piggybacking on his efforts; they all eagerly copied his new template, too. The self-renewing, all-encompassing restrictions used in Armour Hills would become the foundation of nearly every neighborhood built in the Kansas City area from that point forward.

By 1923, Nichols was breaking ground on at least one new subdivision a year, and the sheer mass of his enterprise solidified the symbiotic, public-private relationship he'd been forging with municipal and county government. The city's infrastructure—roads, transit, water, sewerage, gas, and electric—all pivoted and ran south by southwest, pulled by Nichols's center of gravity, custom fit to meet his needs, and all at taxpayer expense. What was good for the Country Club District was good for Kansas City.

....

J. C. Nichols's suburban creation was a masterpiece. Every last detail orchestrated just so, totally insulated from reality, and with plenty of room for parking. It was unlike anything most Americans had seen at the time. *Ladies' Home Journal* called it "a lesson for all cities" to emulate. The president of the U.S. Chamber of Commerce named it "the most beautiful residential section in America."

By the early 1920s, Nichols enjoyed a stature in the business that was without peer. He served as president, booster, or board member for a constellation of industry trade groups. President Calvin Coolidge called him "the father of city planning in the West" and appointed him to serve on the National Capital Park and Planning Commission, responsible for overseeing the development of Washington, D.C. Herbert Hoover, Franklin Roosevelt, and Harry Truman would retain him in that post until 1948. Hoover was a personal dinner guest at the Nichols home, twice.

In 1917, Nichols had also founded and chaired what would be one of the most influential organizations in the history of real estate: the Annual Conference of the Developers of High-Class Residential Property. Membership was open only to the most powerful real estate men in the country. At Nichols's invitation, these men came together at annual confabs to share ideas and establish a set of industry best practices, including—as discussed quite openly and on the record—the best way to implement restrictive covenants to keep neighborhoods all white. Some developers wanted covenants extended to cover Jews, "Orientals," and others. Others were undecided on whether to exclude *all* Jews or to let in the good Jews. There was no debate about blacks.

Prominent in the group was J. C. Nichols's close friend Robert Jemison of Birmingham, Alabama. In 1924, Jemison wrote Nichols that he was planning to build Birmingham's own premier, high-class development and asked if Nichols could, "at his earliest convenience," send templates for "the latest form of deed and restrictions, with the proper provisions for maintenance." Nichols was more than happy to share. Shortly thereafter, Jemison broke ground on his own "Country Club District." He called it Mountain Brook. It was a carbon copy of the Kansas City original—right down to its shopping village, built just for the automobile. In 1947, inspired by Jemison's success, a developer named Charles Byrd went south of Mountain Brook and bought up the ostentatious estate of a recently deceased eccentric. Byrd chopped it up, cordoned it off for white folks, and called it Vestavia Hills.

The High-Class Developers conference included New York City's John Demarest, Detroit's Judson Bradway, Baltimore's Edward Bouton, Dallas's Hugh Prather, San Francisco's Duncan McDuffie, Omaha's J. E. George, Indianapolis's Emerson Chaille. Like Jemison, these men would all leave the conference each year and put their ideas to work. Self-perpetuating restrictive covenants soon found their way into Bloomfield Estates outside Detroit, Highland Park north of Dallas, St. Francis Wood in the heart of San Francisco, and many other high-end subdivisions—plus all their Vestavian imitators—north and south, east and west.

Together, these High-Class Developers made up the brain trust of the

National Association of Real Estate Boards (NAREB), one of the most powerful trade associations in the country. Nichols and the others rotated through the presidency and other high-ranking offices, each gentleman taking his turn. Not by coincidence, in 1924 NAREB made racial discrimination official policy, updating its code of ethics to say, "A Realtor should never be instrumental in introducing into a neighborhood . . . members of any race or nationality . . . whose presence will clearly be detrimental to the property values of that neighborhood. Like termites, they undermine the structure of any neighborhood in which they creep."

All of which was legal.

In 1916, the city of Louisville, Kentucky, had passed a zoning ordinance delineating where blacks could and could not live. In *Buchanan v. Warley*, the NAACP challenged the law, taking their petition all the way to the Supreme Court, which ruled in their favor. The court's opinion cited Louisville's ordinance as a public infringement on private property rights. Ten years later, when the issue of private racial covenants came before the court in the case of *Corrigan v. Buckley*, the justices held that said covenants were legitimate and binding; they represented an arrangement between a private buyer and a private seller, which was not the government's business. The combined effect of these decisions, as pointed out in the *Kansas City Call*, was to say that cities and states could not violate blacks' property rights, but with restrictive covenants, private citizens could unilaterally take those same rights away with nothing but a pen and paper and a trip to the notary public. Soon, thanks to the public-private partnership, the distinction between government policy and corporate policy would cease to matter entirely.

....

The Great Depression nearly killed the residential gold rush. In its first four years, the number of permits issued for new home construction fell by 93 percent nationwide. But out of this crisis came suburbia's great leap forward.

In 1932, as the economic disaster showed no signs of abating, the Hoover administration passed the Federal Home Loan Bank Act. Its goal was to stimulate home building and home buying through government-backed, long-term amortized mortgages,* as well as housing subsidies to stimulate private developers. In 1933, Roosevelt's New Deal extended Hoover's efforts by establishing the Home Owners' Loan Corporation (HOLC), tasked to determine the creditworthiness of home owners the government helped to finance. Roosevelt then chartered the Federal Housing Authority (FHA), whose task was to issue and administer loans and subsidies based on those assessments. And since most politicians aren't experts in land development, they turned to those who were: the National Association of Real Estate Boards and its most prominent representative.

J. C. Nichols was so intimately involved with the formation of the FHA that he was called to consult privately with FDR in the Oval Office. When America's housing policy was drafted, whole chunks were lifted straight out of the Nichols Company handbook, practically word for word. Through the HOLC, the federal government developed a four-tiered classification system for neighborhoods: high-end, all-white neighborhoods were given the highest rating; white working- and middle-class neighborhoods were given a secondary rating; Jewish and ethnically mixed areas were rated third; and the lowest possible rating was given to black neighborhoods—regardless of the quality of the housing stock or the income of the inhabitants. Then the HOLC went through every block on every map of every city in America, giving each neighborhood a color-coded designation. Black neighborhoods were coded red.

The four-tiered rating system devised by the HOLC had been intended as a metric to assess credit risk and therefore assign a proper rate of interest, but black neighborhoods were not simply assigned higher interest rates. They were not assigned anything. In a process that became known as redlining, the FHA cordoned off black neighborhoods and designated them wholly ineligible for federal subsidies and mortgages. According to the federal law of the United States, a black person anywhere was now a threat to property values everywhere. This was a pol-

....

*Prior to this point, there had never been any federal mortgage insurance of any kind, no Fannie Mae or Freddie Mac; without federal backing, new home purchases had required something on the order of 50 percent down just to walk in the door.

icy based on nothing more than the say-so of the men who stood to profit from it.

Once the FHA guidelines were in place, private lending institutions adopted them as their standard, too. So did insurance companies. If the government was unwilling to cover the risk, why should they? Once a neighborhood was redlined, residents found it virtually impossible to get any kind of legitimate mortgage, home owners' insurance, or home improvement loan, even if those instruments weren't federally insured. Inevitably, the legal embargo against fair lending in redlined neighborhoods sped the growth of predatory lending; blacks could get mortgages, but usually at grossly inflated rates and with no consumer protections against fraud.

During the late 1930s and early 1940s, though still hampered by the Depression and World War II rationing, new home construction made a slow and steady return. FDR's New Deal had laid the groundwork for the ultimate public-private partnership: an endless river of construction subsidies and federally backed mortgages, issued with almost no oversight and minimal preconditions. In fact, the only real restriction on FHA monies was that they be used in racially homogenous neighborhoods. The FHA's official underwriting manual explicitly directed its agents to grant subsidies and back mortgages only in areas protected by restrictive covenants. "If a neighborhood is to retain stability," the manual stipulated, "it is necessary that properties shall continue to be occupied by the same racial and social classes. A change in social or racial occupancy generally leads to instability and a reduction in values." In the suburbs, it became completely irrelevant that the government couldn't impose racial zoning laws. Cities no longer planned themselves—corporations did most of the work. Thanks to the FHA, private developers had access to billions of dollars in nearly risk-free capital, which allowed them to buy up vast tracts of land and operate them as they saw fit, with a unilateral say on what could be built and who could live in it.

As the veterans of World War II returned home and the baby boom took off, America's High-Class Developers shifted gears and started cashing in on the surging demand for middle-class housing. The "refinement of the suburban estate" was no longer a luxury for the well-to-do; it was a mass-produced consumer good for everyday use. Developers built two- and three-bedroom starter homes, identical Cape Cods and ranch houses stamped out block after block. America had started to sprawl.

In 1947, the developers of Long Island's Levittown perfected an assembly line technique for home building. FHA subsidies enabled them to clear a bunch of empty potato fields and start plopping down houses at a rate of thirty per day. Outside Los Angeles in 1950, the entire town of Lakewood simply rose up in a matter of months out of an old 3,300-acre lima bean farm. And in Johnson County, Kansas, just adjacent to the million-dollar mansions of Mission Hills, J. C. Nichols opened up Prairie Village, an everyman's Country Club District of modest homes with all the modern conveniences. Nichols even updated his sales pitch for the Cold War generation. "When you rear children in a good neighborhood," he told a reporter from *Time* magazine, "they will go out and fight communism."

After the war, the heroes of Normandy and Okinawa were duly rewarded by their country. The GI Bill gave low-interest, zero-percent-down mortgages to all returning servicemen—a chance to buy a piece of the American Dream. John and Jane Veteran came home from the war and flocked to suburbia, racing to grab their slice of white-picket paradise. At least, that's what America likes to believe about itself. In truth, GI loans were simply FHA loans by another name, subject to the same redlining restrictions. When the whites of the Greatest Generation went looking for a place to call home, it was all but illegal for them to buy a home in a subdivision that didn't exclude blacks. Realtors didn't show white people anything else, because their money wasn't any good anywhere else. Black veterans, on the other hand, could use their housing vouchers only in all-black areas; even with the GI Bill, many were still denied loans.

By 1950, new houses in America were going up at an average rate of four per minute, 75 percent of them in the suburbs, and nearly half of them bought under the GI Bill. By 1960, the population of Levittown had gone from zero to 80,000, all of it white. Lakewood, California, had gone from zero to 67,000, all of it white. And in 1960, Prairie Village, Kansas, was home to just over 50,000 white people. Some form of racial restriction was used in over 50 percent of all subdivisions nationwide. They were so pervasive that when the Supreme Court finally ruled on the matter again, in 1948's *Shelley v. Kraemer*, three of the justices had to recuse themselves because they lived in restricted neighborhoods. So it was by a vote of six to zero that the court finally struck them down.

But the court's narrowly written opinion didn't say that racial covenants couldn't be used, just that they were not enforceable in a court of law—and good luck finding black home owners willing to take that issue to trial in the late 1940s. In the Kansas City metropolitan area, more racial housing covenants were used in the decade after 1948 than in all four decades prior. The last one was written in 1962. The residential color line in suburban Johnson County would not be broken until 1965.

....

In the history of race, slavery and segregation are always called out for what they did to blacks' human and civil rights. Redlining and racial covenants never seem to get the same amount of play, despite the damage they did to blacks' property rights. Slavery and segregation can't be kept out of the history books; they're too big. But the story of real estate is buried in the ground, so it's easier to pretend it never happened. We get to act like all that money out in the suburbs came from nothing but honest, American hard work, and not a big, fat, racist handout from Uncle Sam.

The suburban landgrab of the twentieth century was one of the single greatest engines of wealth creation in human history. It took a country of second- and third-generation white-ethnic immigrants, vaulted them into the middle class, and sent all their kids to college. In 1946, you could buy a brand-new Prairie Village starter home for $6,000. That same home is worth around $375,000 today, which, adjusted for inflation, represents a return of well over 500 percent.

J. C. Nichols died in 1950, but his plan for permanence lives on. His racial covenants are still with us, auto-renewing year after year, like some horrible gym membership we'll never get out of. Illegal and unenforceable, yes, but they can't be stripped out. Not without the unanimous, notarized consent of every single member of every single home owners' association collected and filed five years ahead of the original deed's renewal date. A report by the *Kansas City Star* in 2005 found racial covenants still on the books in more than a dozen Country Club District developments. Acreage-wise, the Country Club District is the largest contiguous parcel of land ever developed by a single company in the history of the United States. As of the mid-1990s, the Nichols Company's assets were valued in excess of $500 million.

For blacks, however, the good times were not nearly so good. Between 1908 and 1948, racial covenants were used to exclude them from 62 percent of all new housing developments in Jackson County, Missouri (home of Kansas City proper). During that same period, racial covenants had excluded them from 96 percent of all new housing developments in Johnson County, Kansas. And between 1934 and 1962, the Federal Housing Authority backed mortgages for more than 77,000 homes in the Kansas City area; less than 1 percent of those loans went to blacks.

And they could have used them. In 1945, a survey showed that 85 percent of housing inhabited by blacks in Kansas City was substandard or borderline uninhabitable. By 1950, the black population of Kansas City had more than doubled once again, to more than 55,000. Eighteenth and Vine was bursting at its seams, yet it had expanded by only a few blocks to the east. There was nowhere for black people to go. Pretty soon, Bob Wood would show up knocking on their door, and he'd make them an offer they couldn't refuse.

[3]

49/63 or Fight

Susan Kurtenbach was still a young girl when the first black family moved to her neighborhood. It was in 1969, or maybe 1970. The Kurtenbachs were a working-class Catholic family. It was Susan, her parents, and her two older brothers, and they lived in the 5100 block of Lydia Avenue in a little tree-lined pocket neighborhood called Troostwood. Troostwood was right on the wrong side of the Berlin Wall of Kansas City, and Lydia Avenue was on the most vulnerable, easternmost frontier. Looking out Susan's backyard, just a block across Paseo, was Norman Rotert's Blue Hills, the neighborhood that was currently "in transition."

At the time, Kansas City had thousands of hardworking black families in need of good housing. The first black family on Susan Kurtenbach's block was not one of them. "They moved onto Paseo," she says, "right behind us, a couple houses up. They would have been unpleasant in any neighborhood. They would throw raw garbage out in the backyard. Back then, this was a place with families, with a lot of children, and the pestilence problem it created was really of concern. They put their old toilet out in the back. The parties they would have and the arguments they would have, the domestic violence and the police being called—that didn't happen in this neighborhood."

That a family such as this would find its way into a place like Troostwood seems unlikely, but they didn't wind up there by accident. That particular family was put in that particular house to scare white people, and the man who put them there was Bob Wood. "It was quite purposeful and quite disturbing," Susan says, "and it was very effective."

Much like Kansas City's more celebrated real estate man, Bob Wood didn't sell houses. Where J. C. Nichols offered the promise of desirable associations, Wood spread the fear of undesirable associations. Nichols built the supply. Wood stoked the demand. One of these men had a standing invitation to the White House, the other lurked in slums and back alleys, but neither could have succeeded without the other.

Between 1950 and 1970, the white population in Kansas City's southeast corridor fell from 126,229 to 33,804. In those same two decades, the black population rose from 41,348 to 102,741. Nineteen census tracts lay in the blockbusted path from Eighteenth and Vine down to Blue Hills. All of them were now over 90 percent black. Bob Wood had run right over Norman Rotert, and now he was coming to Susan Kurtenbach's house. Troostwood would be the next domino to fall.

Only it didn't.

. . . .

Ed and Mary Hood moved to Kansas City in 1969. Ed had been offered a teaching position at the law school of the University of Missouri–Kansas City (UMKC). Both native Iowans, the young couple had spent the late sixties soaking up the spirit of the times, living in New York's downtown bohemia, spending the '67 Summer of Love in San Francisco, and then settling in to raise a family up the coast in Oregon before getting the call from UMKC. Not knowing the Kansas City area at all, they asked the university for some assistance in locating a house.

"The only thing we got back," Mary Hood says, "was this glossy, full-color brochure with the title 'Beautiful Johnson County.' We looked at the map and saw it was way out away from everything and we were like, 'Why would we want to live there?'

"So when we came to town we met with this Realtor. We told her what we liked, and she sat down with a map and literally drew big red lines around whole areas and said, 'Well, you wouldn't want to live here.'

"After a few minutes it dawned on us what she was doing, and finally one of us said, 'No, that *is* where we want to live.'"

With three small children, the Hoods moved into a single-family rental on Rockhill, just west of Troost. Ed could walk to work at the university, their oldest daughter started school at Nelson Elementary just a few blocks away, and they became parishioners at St. Francis Xavier, a Catholic parish located just around the corner at Fifty-second and Troost.

Father Luke Byrne arrived at Xavier in the spring of 1970, and it was clear from the start that something was wrong. A once vibrant church, Xavier was shedding parishioners at an alarming rate; you could almost track it from Sunday to Sunday. Norman Rotert warned Byrne of what was coming his way, and how he had failed to stop it. So Byrne, too, set out to salvage the parish and the neighborhood.

Xavier had a "social action committee." It had been formed after the church's Second Vatican Council with vague intentions of civic involvement, but it wasn't actually engaged in any at the moment. Byrne approached a young, active parishioner who was also a newly arrived UMKC professor, Pat Jesaitis. Like the Hoods, he'd spent the sixties in lefty academic circles—his were at Oberlin and Harvard—and had come to UMKC to teach. "Father Byrne told me they were having problems with shifting neighborhoods, whites selling out of fear," Jesaitis says, "and asked if I would pull the committee together to investigate it." The young professor agreed and reached out to the Xavier people he knew, most significantly the Hoods and Father Jim Bluemeyer, a dean at Rockhurst, a Jesuit university abutting UMKC that was loosely affiliated with Xavier. "I didn't know anything about redlining or blockbusting," Jesaitis admits, "but I was good at running meetings."

A charismatic leader who pulled people together and got them motivated, Jesaitis corralled his team of parishioners into their first meeting in Rockhurst's library basement in October of 1970. Very quickly everyone agreed that the transition wasn't really a parish problem; it was a neighborhood problem. Actually, it was a multineighborhood problem, as the parish stretched over areas like Troostwood and Troost Plateau to the east of Troost, and Crestwood and Rockhill Ridge to the west. To be effective, any solution they created would have to cover the whole area. It would have to hold both sides of Troost together.

By the very next meeting, the group had evolved into the 49/63 Neighborhood Coalition, drawing its boundaries from Oak to Paseo on the east-west axis, and from Forty-ninth Street to Sixty-third Street north to south, an area of approximately 10,000 residents in 3,200 homes: 77 percent white, 20 percent black, and 3 percent everyone else. Ed Hood volunteered to draw up the incorporation papers. The group's first formal meeting was held on February 3, 1971. Its stated mission was to "create a nonexploitative real estate market" and to "sustain a multiracial neighborhood where people, regardless of race or color, can find satisfying conditions." What that actually meant, nobody had a clue. They were making it up as they went along, and the whole seemingly impossible enterprise was straddling the Berlin Wall of Kansas City.

Many neighborhoods east of Troost had tried and failed to arrest the blockbusting, largely because the working-class families who lived there lacked the skills to do anything effective. But when Bob Wood ran up against 49/63, he was wrestling with a bunch of young, passionate left-wingers determined to fight the good fight. These weren't your tune in, turn on kind of hippies, either. They were property tax attorneys, PhDs, business owners. "We were out to save the world," Mary Hood recalls with some nostalgia. But they weren't really out to save the world, just their homes.

Once the coalition was established, it attracted residents from day one, people like Gene and Mary Livingston, white holdouts living east of Troost, and Maureen and Gene Hardy, an interracial couple (he is black; she's white). The coalition started a newsletter. Pat Jesaitis organized block captains. Gene Livingston did the accounting. Father Bluemeyer took the crime and safety committee. In less than a year, the coalition had more than sixty core volunteers. Everyone donated their time, and their monthly budget was however much cash turned up at meetings when they passed the hat.

The Hoods were given the most important assignment of all: heading up the real estate and housing committee. Its first order of business was to stop the panic selling, first by getting rid of the rampant FOR SALE signs. "They were everywhere," Ed says. "We did a survey east of Troost, and there was something like ninety of them."

"The one who stood out was Bob Wood," Mary adds. "He had the most."

In March, the Hoods organized a meeting with all the real estate agents working in the neighborhood. A lot of screaming and yelling ensued, followed by more meetings of the same. Finally, in June, the coalition got six agents to agree to a three-month moratorium on all yard signs and unwanted solicitations. That October, the agreement was extended indefinitely. In March of 1972, the coalition started its own housing office. Through word of mouth, it quickly became the first resource residents turned to in order to sell or rent their homes. Realtors who'd agreed to stop blockbusting were allowed to list their properties through 49/63, and thus were among the first in line for the legitimate home transactions that occurred. "We appealed to their bottom line," Mary says. "They would make more money if property values stayed up. 'Work with us, and you might do better in the long run.'"

While the yard signs were easy to root out, the late-night solicitations were harder to stop. It fell to the block captains to educate everyone, house by house, and encourage them to report any unwanted threats. The housing office staff took the complaints as they came in, and the offending brokers were contacted and urged to halt such practices in the area. For residents most susceptible to scare tactics, like the elderly, the coalition took another tack. "We had a woman who called," Ed recalls, "and she was all upset because a guy had come through saying, 'Listen, I'll give you five thousand cash right now, but if you wait you'll only get two.' Well, the market value of the house was eleven. She was an elderly white woman, and she was scared to death. So the coalition took out two mortgages for the full value of the house, bought it, and then rented it to a younger white family that was willing to stay." As 49/63's budget increased with donations and grant money, it started financing other homes in the same manner. The panic began to subside.

....

Having shut down the predatory speculators, the 49/63 Coalition now turned its attention to the next greatest threat to the neighborhood's housing: the 1968 Fair Housing Act.

In Washington, D.C., the issue of fair housing was radioactive. In 1962, President Kennedy had issued an executive order that "banned" discrimination in publicly subsidized housing, then never lifted a finger to enforce it. President Johnson had worked tirelessly to pass the civil rights and voting rights laws of 1964 and 1965, but as both bills moved through Congress, any measures that dealt with housing or mortgage discrimination were deliberately stripped out. That was the price of getting them through. Critical to the passage of any civil rights legislation was a coalition of Northern Democrats and moderate Republicans, all of whom took the moral high ground on racism alongside Martin Luther King, but only so long as the preacher's crusade remained fixed on the ignorant crackers of the Deep South. Black people were fine, just not in their voting districts. Once King started making noise in the North, marching in the white Bungalow Belt neighborhoods of Chicago to call for fair housing, those same politicians went running for cover. Starting in the congressional elections of 1966, Republicans, in particular, had begun to bank their entire electoral strategy on securing the emerging white majority that lived in the suburbs.*

For his entire presidency, LBJ had failed to pass any kind of fair housing law. Then, on April 4, 1968, while leading a sanitation workers' strike in Memphis, Tennessee, Martin Luther King was assassinated. Riots broke out in over a hundred cities nationwide, and that crisis gave the president one last ounce of leverage to shove a housing bill through Congress. On April 11, Lyndon Johnson signed the Fair Housing Act into law. It contained specific injunctions against blockbusting and redlining; outlawed the use, or even the implication, of racial bias in advertising for property sales; made it illegal for a broker to engage in "steering" (i.e., making false statements about unit availability to steer black residents in

....

*In 1966 and 1968, with the Democrats now owning the incendiary issue of race, the Party of Lincoln would reach back and copy verbatim the race-baiting playbook that had been used against it in Kansas City in 1908. "Every man's home is his castle. Keep it that way. Vote Republican."

one direction or another); and made it unlawful to not rent or sell property on the basis of color. Once again, however, there was a price to getting it passed: Republicans had attached so many amendments stripping away the bill's enforcement mechanisms that it was rendered practically worthless.

Under the Fair Housing Act, the Department of Housing and Urban Development (HUD) had no power to investigate violators, and no authority to issue cease and desist orders. HUD could only pursue grievances brought by individual complainants, the statute of limitations on which was 180 days from the date of the alleged offense. HUD also had no authority to impose penalties; it could only refer a matter to the Justice Department for prosecution. In the case of a successful prosecution, punitive damages were capped at one thousand dollars. And the Justice Department was not allowed to take a case if the state where the offense occurred possessed a "substantially equivalent" fair housing law. So if a state had already enacted meaningless housing legislation of its own, the local government's authority to do nothing superseded the federal government's authority to do nothing. And so it was in Kansas City. After King's murder, citing fear of ongoing unrest, the city council passed a hasty resolution saying, essentially, that the municipal housing authority agreed to abide by the regulations of the national Fair Housing Act. Washington had passed a law that did nothing, and Kansas City agreed to follow it.

Although most parts of the Fair Housing Act did nothing, one part did do something, and did it horribly, horribly wrong. In an effort to remedy the drought of mortgage credit in black neighborhoods, under Section 235 of the act, the FHA was now required to guarantee any mortgage to any person in any neighborhood, with no regard for creditworthiness whatsoever. If the home owner defaulted, the government would insure the lender for all but 1 percent of the interest on the loan. If redlining a neighborhood was bad, some genius decided, the inverse of that must be good. The solution to the drought was a flood.

Denying someone a mortgage is unjust. Saddling him with a mortgage he can't afford is worse, and that's precisely what Section 235 loans did. Up to 1968, the pace of blockbusting had been held to the speed with which brokers could find black applicants who at least had a down payment and maybe a first month's note. Now, no credit? No problem. The federal government had given Bob Wood an unlimited pool of unregulated, risk-free capital.

An ambitious speculator might pick up a row of distressed properties at, say, $4,000 a piece, put $500 worth of cosmetic fixes into each, and then turn around and sell them to black families at $14,000 a piece. In extreme cases, some black owners moved in only to discover they'd purchased a home that had already been condemned. By the time blacks either defaulted on or abandoned these worthless properties, the brokers were long gone with their commissions, and whoever was holding the mortgage note (either the bank or often the broker himself) walked away with a reimbursement check from the FHA for the full value of the property. Blockbusting was suddenly more profitable than ever.

And because 235 loans allowed brokers to scrape the bottom of the socioeconomic barrel, they could go into the ghetto and come back to white neighborhoods with prospects (like Susan Kurtenbach's new neighbors) who fulfilled all the worst stereotypes that white people already believed. Very soon, in places like Blue Hills, every black family that moved in was assumed to be "a 235er," a harbinger of the urban blight that was sure to follow. And urban blight did follow, more often than not—not because of black people, but because blockbusters and school boards were tearing the social fabric of these communities to shreds. Federal housing policy was practically designed to create urban blight. Once a 235-financed house was foreclosed on and repossessed by the government, HUD guidelines mandated that the property remain vacant until the government decided what to do with it, a process that could take months or years. Abandoned homes began cropping up all over formerly vibrant communities. They quickly went to seed, attracting vagrancy and crime. Once a neighborhood began that slide, the rest was self-fulfilling. A study that later came out of Congress would describe the 235 program as a recipe for "instant slums."

By the fall of 1972, Section 235 loans had infested Blue Hills top to bottom. In Troostwood and Troost Plateau, more than fifty homes had already been sold under the program, with a foreclosure rate that was 20 percent and climbing. The 49/63 Coalition joined with Blue Hills and other neighborhood associations, and together they sued the city and federal housing authorities in an effort to shut the program down. That lawsuit was quickly rendered moot, however, as the 235 program proved to be so disastrous on a national scale that Washington pulled the plug on it anyway.* Lending in black neighborhoods dried up again. The drought returned, leaving these new "instant slums" without the financing they needed to reverse the decline that blockbusting had begun.

By the early seventies, America's inner cities had been gutted. In Kansas City, practically everything east of Troost was circling the drain—except for 49/63. In February 1973, after two years of sustained effort, the coalition newsletter reported that virtually all blockbusting activities in the neighborhood had ceased. More than thirty real estate agents had agreed to abide by the neighborhood's fair-business regulations, and the number of FOR SALE signs east of Troost had dropped from ninety to fourteen. One of the most enthusiastic of these cooperators was Bob Wood. The man wasn't stupid. If blockbusting no longer produced a profit, he wasn't going to do it. So he changed his business model. He became a slumlord.

"During that time," Gene Hardy says, "nearly every house that somebody moved out of east of Troost, Bob Wood went in and bought it. He wound up owning so many houses that when blacks did move in, he could charge them whatever rent he wanted and they'd pay it just to be there."

Everything east of Troost had become prime territory for absentee landlords. A survey conducted by the coalition in the summer of 1972 found fifty abandoned properties on the eastern side of the neighborhood. So a new committee was formed and sent out to document every vacant property's code violations, which were then reported to the hous-

....

*In January of 1973, citing the rampant corruption in the 235 program and problems with HUD policy in general, President Nixon announced a moratorium on any and all federally subsidized housing efforts for the next eighteen months in order to "reevaluate the program's effectiveness"—a handy excuse to neutralize any attempts to push integrated public housing into the suburbs.

ing authority. Faced with the cost of bringing those houses up to code, the owners of most of them agreed to sell and move on. Responsible tenants were found through the coalition's listing service. Then, in October of 1973, the coalition petitioned the city to pass a zoning ordinance that would keep houses in 49/63 zoned as single-family residences. With that policy in place, homes couldn't be chopped up into efficiency units, and the slumlord trade got a lot less lucrative. The vigilance of the coalition made it harder and harder for real estate agents to do anything other than fair and legitimate business.

The final piece of the puzzle was the mortgage issue. Despite being "banned" by the Fair Housing Act, redlining was still standard practice because it couldn't be effectively prosecuted; a single rejected loan application wasn't proof of discrimination, as any number of factors could lead to an individual's being turned down.* Redlining, as most people understand it, is a byword for discrimination against blacks—and that was certainly the net effect in most cases. But much of the historical data actually shows a U-shaped pattern: high loan availability for whites on one side, lower availability for blacks on the other, but with the lowest availability coming in the middle, in transitional neighborhoods. Mortgage redlining hurt low-income blacks looking to buy in. Insurance redlining hurt existing white residents, who found their rates inexplicably jacked up. In fact, many of the middle-class whites who wound up in 49/63 initially came to the group because they'd been turned down for home owners' insurance once black neighbors moved in. White families with good credit who wanted to move into Kansas City had their mortgage applications denied; like the Hoods, they were told to try Johnson County.

The FHA had yoked urban neighborhoods from one extreme to the other, either withholding credit or opening a floodgate of it. But one idea had actually never been tried: fair credit for qualified applicants. So

....

*Widespread loan discrimination couldn't even be documented, much less litigated, until the passage of the Home Mortgage Disclosure Act (HMDA) in 1975, which compelled banks to disclose where and to whom they were making loans. Once that information became available, the *Kansas City Star* reported that $642 million in home mortgages were written in the metropolitan area in 1977, less than 1 percent of which was issued east of Troost.

crazy, it just might work. The 49/63 Coalition got the opportunity to try it in April of 1974 with the arrival of Neighborhood Housing Services (NHS), which had started out as a pilot program in Pittsburgh; its founders came to 49/63 seeking a candidate for expansion. NHS was "a local, not-for-profit organization advocating affordable housing, safe living environments, and community revitalization through a variety of federal, state, and local resources." Roughly translated, NHS was George Bailey's Building and Loan Association from the fictional Bedford Falls of Frank Capra's *It's a Wonderful Life*; it provided low-interest, nondiscriminatory mortgage credit to the low-income and black applicants shut out by redlining.

Neighborhood Housing Services even had its own George Bailey: Joe Beckerman. Beckerman had moved to Kansas City from southern Missouri in 1972 to go to law school, and one of his professors, Ed Hood, roped him into serving on 49/63's code violations committee, which eventually led to a job as president of NHS. Tall and lanky with an aw-shucks demeanor, Beckerman even has a Jimmy Stewart kind of way about him. (And for what it's worth, J. C. Nichols looked a lot like Old Man Potter.)

"Neighborhood Housing Services is a partnership of all the people in that demographic area," Beckerman explains. "It's residents, city government, and all the businesses you can get. You bring those three diverse groups together and say, 'Hey, we all have a vested interest here.'" By appealing to that vested interest, NHS raised a pool of operating capital from local businesses and lending institutions, and then assumed the risk of issuing mortgage loans. "We could do anything we wanted with our loans," Beckerman says, "as long as it made sense."

What made sense was to jettison the racist redlining standards and start lending in ways that didn't further destabilize the urban infrastructure. Instead of investing only in "safe" neighborhoods, NHS used capital to make neighborhoods safe to invest in. Low-income prospects willing to take on a fixer-upper could get a flexible, minimal-interest mortgage, part of which could be worked off with sweat equity. Paint your house or resod your lawn, and the appraised value of the capital improvement went to pay down the principal of your original loan. If you hit a rough patch, you went down and talked to Joe Beckerman and he'd work with you on it, person-to-person, to find a solution. Helping you stay and improve your home's value enhanced the value of the house next door and so on down the block, which only brought more business to the area. "Basically, it's the perfect program," Beckerman says, "and that's why it's still around today."

Neighborhood Housing Services worked because it wasn't a bank. Its goal wasn't to maximize the profit on each transaction, but to ensure the viability of the neighborhood, thus lowering the area's overall risk and, ultimately, generating sustainable revenue. In its first year, NHS issued forty-six mortgage loans totaling $246,299, loans that would have been rejected by FHA standards as "high risk." Nonetheless, coalition records show that after two years only five of those loans were thirty days in arrears. No resident was more than sixty days in arrears, and not a single NHS mortgage had resulted in foreclosure. Those same records show that in 1976 the average price of a three-bedroom home east of Troost was around $12,200. Since "the blacks" had moved in, property values had either held or gone up.

"It was so simple," Beckerman says.

....

In the years that followed, 49/63 thrived. While banks were disinvesting from the city as fast as they could, the NHS program was so successful lending east of Troost that its operations soon expanded up to Thirty-ninth Street, and would later expand again. Through lobbying the city, the coalition had secured $60,000 to create a neighborhood park and over $800,000 for infrastructure improvements to curbs, streetlights, and sidewalks. More than five hundred delinquent properties were brought up to code, representing a private capital investment of over $680,000 in the neighborhood (about $2.3 million in today's dollars). The results of this homegrown, seat-of-the-pants experiment took down every single myth on which white flight was based, including the big one. In 1976, the local police precinct reported that crime in the neighborhood, by every index, had gone down.

Gene Hardy still shakes his head about the fears of black crime. "Everyone was saying, 'The blacks are coming in! You're gonna have crime!' Hell, we had less crime in that neighborhood than anywhere else in the city. We didn't lock our doors. Never had any problems as an interracial couple, either. We'd walk down the street, and everybody knew everybody."

If the archives of 49/63's newsletter serve as any kind of barometer, by mid-decade the sense of fear and panic had widely subsided. The bold-type headlines on redlining and abandoned properties fell back to page three, and the front-page features focused on neighborhood arts festivals and Fourth of July barbecue tips. Expanding from its original goal of residential real estate protection, 49/63 launched an after-school tutoring program, a summer recreation program, and a Business Renewal and Redevelopment Corporation to maintain the commercial district on Troost. While the north end of the avenue had been long deserted, the stretch in 49/63 still had two grocery stores, a few drugstores, several college bars, a bowling alley, and a brand-new, black-owned Buick dealership.

In terms of policy, nothing 49/63 did was all that revolutionary. The only thing that set it apart was the willingness to do it. Coalition members made 49/63 their lives, putting in twenty to thirty hours a week, on top of their regular jobs and family duties. It was a grind. "But it was fun," Ed Hood insists. "I liked it." Rallying around the neighborhood had galvanized the group, created a real sense of community that spilled over from council meetings to late-night dinners or drinks at Mike's Tavern, one of the local bars down on Troost. It was the opposite of the neighborhood associations in the Country Club District, which weren't really "neighborhood" associations at all. Those were more like corporate subcommittees, established by J. C. Nichols to maintain the artificial stasis of race and class that would inflate his company's land values. The 49/63 Coalition was everything that a J. C. Nichols subdivision was not. Yet it offered in reality what Nichols had sold as fantasy: a community that fostered strong moral character and desirable associations.

"The biggest thing we did," Gene Hardy says, "was prove to the rest of the city that you could have black and white living in the same neighborhood and it didn't go to pot. We had a ten-year stretch where it was the finest neighborhood there was."

"And we made a lot of friends," Maureen Hardy adds.

There was only one hitch to the whole 49/63 integration experiment: nobody made any black friends.

Turf

Despite being the leading proponent of residential integration in Kansas City, 49/63 itself was white, almost entirely white. Father Jim Bluemeyer remembers exactly what happened when the group first tried to move beyond that. "When we started," he says, "we brought in some black people, good people, and they just thought we were crazy. They said, 'This won't work. Integrated neighborhood? You're dreaming.'"

Even as the coalition ramped up, black residents opted out. The few who did participate did so sparingly, and rarely for very long. "We didn't have a lot," Ed Hood says, "and it was very difficult to get them involved."

"I doubt if we had six," Gene Hardy says of the group's black volunteers, including himself. Most of the time, he was the only one there. "Blacks chose not to participate," he says. "A lot of it was a lack of education and a lack of understanding. Maureen was on the board, but I worked fifteen hours a day, and then I took the time at night and went to the meetings. It's a sacrifice to do something like that."

"There was a big difference in socioeconomic scale," Ed Hood says. "Most of the coalition people were university people, and a lot of the African Americans coming in were on those 235 loans; they were coming out of the projects. Bridging that gap was problematic."

Helen Palmer moved her family onto Virginia Avenue in Troost Plateau in 1963. She was one of the black residents in the area and is still there today. "The woman I bought this house from," Palmer says, "she was the type of person who would never let a black person inside. If she had to let a black person come in to do any kind of work for her, she would have to have another white person in here with her while the black person came in here and did the work. When blacks moved in, she moved out. Myself, I wasn't afraid that it was all white. It was prejudiced, but I never had any harassment."

Nor did she have any involvement, mostly because she was never around. The university professors and stay-at-home moms who formed the backbone of the coalition had a good deal more free time. Helen Palmer, like many blacks working two and three jobs to be "middle class," did not. "At the time I moved in here," she says, "I was working twelve hours a day, seven days a week at a printing shop. Did that for forty-two years. I would come home, have a little sleep, and get back to work. Never really had a day off, so I didn't hear much about 49/63."

But the problem went deeper than conflicting schedules. As reported in coalition meeting minutes and status reports, the group's lopsided racial makeup was a persistent and troubling concern. "We tried to find blacks who were willing to help out," Pat Jesaitis says. "We found a couple. We had one guy from Chicago, this other black woman, Gene Hardy. When we had meetings on individual blocks, you'd get black families there, but that was a very slow process. And then they'd never come to the monthly planning meetings or really participate.

"As the president, when a black family moved in, I'd go knock on their door to talk to them, welcome them, but my impression of it was that there was too much fear, too much 'I don't know if I believe this guy.' We were just getting started, and they couldn't see enough concrete evidence that we were with them, not trying to keep them out. There seemed to be a lot of mistrust." It was more than mistrust.

"49/63 was called racist," says Alvin Brooks.

Alvin Brooks joined the Kansas City Police Department as a patrolman in the early 1950s, one of only a handful of blacks on the force. Today, his career in public service is now entering its seventh decade, and he shows no sign of slowing down. Brooks has been elected to the city council, served for a period as mayor pro tem, and was most recently appointed to the police department's board of commissioners. In the late 1960s, Brooks was serving as director of Kansas City's Department of Human Relations—a vague title that translates roughly to "The Guy Who Handles the Racial Stuff." Not too long after Pat Jesaitis started knocking on doors, Brooks started hearing talk about a group of white people calling themselves 49/63.

"I attended some of the meetings," Brooks recalls, "and you'd hear some very strange, but very familiar, voices from the whites. There was this whole plan of restricting how people could move in. You'd hear about 'stabilizing the community.' Stabilizing? What does that mean? It means keeping it as it is. Blacks had started to come in, and this group was worried about being overrun by blacks, so they were suspect. Integration? All of a sudden white folks *wanted* us to do this? There were some who heard these things and questioned why. Why now? We'd been duped before."

....

The 49/63 Coalition wasn't the only group of well-meaning white folks left standing at the integration altar. At the height of the fair housing movement in Chicago, a group called Home Opportunities Made Equal (HOME) sent direct-response mailers to some eight hundred black organizations, advertising housing opportunities for black families in the suburbs. It received zero replies. In Los Angeles in the mid-seventies, community leaders in the sprawl of the San Fernando Valley thought they'd evade the government's school desegregation dragnet by making their own racial balance, reaching out and encouraging upwardly mobile blacks to move to the area. Through the San Fernando Valley Fair Housing Council, a $92,000 public awareness campaign was launched across local black radio and newspapers, urging city residents, "Move on into the Valley!" The council fielded only a hundred queries from black families. Of those, seven bought homes.

For black America, the right to live wherever they wanted was a moral imperative. The reality of trying to exercise that right had bred a mistrust that bordered on fatalism. For years, blacks who set foot in certain working-class white neighborhoods were often beaten or harassed.

Those who tried to buy had bricks hurled through their windows, their front porches burned. Blacks who made it out to middle-class suburbia endured a more refined and WASPy version of the same—indignant housewives with picket signs and a steady drumbeat of neighborly reminders that "maybe you'd just be more comfortable someplace else." As early as 1926, the publisher of the *Kansas City Call* had written, "It is time wasted to try to prove to whites that they should not refuse to live as neighbors to Negroes."*

Alvin Brooks has spent almost his entire life policing the residential color line of Kansas City's turf war. As a cop in the 1950s, the color line determined where he and other black cops could patrol: first the black neighborhood, then only low-end pockets of immigrants, never the middle-class whites. In 1960, he and his wife rode the first wave of block-busting, buying a house not far from Walt Disney's boyhood home. Only the fifth black family on the block, they were able to finance a mortgage without going through a bank. "I was a cop at the time making $560 a month," he says. "My white counterparts could qualify, and although my credit was good and I had a steady job, if I had gone to a bank we would have had trouble. I would have had to put a lot of money down. We were lucky." Many of his neighbors weren't. Once optimistic about buying their stake in the American Dream, black home owners quickly grew frustrated as the blockbusting con played itself out. "Realtors were pretty slick. Black families were paying higher interest rates, getting sold these balloon mortgages. People got took. Integration wasn't kind to those who it was supposed to be kind to."

Once Alvin Brooks overcame his initial doubts about 49/63, he came to see it as a good working model for other neighborhood groups in the city. But he also had a front-row seat to see the ways in which "integration" failed to be kind, as the government simultaneously did too much and not enough. Brooks watched as the north end of Eighteenth and Vine was plowed under to make way for the Wayne Miner Homes, five vertical towers of ultramodern public housing. Billed as the salvation of the

....

*The black newspaper's official stance at the time was not to fight racial covenants, but to expand Eighteenth and Vine to the east and improve the all-black neighborhood from within.

urban poor, it turned into a vertical slum instead. Brooks was there when HUD opened up the money spigot of housing vouchers for low-income families while providing no safeguards against the systemic discrimination in how they were used—in effect further subsidizing residential segregation. "A few blacks ventured out into white neighborhoods with those Section 8 vouchers," he says, "and they were fought. So most of it went back into the black community. Absentee landlords would fix up the house to Section 8 qualifications and rent it out because they knew it was good income. HUD was as guilty of perpetuating segregation as anyone."

Well before the 1960s stumbled to a close, faith in Martin Luther King's idealistic, integrationist crusade had waned. Black frustration boiled over in the urban riots of Watts and Newark and Detroit. That frustration found a symbol and a voice when the young Stokely Carmichael raised his fist and issued a rallying cry of "Black Power!" during a Mississippi march in the summer of 1966. Integration, Carmichael and his coauthor Charles Hamilton wrote in their seminal *Black Power* manifesto, was simply an "insidious subterfuge for the maintenance of white supremacy." It was a kind of cultural genocide, forcing blacks to assimilate—to "give up their identity" and "deny their heritage" in a servile, slavish imitation of white society—and all for naught as well. The white establishment, immune to appeals of conscience, was eternally racist, entirely dependent on exploiting the black underclass, and would never accept blacks as equals. "Before a group can enter the open society, it must first close ranks," went *Black Power*'s central thesis, comparing blacks to Jews and Italians, groups that had thrived in America through ethnic loyalty and solidarity. "Black people must lead and run their own organizations . . . consolidate behind their own, so that they can bargain from a position of strength."

This defiant, self-reliant streak of black nationalism had been present all along, from Marcus Garvey's Back to Africa movement to Malcolm X's Nation of Islam. Now, with white America so clearly acting in bad faith, assertive calls for solidarity and self-empowerment struck a chord with many in the black community, especially the young. But at the same time, the power of King's vision of a color-blind society proved enduring as well; it wasn't so easily dismissed. In truth, the majority of black Americans at the time were not so committed one way or the other. They didn't want an ideology. They wanted jobs, housing, fair treatment under the law, opportunities for their children—they were going to throw in their lot with whoever or whatever delivered results. If integrated labor unions provided better wages, great. If integrated schools treated black principals like janitors, thanks but we'll pass. According to one *Ebony* magazine poll in 1973, only 7 percent of blacks considered themselves "radicals" in the paramilitary Black Panther mold. A good 47 percent still wanted "traditional integration," but a majority, close to 60 percent, also believed that some forms of separatism and solidarity were necessary to bolster the race and provide material progress. Strung between the poles of integration and separation, black America found itself in the very awkward position of needing both.

....

In Kansas City, black citizens closed ranks through a coalition called Freedom, Inc. Originally a grassroots activist group, as the civil rights movement shifted from marching in the streets to working in city hall, Freedom, Inc. evolved into an urban political machine. "It became a real force to reckon with in the sixties, seventies, and eighties," says Brooks, who has enjoyed the coalition's backing in his runs for elected office. "They were able to negotiate, to get the first blacks elected to the city council."

The group has racked up a long list of African-American "firsts" in Kansas City: the first black city council members in 1962, the first black school board member in 1970, the first black mayor, Emanuel Cleaver, in the 1990s. The group has engineered more than a few electoral victories at the state and federal level as well. But like many all-black organizations, Freedom, Inc. was caught in the paradox of the moment. Even as the group lobbied for fair housing, school desegregation, and all the rest of it, the group's power was rooted in maintaining a solid, majority-black voting bloc, which meant keeping black people right where they were.

Black Power began with the premise that the community needed to control its own turf. In its more radical and fantastical conceptions, this idea manifested itself in calls to break off part of the continental United States and form a Republic of New Africa. At the more practical end of the spectrum, urban leaders simply called for rejecting the obtuse white paternalism that had botched all the school and housing issues in the first place. Black America's needs were such that only black America knew how to fix them. In urban communities across the country, black-run organizations sprang up, advocating for a community-based nationalism: black consumers shopping in black business districts with black dollars. Through collective action they would police their own neighborhoods, teach their own school curriculum, organize tenants to lobby for better living conditions—control their own destiny in every regard. Given the aims that racial solidarity intended to achieve, any notion of integrated housing was anathema. Blacks should have the right to live anywhere, of course, but given that right, it was still politically and culturally advantageous to stick together. Integration meant dispersal, being dissolved into white America, destroying the black community as they knew it.

The idea that black America should control its own turf fell apart, unfortunately, when faced with an inconvenient truth: black people didn't have enough turf. In 1970, black families held just 3.5 percent of the total housing equity in the country, and their holdings in commercial real estate were far less than that. In the great American game of Monopoly, Black Power essentially told white people we could keep all our hotels on Broadway and Park Place because blacks were going to take back Baltic and Mediterranean, and that would show everybody. But as one open-housing advocate pointed out, "If there were any relationship between blacks per square foot and power enjoyed, ghetto people would be the most powerful people in the world."

If black America wanted to assert control over black turf, it would have to surrender the fight over how business was done on the white turf, which was pretty much all of the turf. That was the devil's deal that black politicians and community groups had to make, and that's the deal Freedom, Inc. made in Kansas City, Missouri. "It was the same as in Detroit or Birmingham or other cities where blacks were either in the majority or near the majority," Brooks explains. "People were saying the only way to hold this stronghold was to let white folks run and flee—it was pretty much said without saying it. If it had not been for that, Freedom, Inc. would not have been as strong as it was."

Behind its long list of successfully elected officials, Freedom, Inc.'s official bio boasts of having built strong coalitions in Kansas City's second, third, seventh, fourteenth, fifteenth, sixteenth, seventeenth, eighteenth, and nineteenth voting wards. This is touted as a sign of strength, but if you take a ruler to a map of those districts and draw a straight line north to south along their western boundaries, you'll find that it runs right down the middle of Troost Avenue. Black solidarity required not only accepting the Berlin Wall but reinforcing it from the inside.

Over on the white turf, largely unchallenged, housing discrimination just kept right on. With opposition-free, white Republican majorities, the suburbs of Johnson County voted to cordon themselves off from "undesirable" residents in ways that weren't explicitly discriminatory: jacking up property taxes, opting out of public transit systems, restricting their zoning codes to prohibitively expensive homes, etc. Redlining by banks and racial steering by brokers lived on well into the eighties and nineties (and they continue in more subtle forms right up to the present). In those rare cases where suburban developers were legally compelled to create mixed-race or low-income housing, it was generally clustered, "warehoused," shunted off to some part of the county where there was no chance it would spoil the view from the eighteenth fairway. Back in Kansas City proper, with so little done to stem the tide of white flight, property values cratered. In the 1980s, the Nichols Company and other developers went on a buying spree, scooping up land that buffered the Plaza and the Country Club District. Whole neighborhoods were bought for pennies on the dollar, then leveled to make way for high-end condos, office towers, and luxury hotels. Meanwhile, the black side of town remained the black side of town. The only time white people had to think about east of Troost was to remind themselves not to go there.

....

Gene Hardy was quite right about the 49/63 Coalition: the biggest thing they accomplished was proving that "you could have black and white living in the same neighborhood and it didn't go to pot." Which sounds good, but "not going to pot" is pretty much the baseline of what should be expected from a functional human society.

Blacks and whites in 49/63 shared the same zip code but they didn't share much else; it would be a stretch to call them "neighbors" in the true sense of the word. White social life oriented west, toward the university. Black social life oriented east and north, to the churches and clubs that had always sustained the black community. The races coexisted; they did not coalesce. And even though the left-wing intellectuals were running 49/63, not every white person on the block was nearly so progressive. There were more than a few Archie Bunkers still hanging around.

Blacks who resisted integration were not being unreasonable. Where exactly was the average black person in Kansas City supposed to go to integrate himself when the only successfully integrated neighborhood in town was not, in fact, an integrated neighborhood? Back when he was The Guy Who Handled the Racial Stuff, Alvin Brooks found no shortage of racial stuff to deal with in 49/63. "They had problems," he says. White folks were still testy, still beefing over turf. It was generally some trivial matter, too, the kind of thing normal neighbors could have settled with a talk across the fence. "You'd have older white neighbors without any kids," Brooks says, "and you'd have a young black couple in their thirties with a couple of kids and their bicycles and tricycles, the dog pissing and crapping in the white person's yard. And I was the one who got the complaints. I had a feeling in many cases there was an underlying reason of race; it was race in terms of what they made it. It was inevitable. I think there were whites who were afraid of being called nigger lovers, blacks who were fearful of being called Uncle Toms for aiding and abetting the whites. It was a trying experience for both to try and deal with that— damned if you do, damned if you don't."

In the end, most people didn't. Ed Hood spent years at the center of one of the most carefully and conscientiously integrated neighborhoods in the country. Today he can sum up a decade's worth of social interaction between blacks and whites in a single word: "Limited."

But that was the parents. Their children tell a different story.

Despite enduring the worst of the blockbusting on the area's eastern frontier, Susan Kurtenbach's family had stayed on Lydia Avenue. Most of her neighbors were black. "I remember right next door to me there was a girl maybe a year younger than me," Susan says. "I used to love going over to her house. It was the first black family on the block that had kids. The music, the life there. I was just in awe. It always smelled wonderful, just a little different than our house, and I was always welcome because I was their daughter's little friend.

"Our parents didn't socialize. I don't remember the grown-ups ever having dinner at each other's houses or that type of thing, but the kids would play together without any problem. I remember going to a birthday party where everyone was dancing, and thinking, Wow, this is *so cool*. This doesn't happen at my birthday parties. I think we really liked exploring some of the differences."

From the other side of the color line, Helen Palmer reports the same. She might not have been involved in the neighborhood, but "my kids got along fine with everybody," she says, "and today they all have more white friends than they do black."

In those years, 49/63 had two elementary schools, Nelson and Troost. Located in the southeast corner of the neighborhood, Troost had taken the brunt of the blockbusting. Plus its boundaries stretched east of Paseo, so it had flipped from 5 percent black in 1969 to 72 percent black in 1973. By the end of the decade it had maybe a few token whites. By contrast, Nelson served the area of the community where housing had stabilized the most. Nelson's classes averaged between 20 and 30 percent black, but the school wasn't just racially balanced. It was integrated. It had a black principal, Yvonne Wilson, and black and white parents serving together on the PTA. Pat Jesaitis's daughter, Colleen, went to Nelson, and, to her memory, everyone got along swell. It was all very mixed. Most of the black kids still lived east of Troost, she says, and they would play together on either side without any understanding of what that meant. The only thing she recalls being a point of racial contention was whether you wanted an Osmonds poster or a Jackson 5 poster for your bedroom. "I had the Jacksons," Colleen says.

The 49/63 area was hardly a model of racial harmony. What its home owners achieved, on their best day, was a wary, arm's-length cease-fire.

But what they created was a place where children maybe, possibly, had a chance to shed the racial baggage of their fathers. To the kids who grew up here, all you needed to get across the Berlin Wall was a bicycle. A world of mixed-race peers was perfectly normal. Very few children in Kansas City had that chance. Every "racially balanced" public school in the city had been artificially engineered by court-ordered busing. Pandas in captivity, every single one. Except at Nelson. There, all the kids felt that this was their school because all the kids, black and white, walked to school. Through years of dedicated effort, 49/63 had created the only residentially integrated school in the entire district.

Then the city shut it down.

....

Once school busing moved from the small towns of the South to the major metropolitan areas of the North, it stopped making sense. The Supreme Court's mandate for America's schools was to eliminate the last vestiges of state-sponsored segregation "root and branch." But the root of the school problem was always the housing problem. Since nothing was done to fix the housing problem, by the time school desegregation plans became law, everybody was already running for the exits. Trying to corral the suburban stampede with a bunch of school buses was like herding cats. Actually, it was worse than herding cats. It was herding white people, earth's only species with a greater sense of entitlement than a cat.

Though legally required, busing was logistically impossible, especially since so many whites had already fled. For Detroit to have met the standard of racial balance set by HEW in the late 1960s, it would have had to expand its bus fleet by 295 new vehicles at a cost of over $12,000 each in order to move 310,000 children across 53 independent school districts at a hard cost of $25 per student per month—at a time when the Detroit school system was already several million dollars in debt. The city of Los Angeles, to meet its court-ordered desegregation remedy, would have had to redistribute 60,000 students across a school district that covered 710 square miles.

To comply with HEW's mandates, Kansas City had adopted its first desegregation plan in 1969. By the mid-1970s, the district's enrollment had already fallen by a third, from 75,000 pupils to less than 50,000. More students were leaving each year, meaning more busing was needed to even out the racial balance, which then prompted more people to leave, which meant even more busing the year after that. It was a program built to self-destruct.

Stuck in the middle of this madness was Nelson Elementary. Nelson remained stable and integrated because of a release valve, a transfer policy that allowed 49/63's high schoolers to attend the majority-white Southwest High rather than the east side schools they were technically zoned for, all of which had flipped to 99 percent black. In the summer of 1974, the school board announced that all transfers sending white students west of Troost were suspended; those students had to be used to balance out the attendance rolls on the east side. So 49/63 sued.

"Here we are," Ed Hood says, "we're obviously having tension between the races, and these white kids would have to go to a 99 percent black school? People weren't going to do it. They would move. We filed the lawsuit to stop the federal desegregation effort because it was short-sighted. It countered what we were trying to do residentially, which was working." After the suit, the school board reversed itself, allowing 49/63's kids to stay at Southwest. Then, the following February, HEW came down harder, threatening to cut off $1.6 million in school funding if whites were allowed transfers. The board reversed its reversal and announced—on just a few days' notice, in the middle of the school year—that hundreds of children would be taken from their classrooms and bused to completely different schools. Still today, Ed Hood is dumbfounded at the memory of it. "Pull 'em out in February and send 'em to a different school? It made no sense. Not only did it adversely affect our de facto integrated neighborhood, it would damage the kids. But the district was in a bind. HEW would not relent. They were stupid. They didn't realize it would make things worse."

The coalition won an injunction and kept the transfers in place, but it was only a temporary reprieve. By the end of the 1980–1981 school year, between the plummeting enrollment, the shrinking tax base, and the $5.5 million a year it cost to cart all those kids around to comply with HEW, the district was broke. It was time to start closing schools, and Nelson was on the chopping block. With 171 pupils, Nelson was up against the nearest elementary school to the west, Border Star. Upon review, the committee charged with assessing each school's performance decided that Border Star should remain open; with 318 students, it was the larger school and therefore the more viable choice, the committee said. Nelson's parents fought back, asking that their school be considered an exception. Border Star was larger, yes, but only artificially. Most of the neighborhood kids there had already been spirited away to private school. Two-thirds of Border Star's enrollment came through busing at a cost of $287 per kid per year. The cost of busing at Nelson was zero dollars, and the cost to bus 171 kids out of Nelson was nearly $50,000 a year. And Nelson was actually integrated. With the district under court order to produce integration, surely that had to count for something.

All through the summer, 49/63's parents were kept in limbo, wondering if their school would stay open. They held bake sales, sold bumper stickers—everything they could think of to raise money to fight on. But by the fall of 1981, when the morning bell rang on the first day of school, the district had stuck by its decision to close the only integrated school in Kansas City, pack its children onto buses, and send them across town to create racial balance at some other schools someplace else.

[5]

Desirable Associations

The fate of any residential neighborhood is bound to the fate of its schools. After Nelson closed, the center of 49/63 couldn't hold. The coalition stayed active, but the headlines in its monthly newsletter once again chart a fairly extreme change in priorities. Around the mid-eighties, "DONATIONS FOR SPRING RUMMAGE SALE!" gradually gives way to "DRUG HOUSES: A SCOURGE ON OUR NEIGHBORHOOD."

In 1987, after two terms of Reagan-era prosperity, 49/63's annual crime report listed 2 murders, 4 rapes, 5 acts of arson, 53 assaults, 292 residential burglaries, 67 nonresidential burglaries, and 296 incidents of auto theft. And that was a 3 percent decrease from the year before. The decade of crack cocaine and the "War on Drugs" brought a slow, grinding decline. Kinko's had opened a location on Troost, but its free business-phone service quickly proved an effective communications hub for crack dealers to answer their pagers. That closed. So did the Blockbuster and the Kroger. The new black-owned Buick dealership shut down. Soon the neighborhood's main commercial anchors were an auto garage and Go Chicken Go, a drive-through takeout for wings.

In the mid-1980s, Kansas City was still beholden to HEW's racial balance mandates, but the city had long since run out of white kids to go around. The courts ordered the city to ramp up its desegregation efforts even further, pushing a busing and magnet school program that would ultimately cost $1.7 billion and leave the district on the verge of bank-ruptcy. By the time the Supreme Court invalidated the plan in 1995, the population of white students had declined even further, and pretty soon black flight was under way, too. Integration fatigue. Black people were tired of chasing white people. Whites went west to Johnson County. Blacks went east into new, middle-class black suburbs like Raytown.

In 49/63, Susan Kurtenbach stayed. So did Helen Palmer. But Pat Je-saitis got a divorce and moved on. Gene and Maureen Hardy left, too, their equity taking a hit as the neighborhood went down. "We stayed too long," Gene says.

Ed and Mary Hood eventually packed it in as well. "We were heavily involved for six or seven years," Ed says. "I know personally we must have spent thirty hours a week on it, each, while she was trying to raise kids and I was teaching at the law school. It ate up our lives."

By the end, even Joe Beckerman said good-bye—Jimmy Stewart gave up on Bedford Falls. The rampant crime, the empty houses. Staying didn't make sense. By that point Beckerman had done well for himself, he says. He could afford to live anywhere he wanted. So when he remar-ried in 1987, he rented out his house on Forest Avenue, and he and his new wife bought a home in the Country Club District's Mission Hills. "It's the real la-di-da part of town, of course," Beckerman says. "I lived over there in this nice, fancy place. But after three years of that, I eventu-ally looked around and said to myself, 'What the *heck* am I doin' here?' And I moved back east of Troost."

....

In 2009, Kansas City snagged a big chunk of federal stimulus funds for the Green Impact Zone, an urban planning initiative to rehabilitate east of Troost with energy-efficient, green technology. The first thing pro-duced by the study was a block-level survey of every lot in the scorched-earth path created by blockbusting and redlining. The report shows huge swaths of foreclosures and abandoned houses, tear-downs with rotted roofs and cracked foundations. On some blocks, two-thirds of the houses are gone. That's what was left of Walt Disney's America after J. C. Nich-ols and Bob Wood were done with it.

Michael Duffy, managing attorney at Legal Aid of Western Missouri, has been working on Kansas City housing issues since the late seventies. "Redlining caused a lot of homes to go into complete inhabitability," Duffy explains. "There are some neighborhoods where 50 to 60 percent of the original homes have been torn down as being uninhabitable. The people who left are the people who could leave, leaving the people who stayed in the crappiest housing. They play musical chairs to stay in the viable houses, and the houses that need credit the most are the ones that get torn down.

"We spent a lot of time going after banks who literally said that the black area of town was not where they wanted to make loans. 'We're not going to do business there, period.' You look at the lending maps and they made loans all in Johnson County, of course, and in the southwest quarter of Kansas City right up to Troost—just thick with loans—and then at Troost it just fell off to zero."

And, once again, the racist embargo on fair lending just sped the growth of predatory lending. In 1993, along came the subprime mortgage industry. "The subprime lenders saw a real opportunity," Duffy says. "They came in and said, 'Well, these inner-city black neighborhoods are not being given access to credit. There's a demand for credit. We'll supply that demand.' They started pouring money into the inner city, taking what had been depressed values and inflating them beyond their real value, which led to people getting into debt way over their heads—crappy debt with huge fees, penalties for early payment, kickbacks to brokers, and, of course, these exploding interest rates that would go up, guaranteeing defaults. The fact that we had these redlined neighborhoods deprived of credit for so long left them wide open. The whole subprime lending thing was the final coup de grâce."

In the Green Impact Zone's grim report, only one area stands out. The southwest corner of the zone overlaps with the northeast corner of 49/63: Susan Kurtenbach's Troostwood. It's the only area in the report where redlining and blockbusting were stopped, and by every measure nearly all of the homes in Troostwood are top-notch. Solid roofs, good foundations, almost no foreclosures. Whatever else 49/63 did, they saved the houses. With that, the work of rebuilding the neighborhood could begin.

Cue the lesbians.

"Troostwood made it through the lesbian pipeline and they jumped all over it and the word spread fast," says neighborhood resident Calvin Williford. "A lot of lesbians moved in—so many that they could host an *Ellen* coming-out episode party in 1997, which was very unusual for Kansas City, east of Troost."

In addition to being a Troostwood resident, Calvin Williford works in the Kansas City government as chief of Intergovernmental Operations and Communications. Formerly a closeted gay, alcoholic black Republican, today he's an openly gay, sober black Independent. "Coming from California," he says, "I had landed in Olathe, Kansas, where my sister and my mother were. After a while I looked around and realized that I lived in the Wonder Bread factory. Everybody was white. Wonderful people, but I wanted to see some people with purple hair and earrings. Give me *something*, you know?"

Williford found that something the first time he visited Troostwood— for an *Ellen* coming-out episode party in 1997. Taken with the area's diversity and its affordable housing, he decided to buy in and adjust to the hardships of living east of Troost. "Still to this day," he says, "I call for pizza and they won't deliver."

Around that same time, architect Josh Hamm and his partner, David Meinhold, moved here from Atlanta and bought a six-bedroom, 4,000-square-foot Victorian, one of the larger homes in the area, for just $128,000. "It would have gone in the mid-two's across the street," Meinhold says, meaning across Troost.

"Real estate agents wouldn't even show us anything east of Troost," Hamm adds. "We saw the listing and had to ask to see the house. We went and looked at it and thought, Well, there's nothing wrong with this neighborhood." Being from out of town, Hamm and Meinhold had no idea what Troost Avenue was; they learned the history of it only after the fact. "It's amazing that that idea still persists fifty years later," Hamm says, "but it does."

Now living in a bungalow in Troost Plateau, Hamm and Meinhold have bought, renovated, and sold ten houses in the area. One of those homes was sold to Jason Peters and his partner, Eric, a younger couple who'd moved up from St. Louis in the mid-2000s. "The same day we came to look at the house," Peters tells me, "one of the neighbors that lived down the street came up and we talked for the better part of an hour, and I'm thinking, Here's a man that we've never even met and we haven't even been in the neighborhood for a day and they're already approaching us and talking to us. We just got a good vibe."

Today, Jason Peters, David Meinhold, and Josh Hamm are all on the board of 49/63. Peters is the president of the Troostwood Association; Meinhold is president of Troost Plateau Association. Hamm runs the 49/63 newsletter and, as of very recently, the new 49/63 Facebook group.

From the lesbians came the gays. From the gays came beautifully renovated homes. And with homes came renewal. Baby strollers, not seen in the neighborhood for years, now roll up and down the sidewalks once again. Black and white, young families with children have returned.

....

Today, Troostwood and Troost Plateau are drawing those families in spite of the two biggest obstacles any neighborhood can have: dismal schools and the fear of crime. And while no one can argue about the state of the schools, the fact is that crime in these neighborhoods is almost indistinguishable from neighborhoods to the west. Statistically, you're just as likely to get mugged at the Country Club Plaza as you are here. People just think it's less safe, because it's east of Troost.

"The crime level is the same," Josh Hamm sighs, "but the perception is that this is not a safe neighborhood—drives me crazy. We have a good friend who lives at the 5700 block of Harrison, about four or five blocks west, and she always asks if we're safe over here. I'm like, 'It's four blocks. How is it any different?!'"

Hamm is right about Troost Plateau. It's not so different. But he's wrong about the four blocks. Four blocks can make all the difference in the world. Go four more blocks east, across Paseo, and you'll be getting your mail addressed to 64130. The Murder Factory is just next door, in Blue Hills.

By the time Bob Wood and his colleagues were done with Blue Hills, it was shot through with more than three hundred vacant houses. Standing in the middle of that wreckage was Father Norman Rotert at St. Therese of the Little Flower. Rotert realized that saving his parish would require him to be more than your typical man of the cloth. So he sent himself to night school in real estate. He passed his boards, got a broker's license, and would spend the next thirty years fighting to pull his community back from the brink. Is he a priest with a broker's license or a broker in a priest's collar? To hear him reel off HUD statistics, it's hard to tell. But given Rotert's experience, I figured he would be best able to answer the very simple question that eighty years of federal housing policy has utterly failed to grasp: what makes a neighborhood a neighborhood?

"Relationships," he said. "Relationships make a neighborhood, to a very great degree."

It's no coincidence that Kansas City's Murder Factory sits right in the scorched-earth path of blockbusting. Black families that moved into Blue Hills thought they were buying their way out of the ghetto, but they were really buying into a different kind of ghetto. One that, by some measures, was worse. Eighteenth and Vine, for all its ills, was a community. It grew naturally out of families and social networks that migrated west and built churches and schools. But the black tenants being randomly shuffled into these blockbusted zones weren't joining communities. They were buying into neighborhoods that were no longer neighborhoods, where the social fabric was in tatters.

"We had a flood of new people into Blue Hills," Rotert says. "They didn't know each other. Some of them did, had previous connections in the African-American community, but surprisingly a lot of them did not. And they had no institutions. They didn't belong to our churches; they were still going to their churches back north. Their kids were being sent to schools all across town, and so for a long time there was nothing to pull the community together. It became clear to us early on that we could rebuild every single house in the neighborhood and we still wouldn't have rebuilt the neighborhood."

Four blocks over, relationships are the very thing keeping 49/63 viable. Starting in the early nineties, one of the area's first new residents was Ruth Austin. Older and semiretired, Austin, who is white, was looking in the area for investment properties. "I was going to be an absentee landlord," she says. Instead, she decided she liked the place, got involved with the coalition, and signed on to head its new COMBAT program, part of a new county-funded effort to root out drug-related crime.

According to neighborhood legend, Austin was like a one-woman SWAT team, sort of *Golden Girls* meets *Miami Vice*. "When I was working full-time at this, I knew lots of people in our African-American community," she says. "And that's where I got so much information. We were the first neighborhood that worked with the street narcotics and investigative units to do multiple busts on one block. We had five busts one day and two the next, and that was a big deal. And it was hard work." Austin didn't limit her social networking to the home owners, either. "I had relationships with a lot of the drug dealers, too—naturally you do when you get to know people," she explains. "I went behind the cops whenever there was a bust, and I told the dealers, 'You better stop now, because your name's on the list.'"

Working with the police and concerned residents, Austin and 49/63 drove out the worst of the crime, which was the first stage of bringing the neighborhood back. Today, the cops do their part, meeting and coordinating with the coalition every week. But to a large extent the neighborhood looks out for itself. On the 49/63 Facebook page, there's a posting anytime someone has a break-in or sees something suspicious. Each posting usually generates numerous responses, saying that the authorities have been called or offering a different report on the same thing from across the block.

Jason Peters's neighbor Herbert Kelly is one of Troostwood's older lower-income black residents. One night, Jason tells me, when his partner, Eric, was walking home up their street, two young black men circled up behind him in a car, a drive-by mugging. The passenger jumped out and grabbed Eric on the sidewalk. One neighbor yelled for help from his front porch, and Herbert Kelly came flying out his front door with a shotgun, locked and loaded. Then the old black guy drew a bead on the young black punk and told him to leave the little white gay kid alone.

Turns out if you want to stop crime, you don't need a white neighborhood. You just need a functioning one. "We know probably about 80 percent of the people that live on our block," Peters says. "We all look out for each other. If something happens, I have no problem calling anyone in the circle and they'll come over and take a look and make sure every-thing's okay. It's that whole mentality people move to the suburbs for, but that doesn't actually exist. We still have it."

But is it integrated? The best proxy anyone's come up with for integra-tion, still, is "racial balance." Every ten years the census numbers come out and we haul out the spreadsheets and check to make sure all the black people are in the right place. The borders of 49/63 don't line up with any of the census tracts where racial balance is tallied. But if you were to eyeball it, Troostwood is about 70–30 white to black, Troost Pla-teau is about 70–30 the other way, and everything west of Troost is still around 80 percent white. And that varies block by block. Some lean black, some lean white, and some are a mixed bag. So what do those num-bers tell you? They tell you nothing. In the aggregate, of course, the numbers are atrocious. Look at the census maps and all you see are big, racially homogenous blobs with little multicultural dots sprinkled here and there. But what do the little dots actually mean? Do the dots like each other? Do they ever hang out and play Scrabble together? How often do the dots rush to each other's aid with shotguns in the night?

The real story is inside the dots, and every person's got a different story to tell. As one of the first blacks in the area, Helen Palmer has been in the same house on Virginia Avenue since the 1960s. She's close with all the folks up and down her block, black and white alike. "It was a little prejudiced back then," Palmer says, "but now it's fantastic. I would rather live in an integrated neighborhood. Most of the people are friendlier. No prejudice at all in the neighborhood and mostly all white, and they are *beautiful* people."

Calvin Williford agrees. He sees diversity, rather than homogene-ity, as the thing bringing people together. "In a cul-de-sac in Johnson County," he says, "you may get to know each other through some pro-cess, but by and large the only commonality is that you belong to the same racial group. That would be true in an African-American commu-nity or a Latino community. But when you make the choice to move into a multicultural neighborhood, then you are making a conscious decision to become a part of something. By my living there and my having a dog and all of us having front porches, we see each other. It's just a neighborhood with real people that actually talk to each other and genuinely like each other and occasionally feud over parking."

But those are the optimistic voices. Every block in a neighborhood is really its own subneighborhood, a microclimate. Attitudes vary, and not all of them are positive. White home owners living on the well-off, western frontier of 49/63 rarely deign to participate in community affairs; they tend to orient their lives toward the commercial hubs of the Country Club District and probably wouldn't use "mixed-race neighborhood" as a primary selling point when putting their homes on the market.

Conversely, many black residents to the east still keep the white-run coalition at arm's length. Jason Peters recently found himself trying to reach out to an older black woman who had emailed Ruth Austin to complain that college students were littering on her lawn and she "knew it was because she was black." As the neighborhood group president, Peters says, he wrote back, offered her his phone number, and "assured her that we (Troostwood) would do what we could to resolve this for her." The woman never contacted him, and never came to a neighborhood meeting. All she did was send another email to Ruth Austin, saying if the littering didn't stop she was going to contact "a group that helps black folks with issues like these." The problem went unresolved.

Decades have gone by and black folks and white folks still can't manage a constructive conversation about whose dog crapped on the lawn. The present-day 49/63 Coalition (finally) has one black council member, Maryanne Youngblood, and the occasional black volunteer. But overall the group is still persistently, intractably white. "We've struggled to get our African-American community to participate in the organization," Ruth Austin says, "and it's still a problem. Lots of efforts were made through the years, knocking on doors of people that we knew, because we knew a lot of wonderful people. I would beg them with tears in my eyes, and they'd do anything but come to a meeting.

"It's understandable in a sense because cultures are different and interests are different. People that get highly involved in an organization often do it as a social thing. I got involved because I'm really interested in the growth of our city and crime and drugs and other stuff, but on the other hand, it's social for me, too. And we have two different cultures here that, generally speaking, socialize in different ways. We may be friendly with each other, but those that are going to be actively involved in an organization have different ways they wish to do it."

So is it integrated? Yes and no. The point of 49/63 is not that it's produced some golden mean of racial balance. It hasn't. It can't. The point is that the coalition stepped in, restored a sense of order to the marketplace, and provided for the equal protection of residents' property rights, creating a stable and open environment. Within that, it's up to the people who live there. They can either form a community or not form a community.

"My sense is that it's about choices," Calvin Williford says. "People are going to gravitate to wherever they gravitate; you're always going to find clustering. I see government's role as providing choice and opportunity, making sure that there are no barriers to residential mobility, and that whatever incentives are being granted actually allow people to make choices about where they want to be." Unfortunately, as Williford has seen though his work in local politics, city hall tends to work just the opposite. It takes choices away. Real communities are fragile, hard to hold together; they ebb and flow with cultural and generational change. That's not what the people in charge want. Politicians want guaranteed incumbency. They want voting districts with fixed social, racial, and political bearings. Inner-city slumlords want low-income tenants stacked by the square foot to cash in on the easy money of federal housing subsidies. Out in the suburbs, developers want all the high-end, good-credit families clustered, too.

Today, the J. C. Nichols empire has become a wholly owned subsidiary of the disturbingly named HomeServices of America, Inc., a conglomeration of twenty-some different realty companies covering twenty different states. In the early 1990s, the Walt Disney Company broke ground on its very own town, a suburb of Orlando called "Celebration, Florida," marketed as "a place that takes you back to that time of innocence." Just like the Country Club District, Celebration is a suburban dream factory manicured down to the last blade of grass. In the twentieth century, Kansas City produced two true geniuses. In the twenty-first century, the visions of J. C. Nichols and Walt Disney have come full circle and joined. "Neighborhoods" are increasingly "developments," corporate theme parks. But corporations aren't interested in the messy ebb and flow of humanity. They want stability and predictable rates of return. And although racial discrimination is no longer a stated policy for real estate brokers and developers, racial and social homogeneity are still firmly embedded in America's collective idea of stability; that's what our new corporate landlords are thinking even if they're not saying it. And as long as black people and white people are still arguing about whose dog crapped on the lawn, why should those companies think any different?

America has lived for decades with this myth that mixing races lowers property values. In fact, the opposite may be true. Some studies from the 1970s showed that mixed-race neighborhoods, if they could stabilize, held their property values better than homogenous ones. If anyone can live in a particular neighborhood, then it has a larger customer base. On top of which, quality mixed-race housing is an incredibly scarce resource. When demand is greater than supply, prices go up. Joe Beckerman bought his place at $25,000, furnished, and now he's sitting on a quarter million in equity. Other residents attest to home values that have increased five- and tenfold as well. "Best investment I ever made" is a phrase you hear a lot around here. "If I put up a sign listing my house for $140,000," Calvin Williford says, "I would have an offer in a couple of days. If I put it at $130,000, my phone would ring off the hook. My neighbor sold her house in forty-five minutes."

Capitalism: it actually works sometimes. If only America would let it.

....

Before leaving Kansas City, I thumb through the local white pages on a whim and discover, somewhat to my surprise, that I have one last stop to make. I check out of my hotel, drive into town, and head south in search of 7530 Troost Avenue, still listed as the home of Bob Wood Realty.

From the outside, it's what you'd expect: a run-down, two-story office building. Red brick with a tacked-on facade of columns, the whitewash cracked and peeling. Inside, the cramped hallways are a sad and dingy shade of beige. All the offices seem either closed or vacant, but there's activity on the second floor. I go up and poke my head into the only room with any lights on. Half-opened boxes line the floor. Bubble-wrapped shelving units lean against the wall, awaiting assembly. New tenants. Behind the reception desk, a black guy about my age is busy unpacking and setting up a fax machine. "Can I help you?" he asks as I wander in.

"Yeah," I say. "I'm looking for Bob Wood."

"The Realtors?" he says. "They're gone. But I can tell you all about Bob Wood."

"How's that?"

"Because I lost my house in a subprime balloon mortgage Bob Wood sold me ten years ago."

Wood's been dead a few years now, it turns out, still hanging around the white pages like an infection. The properties he managed in his slumlord days are still around, too—run-down houses that attract marginal tenants and cause headaches for the neighborhood. I talked to some of the neighborhood cops on 49/63's safety committee, and they say whenever they get a call for a domestic disturbance or some other unpleasantness, odds are good it's coming from an old Bob Wood house.

Despicable as Wood may be, it's important to make one small point in the man's defense: from blockbusting to slumlording to subprime lending, most of what he was doing was perfectly legal at the time he was doing it—not just legal, but explicitly encouraged by the federal government and the real estate industry's leading trade organization. And even where Wood's actions were illegal on paper, authorities were purposefully denied the enforcement tools that might have shut him down. The problem was with the housing market and the people we elected to regulate it for us. Bob Wood was just an asshole.

"It takes a long time," Joe Beckerman says. "As you can see today, it takes generations to get people thinking differently about their fellow man. All the country clubs I've ever belonged to, people always say, 'You live *where*?' Or, 'Do I have to bring a gun over there?' But I tell them I live in a great neighborhood. I've got black neighbors, Asian neighbors, a socioeconomic strata from people on food stamps to people that make a quarter of a million dollars a year, and that's the way the world is. That's very important to me and my kids, who are very much that way, too. Forget about the neighborhood, it's about how you think about the other person."

To sift through the census data for 49/63 and ask "Is the neighborhood integrated?" is to pose the wrong question. The only question you can ask is "Who in the neighborhood has integrated?" Ruth Austin has. Helen Palmer has. The woman with the littering problem has not. A lot of the white folks west of Troost haven't, either. It's entirely possible that 49/63 will gentrify, drive out older residents, and lose all its character. It could also backslide into urban decay, sending families with children out the door. The relationships in the neighborhood will decide. "True integration," as Martin Luther King said, "will be achieved by true neighbors who are willingly obedient to unenforceable obligations."

If you turn on your television these days, you hear a lot of old white people talking about this "real America," some apple-pie, Bedford Falls, Walt Disneyfied idea of a simpler country, a "time of innocence" that we've lost. They're right. It's gone. We destroyed it so we wouldn't have to share it with black people. We gave up real neighborhoods in real cities so we could pay more to have "protection" inside the regional profit silos of HomeServices of America. We gutted Blue Hills, and now you have to go to Orlando to buy it back. Only that's the big lie at the heart of the J. C. Nichols dream. Desirable associations aren't something you can buy. They're something you have to make.

There's only one way America's neighborhoods will begin to integrate: people have to want it more than vested public and corporate interests are opposed to it. And more people should want it. Mixed-race, mixed-income housing is a product we need on the market. It's the only real solution to segregated schools, for one. So how do you sell that idea to a country still beholden to outdated stereotypes and fears? The same way J. C. Nichols did. You advertise it.

PART 3

WHY DO BLACK PEOPLE DRINK HAWAIIAN PUNCH?

[1]

The Old Boys' Network

"Some fifty years ago, the late, great Nat King Cole, when Madison Avenue had canceled his groundbreaking TV show, said that Madison Avenue was afraid of the dark. Well, it's 2009, and dark still ain't gettin' it on Madison Avenue."

Big applause.

"Madison Avenue is like the segregated graveyards of the South where unrecognized and unnamed black people and their talent and ambitions lie buried."

"Amen!"

"The money that we spend as consumers drops to the bottom line of the companies that we support, these Pepsis, these AT&Ts, these Johnson & Johnsons, these Procter & Gambles. They take that money and it becomes their advertising budget and with that money they subsidize the growth, proliferation, and ascendancy of white media, which does nothing more than advance and perpetualize and institutionalize white supremacy in America!"

"Tell it!"

I'm not in church. It's July 12, 2009, and I'm in a conference room at New York's midtown Hilton Hotel for the centennial convention of the NAACP, the nation's oldest civil rights organization, legal architects of *Brown v. Board*. In the coming days, dozens of panels and seminars will convene here to reflect on the past hundred years of race relations in America—and to plan for the next hundred. The week will end with a roof-raising speech from the freshly inaugurated President Obama. The event I'm attending at this moment is a Continuing Legal Education seminar. The topic at hand is workplace discrimination in America's advertising industry.

"You've heard of a show called Mad Men? *Well, I think it should be* Gone With the Wind, *'cause there ain't no difference."*

Up on the dais, a panel of lawyers, activists, and disgruntled former advertising employees are all taking turns lambasting the hostile, unconscionable racism they've experienced in the business. At the microphone just now is Sanford Moore, onetime account executive at the BBDO ad agency.

"Madison Avenue is the last bastion of corporate segregation in America. They're the Men in the Gray Flannel Sheets, and it's time to take the hoods off!"

Crazy applause. Emotions in the room are running high, because the NAACP is getting ready to sue the crap out of some white people.

From the late 1960s to the late 1990s, the dearth of black faces in the ad business was not a matter that received much public attention. Part of the problem, as one lawyer here explains it, is that there weren't enough black people in advertising to get mad about the fact that there weren't enough black people in advertising. Over the past decade, that has changed. (The getting-mad part, not the having-enough-black-people part.) In January 2009, the NAACP launched the Madison Avenue Project, which is having a coming-out party here at the centennial convention with the very ambitious slogan "Ending racial discrimination in America's advertising industry."

"Madison Avenue" is the colloquial catchall term for the advertising industry; the name derives from the fact that the nucleus of the industry was once located along that particular stretch of midtown Manhattan, much like investment banks are associated with Wall Street. Today, the industry is no longer clustered geographically. It's clustered corporately. Eighty percent of America's ad agencies are consolidated within four major holding companies—WPP, Publicis, Interpublic, and Omnicom. They're the ones on the hook, as far as the NAACP is concerned.

A few months back, the Madison Avenue Project published an extensive report on minority hiring patterns in the four conglomerates. The median share of employment for black managers and professionals in advertising is 5.2 percent, but that includes black-owned agencies that specifically target the black consumer market. Once you factor the black agencies out, the percentage is substantially lower. Then, once you move beyond the back office and into the upper-level creative and client-facing positions—the writers and art directors who actually make the advertising, and who make the real money—the numbers fall off a cliff. According to the economists who compiled the NAACP's report, the black-white employment gap in advertising is 38 percent worse than the U.S. labor market as a whole. When the study was published, *USA Today* called Madison Avenue "the poster child for the death of diversity."

Employment figures aside, what advertising has, ironically, is an image problem. It is seen as a "racist industry" in the same way Vestavia Hills is seen as a "racist suburb"; the business doesn't so much *practice* discrimination as it *is* discriminatory in its nature. Today's hit TV show *Mad Men*, about the lives of advertising professionals in the 1960s, has drawn critical raves for its portrayal of that era's retrograde racial and gender politics. It's also proven to be a handy visual aide for those who insist that the business has barely changed since. Whole websites exist just to vent frustration about the deplorable state of race and advertising.

Madison Avenue is Whiteytown. It is, according to Sanford Moore, "The last business where undereducated, undercredentialed white people can make big money." On this point he is certainly correct. I should know. The poster child for undereducated, undercredentialed white people making big money in advertising is the author of this book.

....

Advertising used to be a closed shop. On the creative side, agencies took on very few entry-level hires, weeding out most of them with a brutal apprenticeship process. Anyone who got in the door to begin with probably came from one of a handful of places: the expensive portfolio schools that feed the industry or the social class of friends and relatives of people already in the industry.

In 1964, the Civil Rights Act banned discrimination in the workplace "on the basis of race, color, religion, sex, or national origin." But the law didn't say what discrimination *was*, just that you couldn't do it. Since the act of hiring or promoting someone is discriminating in and of itself (i.e., choosing one person over another), arresting bias in the workplace has always been a hit-and-miss proposition. And as racial attitudes have slowly improved, overt discrimination has become that much harder to document and prosecute. For the fight against workplace discrimination to continue, new legal standards are constantly seeking judicial precedent.

Lawyers for the NAACP are offering a standard they call "second-generation discrimination," hiring based on "informal social groups that over time tend to exclude nondominant groups." The NAACP isn't really after the four media conglomerates. They're after the old boys' network that feeds them. The guy they're after, really, is me.

I wasn't born a member of Madison Avenue's elite club. "Tanner Colby" is really just poor white trash who cleans up okay. My working-class grandparents were born to Louisiana sharecroppers; I'm only two generations and a college diploma away from a life of subsistence farming in the swamp. But eighty years and a piece of paper will get a white guy in America pretty far. I graduated from college in the 1990s, the early Stone Age of the Internet. Media outlets and major retailers were just making their first tentative forays onto the web. Few, if any, were turning a profit. Still, certain visionaries proclaimed, if people can look at it then you can sell advertising on it, which means eventually it has to start making money. "Interactive advertising," people were calling it. Clients wanted it, and since nobody really knew what it was, if you were standing in the right place at the right time, people would throw money at you for no reason at all. Compared with the hardship of today's job market, it seems almost criminal that we had as much luck and opportunity as we did.

In 1999, I lived in New York. I had a history degree and not a whole lot going on. I knew almost nothing about the Internet and even less about advertising. I did know one thing, though: I knew somebody who knew somebody. I knew an actress who was dating my college roommate and who happened to be temping as an admin at the Ogilvy & Mather agency. When she heard that the interactive advertising department was looking for writers, she offered to pass on my résumé and writing samples. Two weeks later I was a copywriter at an ad agency.

For a brief window, Madison Avenue's closed shop was wide open.

You could get a job in interactive advertising if you could write your name in the sand with a stick. And once you were in, you were in. My cubicle-mate had a degree in furniture design, not web design. Didn't matter. He knew somebody who knew somebody, too. One colleague of ours got in because somebody remembered him as "that guy who writes those funny emails." One of our art directors had some experience in traditional advertising, but wasn't really up on the web stuff when she got hired for interactive. "I remember designing an email for Sears," she tells me. "I didn't know what an email was."

And if you did know computer stuff, you could pretty much write your own ticket. I had one friend who'd taught himself those digital animation programs while he was trying to get his rock band off the ground. With that, he was billing the agency as a computer animator at four grand a week. And since he was hired by a pal, he'd never even given anybody a résumé. "For all anyone knew," he says, "I might not have graduated from high school." Of course, all of us had graduated from high school. And college. But nobody really needed to check because we'd all gone to the right colleges, which is how we all knew one another. Everybody hired everybody they knew, and everybody that everybody knew was white. Or Asian.

At the exact same time this was happening, in the spring of 1999, Representatives Carolyn Kilpatrick (D-MI) and James Clyburn (D-SC) of the Congressional Black Caucus began publicly denouncing Ogilvy & Mather, expressing "alarm" over the agency's "lack of diversity." Ogilvy was, at that point, a contractor for the federal government, responsible for making all those commercials to get kids off drugs that don't actually get kids off drugs; as such, affirmative action law mandated that a percentage of the agency's workforce be composed of minorities and that a percentage of all government accounts be subcontracted to minority-owned businesses. Whatever Ogilvy was doing, it wasn't enough. In 2000, President Bill Clinton signed an executive order mandating that the allocation of government ad dollars be "fully reflective of the nation's diversity." And in 2004, the New York City Commission on Human Rights (NYCCHR) led a protest in front of Ogilvy's world headquarters in midtown calling for "an end to Jim Crow on Madison Avenue."

Ogilvy, of course, was just being made the example for a problem that was industry-wide. Shortly after the protests, the four holding companies agreed to submit to hearings with the NYCCHR. In 2006, sixteen major agencies came to a voluntary agreement with the city, vowing to increase hiring goals for minorities, particularly in the creative, professional, and managerial ranks. One of the conglomerates, Omnicom, even pledged $1.2 million to fund an executive-level Diversity Development Advisory Committee. Various agencies announced new programs for diversity training and diversity outreach. And come Black History Month, the industry trade papers *Advertising Age* and *AdWeek* were all flush with wall-to-wall, full-page ads from ad agencies advertising their passion for, and commitment to, diversity. Two years later, despite its newfound love for diversity, Madison Avenue was still the poster child for its demise, and the NAACP stepped in.

"We think the advertising industry is laughing at black people," says the NAACP's interim general counsel, Angela Ciccolo. "I think they're laughing because it goes back to 'We're special and this is a special club and we're so talented and smart and we're entitled to this lifestyle.' It's great that people have friends and connections, but when you have public companies, you have laws that are designed to protect people and give people opportunity, and they should be obeyed. Men in particular have preserved their social standing and economic status by perpetuating networks. 'We're gonna bring in who we want to bring in and goddamn anybody else who wants to challenge that.' The whole industry is like they've never heard of the EEOC or equal opportunity. It may turn out that they have to be sued. Sometimes, that's the only way you can get someone to listen."

....

By 2008, my last year in advertising, I was mostly freelancing part-time, but I'd spent close to nine years working on and off at a total of five different agencies, all of it during a time of mounting legal and public pressure to hire minorities. Yet I can count the number of black people I worked with on one hand—not including the ones who emptied the wastebaskets or installed the telephones.

Moving from full-time to freelance and back again, from one agency to the next, I never had to sit for a single performance evaluation or go on a single job interview save the first one. I never had to produce a résumé, a portfolio, or fill out any sort of application. I just kept getting work because I knew the people doing the hiring because they'd known the people who'd hired them; just a few years in and some of us were already management. All that time I had one foot out the door because what I really wanted was to "be a writer." Yet by the end of my run, I'd tripled my pay rate, was using a window office overlooking the Hudson River, and had been offered a managerial slot that came with a very decent low-six-figure salary. My cubicle-mate? The guy with the degree in furniture design? He was running the department. He's the guy who offered me the job.

I've since been told—by those who defend Madison Avenue's hiring practices—that my experience in the industry was some sort of anomaly, that you're not supposed to be able to skate through the system and get as far as I did the way that I did. Maybe. But I'm pretty sure I'm not that clever, and I know I'm not that charming. The truth is that a bunch of kids out of college happened to be in the right place at the right time and the world started dumping money in our laps.

Which, come to think of it, is a pretty good summary of how the entire modern advertising industry was born. After World War II, a bunch of white guys in New York happened to be in the right place at the right time the last time the next big thing came along. And, no, it wasn't television. Madison Avenue became what it is today—incredibly lucrative and permanently divided—thanks to the federally subsidized, racially restricted suburb.

Mad Black Men

In the early 1950s, BBDO hired Clarence Holte, the first black man ever to hold a professional position at a major ad agency. But Holte was hired solely to cover the Negro market, handling accounts that bought media in black newspapers and on black radio. It was a niche position, as few advertisers were genuinely interested in marketing to black consumers to begin with; they were too poor to merit attention, companies felt. At the time, most every black person who worked in sales and media was relegated to a position like Holte's. It was assumed that the Negro market would forever stay the Negro market, and that niche was the only place blacks were qualified to work. No black person could get hired to write or manage general-market (i.e., white) advertising, because what black person would possibly know how to talk to all those white suburban housewives?

Television changed the way we communicate, but it was suburbia that drove the demand for the advertising that paid for what was on television. To make money for J. C. Nichols, the Federal Housing Authority had sent the Greatest Generation out to live in a bunch of empty houses in the middle of nowhere, and now all those empty houses had to be filled up with stuff. New dishwashers. New carpet cleaners. New lawn furniture. New everything. In the 1950s, the total dollars spent on advertising grew by 75 percent, rising faster than average household income and faster than the gross national product.

We all know that advertising is a big con to get us to spend money we don't have on things we don't need. It works on us anyway. Ads work because they're aspirational. They tap into some unsatisfied desire and then sell you the solution for it. Buy this product, take it home, and you'll be safer, happier, and more attractive. And therein lay the root of the industry's problem with race, both in the office and on the airwaves. If advertising is aspirational, who in the 1950s aspired to be black? No one, as far as major corporations were concerned. The big money was in selling suburbia, and the appeal of suburbia was rooted in its racial and social exclusivity. Maytag wasn't going to sell washing machines to Susie Homemaker by showing a prosperous black family moving in with one next door. Blacks played only one role in white America: they were the help. And that was the only role they played in advertising as well. Aunt Jemima stopped by at breakfast to serve pancakes, but otherwise black America was kept well out of sight.

For much of the twentieth century, it was even a novel idea that black people should aspire to be black. Black newspapers and radio stations were filled with ads for skin bleachers and hair straighteners. Relative to their income, blacks overspent on fine clothes and Cadillacs, buying the markers of white status to compensate for the daily insults to their own. But with the civil rights movement gaining steam, blacks were becoming an increasingly self-assertive and self-respecting demographic; the postwar economic boom had given them more disposable income than ever before. Companies began to realize there was profit in getting a share of black dollars, which meant that advertisers had to be able to talk to black consumers without talking down to them. That opened up jobs for people like Clarence Holte to serve the Negro market. But the color line on Madison Avenue was impermeable. So impermeable that it was broken only by a man who wandered across it by accident.

....

Roy Eaton grew up in the Sugar Hill neighborhood of Harlem, the son of Jamaican immigrants, a domestic worker and a mechanic. Despite losing part of one of his right fingers in a childhood accident, Roy wanted to learn to play piano. He first sat down at the keys when he was six years old. Nine months later he played Carnegie Hall—a prodigy. After graduating magna cum laude and Phi Beta Kappa from City College of New York while earning a dual degree from the Manhattan School of Music, he was awarded a scholarship to study classical piano at the University of Zurich. After study in Europe, he later returned to the states to make concert debuts at the Chicago Symphony Orchestra and at New York's Town Hall.

Eaton's musical career stalled, however, when the army drafted him to serve in Korea. After his tour overseas, he returned to Manhattan and struggled to find work. While searching for a teaching job in academia, he also looked into broadcasting; many of the radio and television programs of the era used live musical accompaniment. One of Eaton's favorites was *Goodyear Playhouse*, but all he knew about the show was that a company called Young & Rubicam was involved in its production. He didn't know what Young & Rubicam was. "Ignorance," Eaton says, led him to Madison Avenue.

"I was visiting an employment agency on Forty-second Street. I walked into the telephone booth, looked at the phone book, and realized that Y&R was only two blocks away from where I was. It was a hot day in July. I just walked into the agency, walked up to personnel, and told them that I'd like to see the director. They took my résumé—it was a slow day, nothing was happening—and when the personnel manager saw all my academic and music credentials, he was very curious as to why I was there. He came out and said, 'How can I help you?' Which, by the way, is code for 'What's that black doing in here?'

"I said, 'I know you do *Goodyear Playhouse*, and I was wondering if there might be an opening for someone to work in that area.'

"He said, 'We don't actually produce *Goodyear Playhouse*. Goodyear is the sponsor. We do advertising, but you wouldn't be interested in that.'

"'Well, I wouldn't know if I was interested in anything unless I tried it,' I said.

"'Okay. Go home and write some ads, and I'll submit them.'

"He figured that would probably get rid of me. But I went home and looked at ads in *Life* magazine and over that weekend I wrote ten commercials; I didn't know I wasn't supposed to do that many. One of the commercials I wrote used a concept that was already in production at Y&R. I wrote it for Hunt's tomato paste. You're in Italy, close up on the food, pull back, and you're in America. The idea being to get Italian flavor in America. The creative director, Charlie Feldman, called me in for an interview. He was Jewish, had broken that barrier himself several years before. So he was interested in me. When I first interviewed, he said, 'If you were white, you'd be at the desk right now. But you're not, and I want a Jackie Robinson.'"

As it happened, Charlie Feldman was a classically trained musician himself. He asked Eaton to compose a few sample songs, commercial jingles. Eaton went home and cranked out seven of them. The next day he became the first black man ever hired to write advertising for white people in America. He quickly mastered the lowbrow art form. His tunes for Texaco (*"Trust your car . . . to the man who wears the star . . ."*) and Chef Boyardee (*"We're having Beefaroni . . . it's beef and macaroni . . ."*) would soon become woven into the country's cultural fabric. For Kent cigarettes, he composed a jingle that incorporated the Bebop Jazz sounds recently pioneered by Charlie Parker and Dizzy Gillespie. Without anyone knowing, Eaton had slipped the avant-garde of black music right into white America's living room. The Kent tune became a hit single, garnering a ton of radio play on its own. The very happy client upped its billings with Y&R by over a million dollars a year. Eaton's annual salary was $8,000. "They got a bargain," he laughs.

Yet Eaton's salary was on par with, even slightly higher than, his white colleagues because of his musical expertise. "People with no experience usually started at six," he says. "It was very fair. Once I was in, it was strictly about the work. With the exception of a few people who just hated blacks—and I knew who they were—I had no difficulties at all. People respected my talent, needed my talent, and that was it. Among my peers I made friendships that are lasting even to this day." Charlie Feldman and Eaton would often play chamber music together. In 1957, a car accident in Utah left Eaton in a coma and killed his young wife. Being a black man, alone, in a coma, *in Utah*, Eaton was certainly not in line to get the best medical services the hospital had to offer. But Charlie Feldman flew out, made sure his friend received every treatment possible, and stayed for his entire recovery. When the hospital bill came, Eaton's colleagues all stepped in, pooled money, and picked up the tab.

Eaton was treated well on Madison Avenue. In 1960, the young black composer was even lured away from Y&R by Benton & Bowles, which promoted him to vice president and music director. But Roy Eaton was the Jackie Robinson who wasn't. He'd only slipped around the color line. It was still firmly in place, and black America was still locked out of the major leagues.

....

In April of 1963, just as the Children's Crusade was laying siege to the segregated department stores of downtown Birmingham, America's three largest civil rights groups, the NAACP, the Urban League, and the Congress on Racial Equality (CORE), had all converged on New York in an attempt to break through the color line on Madison Avenue. At the time, after nearly two decades of sustained postwar economic growth, 55 percent of blacks in America lived below the poverty line, blacks made fifty-three cents to every dollar that whites made, and over 10 percent of blacks were unemployed, nearly double the rate for the general population. A path into the American workplace had to be found.

On April 22, 1963, *Advertising Age* released the results of a three-year study done by the Urban League on employment practices at the ten largest ad agencies in New York City. It showed that out of some twenty thousand employees, only twenty-five blacks held positions in any kind of creative or managerial capacity. Of those twenty-five, like Clarence Holte at BBDO, many were consigned to work exclusively on the Negro market, which the Urban League denounced as a form of "internal segregation."

Finally called to account for their years of discrimination, advertising executives tried to fend off protests, trotting out one excuse after the next. It was the clients, agencies said, who didn't want blacks in their ads or associated with their products. Moreover, there simply weren't any black applicants out there to choose from. This was not entirely false. In the early 1960s, the best minds of the civil rights generation weren't going into business; they were going into law, politics, government, and teaching, professions that they saw as part of the freedom struggle. And of those blacks who were blazing trails in corporate America, few even considered advertising—its reputation for discrimination was just that bad. Ad agencies didn't hire black people because black people didn't apply to ad agencies because ad agencies didn't hire black people.

And advertising already had too many white people. Despite its ubiquitous presence in our lives, advertising is a small industry. In 1962, the six biggest agencies received some twenty-three thousand applications, four times as many candidates as they had employees, let alone job openings; there just weren't a whole lot of vacancies to fill. To give every ad agency proportional black representation top to bottom in 1963 would have required just a few hundred jobs total. But what the agencies didn't get, at first, was that this wasn't only about jobs. It was a fight to control the cultural narrative of the country.

Advertising distorts and amplifies culture. It's a fun-house mirror. It takes ideas and images out of our real lives, exaggerates them for comic or dramatic effect, and then reflects them back to us. Susie Homemaker and Aunt Jemima—the perfect housewife and the loyal help—were part of the same distorted depiction of aspirational upper-middle-class status. Both were cartoons, and both needed to go if America was going to get its head right. Civil rights leaders wanted advertising to show that all consumers were created equal. They wanted Madison Avenue to buy the world a Coke and teach it how to sing. The boys on Madison Avenue had no idea what they were talking about.

Most of corporate America was white in those days, certainly, but advertising was white on a whole different level, so white that there were shades of white in its whiteness. The industry was tribal, incestuous. It was territory you couldn't hope to navigate if you weren't already a member. The biggest agencies, like J. Walter Thompson, McCann-Erickson, and Young & Rubicam, were filled with the scions of the WASPy East Coast establishment. Certain Ivy League grads gathered here, others gathered there. The Irish Catholics had carved out a niche at BBDO. Jews worked at Grey. If there was an outlier, it was the young, scrappy DDB—Doyle Dane Bernbach, Irish and Jewish with a few Italians starting to filter in to the creative ranks.

Throughout the spring and summer of 1963, activists laid siege to Madison Avenue with picket marches and demonstrations. By August, agency executives had agreed to sit down for talks with the NAACP. And in November, NAACP executive secretary Roy Wilkins was invited to give the keynote at that year's annual conference of the American Association of Advertising Agencies (the 4A's), the industry's largest trade organization. At the convention, Wilkins gave a stirring speech on the damage done by advertising's depictions of, and discrimination against, black Americans. Following his address, Madison Avenue promised to take action.

They took out an ad.

On November 11, 1963, the 4A's took out a full-page in the *New York Times*, sending out "AN INVITATION TO ALL BRIGHT YOUNG MEN AND WOMEN TO CONSIDER ADVERTISING AS A CAREER." Hovering above the headline was an illustration now familiar to modern readers: a group of eager young professionals, with a black man and woman in the mix, looking bright-eyed and professional, just like the white folks. "Diversity advertising" was born.

It was as useless then as it is now. Voluntary measures and "We'll do better" pledges were used by the industry to stave off pressure from civil rights groups, but it mostly amounted to stonewalling and tokenism. Madison Avenue's foot-dragging was egregious enough to trigger an investigation by the New York City Commission on Human Rights. Another survey of minority employment in advertising was done. As of August of 1967, out of close to 18,000 employees at several dozen agencies, the commission counted only 635 blacks, most all of them working in the back office or at the clerical or mail room level. Only fifteen were working in any kind of creative, client-facing capacity. Even more damning, close to 40 percent of those black hires were housed in a handful of agencies, the few who had made a sincere effort, which showed that the rest of them weren't trying at all.

Despite its dim outlook, the NYCCHR report did highlight one important fact: companies that wanted to change, could. Benton & Bowles, where Roy Eaton was now music director, led the industry with 8.5 percent black employment overall.* The award for most-improved went to J. Walter Thompson. In four years, JWT's New York office had gone from 0.6 percent black to 4.9 percent black. At the behest of the agency's chairman, JWT had made a sincere, forward-leaning effort. Partnering with civil rights groups, they went out and found the black candidates who couldn't be found. They recruited from black colleges and publicized job openings in black media. A special training program was created to groom clerical hires for professional positions. Management made a decision, and it got done.

Black employees were also encouraged to recruit and recommend any qualified candidates they might know personally. Bring your friends. If you can't beat the old boys' network, start making one.

....

The old boys' network has proven to be nothing if not resilient. In 1941, President Franklin Roosevelt signed Executive Order 8802, which outlawed discrimination in companies applying for government contracts during the buildup to World War II. In August of 1953, President Dwight Eisenhower signed Executive Order 10479, which established the Government Contract Committee to oversee the enforcement of Executive Order 8802, since few companies had bothered to pay it much mind. Almost ten years later, in March of 1961, President John F. Kennedy signed Executive Order 10925, which, again, outlawed discrimination by government contractors based on race, creed, color, or national origin. Kennedy called for "affirmative action" to be taken, not for racial preference, but to ensure that purposeful discrimination would be rooted out.

It wasn't. In 1964, President Lyndon Johnson signed the Civil Rights Act into law. Title VI of the bill (one more time, for good measure) outlawed discrimination in government contracting. Title VII went one step further and outlawed discrimination among all private employers as well—a bold reach, considering how little the law had done to stop discrimination in government contracting thus far. Title VII also established

....

*When protesters picketed B&B's office, Eaton went out to the street to tell them they had the wrong agency. "You should be picketing McCann," he said; McCann had ten blacks to B&B's eighty-three.

the Equal Employment Opportunity Commission (EEOC), a federal agency to enforce all of the above, seeing as how, to date, no one ever had. Then, in September of 1965, Johnson rolled out Executive Order 11246, which outlawed discrimination in government contracts worth more than $10,000 per year, because, somehow, that wasn't covered when discrimination in *all* government contracts was outlawed in Executive Orders 8802, 10479, 10925, and Title VI of the Civil Rights Act passed just one year before. Through all this, between 1962 and 1967, in at least twenty-two of America's fifty states, black employment either remained stagnant or declined.

Same as it did with demands for fair housing, America responded with the right laws and lots of committees and panels, but the authority vested in those entities was laughable in the larger context of the problem. Like HUD, the EEOC was empowered only to engage in "conference, conciliation, and persuasion" with offending companies, or recommend them to the Justice Department for prosecution. Shortly after its forming, the EEOC was flooded with more than forty-four thousand discrimination complaints. Only nine hundred of them were ever brought to trial.

In March of 1968, after the results of its investigation into Madison Avenue were published, the NYCCHR dragged all the agency heads back in front of the cameras for several days of hearings. More excuses were given, more promises made. "We're overreacting to this Negro thing," one exec was overheard saying to another. "It'll go away." Which more or less captured the industry's attitude toward the whole affair. Why get bent out of shape? The most severe penalty the commission could threaten them with was a five-hundred-dollar fine.

Two months after the hearings, the NYCCHR filed suit against the two worst-offending agencies to make examples of them, and Madison Avenue finally got off its ass—and not because of the five hundred dollars. In the weeks between the hearings and the charges, Martin Luther King had been murdered, and over a hundred of America's cities had broken out in riots. After two decades of "progress," the material well-being of the average black citizen had barely improved. The unrest that came in the wake of King's death made it plain that this wasn't a Watts problem, a Newark problem, or a Detroit problem. It was systemic, and it was bad for business. Riots stopped construction. Man-hours were lost. Property was damaged. Worst of all, terrified shoppers and their wallets stayed home, and anytime Americans aren't spending money they don't have on stuff they don't need, the world's largest economy grinds to a halt. The black revolution had finally hit the only nerve that really mattered: the bottom line.

Miraculously, after decades of "not being able to find" qualified black employees, America was on a hiring binge. Some companies were way out in front. Spurred by the 1967 riots in Newark and Detroit, execs from Alcoa, Chase Manhattan Bank, and dozens of other companies had formed the Urban Coalition, calling for an "all-out attack on urban unemployment." The King riots sent those efforts into overdrive. By the end of 1968, the *New York Times* reported that a list of companies running minority outreach programs would probably run "just about as long" as the listing of the New York Stock Exchange itself.

Madison Avenue was late to the party. Advertising is not a business that deals directly with the public. It has no stores to burn, no products to boycott, making it slow to absorb the full implications of "this Negro thing." By the time the agencies went looking, there weren't any black people left. After the Fortune 500 scramble, pretty much every black person in America who would have been qualified to work in advertising was already sitting behind a desk somewhere else. Officials at the Urban League even admitted as much: all the college-educated, white-collar candidates were spoken for. And entry-level salaries in advertising were so low that it was impossible to lure candidates away from jobs they had already taken. In a twist, young black professionals started turning the agencies down, because they were already making twice as much at Xerox or General Mills.

The legal and public pressure on the agencies, meanwhile, had only intensified. No more tokenism and no more stonewalling. And despite the hiring crunch, the NAACP and the Urban League were emphatic that the agencies not hire unqualified candidates, as low-performing employees would only exacerbate existing stereotypes. So as the 1960s drew to a close, Madison Avenue was stuck at the bottom of a sad little hole it had dug for itself. Under the threat of government sanction and public reprisal, the agencies had to hire black employees, but could hire only qualified black employees, even though there were no qualified black employees—and they had to do it now.

....

Madison Avenue launched internship programs, inner-city outreach seminars, summer training courses—anything that would bring black hires in the door. Some initiatives were industry-wide, but most of the agencies were off starting their own. In fact, the sheer volume of competing and overlapping initiatives serves as a pretty good indicator of just how little thought, coordination, and foresight went into their execution. DDB joined with the New York State Employment Service to create a training program aimed at "the hard-core unemployed." Under the program's open-enrollment policy, only a tenth-grade reading proficiency was required to join; some applicants came in at only third- or fourth-grade reading levels. JWT haphazardly sped up its efforts as well. Where the agency had once tried to be thoughtful and diligent in its minority recruiting, now it, too, was taking all comers, even those without a high school diploma. GED classes were folded into its training programs. In the morning, students studied toward a high school equivalency exam, and in the afternoon they took advertising courses. (The men did, at least; women were trained in typing and secretarial skills.)

Given the lack of objective professional and educational qualifications, the program administrators looked mostly for positive attitude, and many young blacks took to the programs with just that. "We are no longer 'boys' but men," said one proud recruit, "and soon, hopefully, advertising men." Another compared the program to finding "a gold mine." Young people came from across the city, and almost overnight there were literally hundreds of new black hires on Madison Avenue. By the end of 1970, in less than two years, the number of blacks in advertising had more than doubled. Ogilvy & Mather had hired fifty; BBDO, fifty-three. The widest nets were cast at JWT and Y&R, which took on eighty-seven and a hundred and seven new black hires, respectively.

Then enthusiasm ran into reality. What company needs a hundred entry-level hires on Tuesday that it didn't need on Monday? Most of the new recruits weren't there to become advertising men; they were there to pad the numbers, to make the issue go away. Now the industry really did have a problem: hundreds of black employees and not a clue what to do with them. At the low end, the washout rate was high. The hard-core unemployed and the high-school drop-outs never really stood a chance; the industry was just inflating their hopes and, very cynically, wasting their time. When it came to the middle-ranking black hires, the average but enthusiastic, the industry just had no room for them. As in most corporate offices, mediocre white people already had the mediocrity tier all sewn up. Many blacks realized that their role was primarily decorative, a nonwhite face to put by the elevator in case the city regulators stopped by. They didn't stay long.

Like Roy Eaton, the only way for blacks to get recognized in advertising was to be absurdly overqualified. And many of the young black hires were. They were smart, talented, eager, and driven. And *that* was the problem. What do you do with the qualified blacks? The ones who did good work and expected to be fairly rewarded and promoted in return? Madison Avenue hadn't really thought that far ahead. The power structure at the agencies was already in place. Every manager had his own turf, his own people, and no one was giving that up. Certainly not to the black guy. "There were some great talents," Eaton says. "But even after many of them had demonstrated their skills, there was a ceiling. There were instances that infuriated me—a copy supervisor who was just brilliant in his concepts and creative ideas, and yet when it came to moving up they chose someone far inferior. It made him so mad he just left."

Those who didn't hit the corporate glass ceiling ran headlong into the cultural one—the stifling WASPiness that dominated the industry. If you couldn't conform to it, drop the right names, wear the right clothes, you weren't going anywhere. Some blacks never learned how to navigate the cultural divide. Others simply chafed at it. "We have to become black Anglo-Saxons to make it," one black account exec bitterly complained.

Advertising isn't baseball. America's pastime is the ultimate meritocracy, with every stat measured and every player ranked accordingly. Advertising is the opposite of that. "Where's the Beef?" "My baloney has a first name . . ." "Plop, plop, fizz, fizz—oh, what a relief it is." They're all pretty stupid sounding when you hear them out of context. How these ideas actually get people in stores to buy products—no one has a clue. The agencies pitch clients on focus-tested solutions and demographic market research, but every idea is a shot in the dark. Advertising sells itself like it's a business model, when it's really just being good at guessing.

Madison Avenue isn't an old boys' network for no reason. "It's a relationship business," people tell you, which is true. On the creative side, writers and art directors work together the same way any creative group does. Like a rock band. Either you jam well together, or you don't. You could be great but maybe I just don't like your sound. A day in the life of advertising might be nothing more than you and your creative partner throwing Nerf balls at the ceiling while talking about your favorite TV shows. A little bit of friction is good to mix things up, but if you really don't like each other, one of you isn't going to stay.

On the business side of things—account management—advertising is literally nothing but relationships. Building them and maintaining them. Knowing whose ass to kiss and when to kiss it—because if you don't, the Cheerios people are going to take their millions of dollars and go to the next guy. And when a client hires an agency, the relationship is really all that they're buying, because it's the only thing that's tangible. And in a relationship business, loyalty and familiarity trump most everything else. Advertising is making friends. That's what the job is. The rest of it is just what you do between lunch breaks.

"The difference between blacks who built success within the industry and those who didn't," Eaton explains, "was this matter of social networking, not talent. The head of production at Foote, Cone in San Francisco, he was black. But his father was a film editor at a major movie studio; he was already a part of that world. The dinner table conversations—it was not an alien experience for him.

"For me, even though I had this high level of education, I always felt an insecurity that I was not as sophisticated as someone who had lived on Ninety-second Street. There's this socialization that happens, a class issue. Even if people never said anything, there was an awareness that there was a life and a station that I was not privy to. That's a barrier, if you let it be. My personality, I'm egocentric. Whatever it is, I'll figure it out. Not everyone has that level of aggressive self-awareness."

However, he adds, "I must also plead guilty to buying into the subterfuge of the industry. Of being ignorant, really. It was almost as if, until I looked in the mirror, I didn't consider myself black. Everybody else was white, and so was I. The nice things they were doing for me and the progress that I was making indicated, in my ignorance, that this was something anyone could do if they worked hard enough. My feeling frequently has been, 'If I can do it, you can do it. Why the fuck *aren't* you doing it?' I was just as critical and judgmental as Bill Cosby, for example.

"Racism is not a white malaise. It is there within the black population, too. It is there in self-image and in critical appraisal. You cannot say that the effect of two hundred years of pile drivers in your head will not have an impact. It must, and it does. I don't have the answer to it. I just know that it has to come from both sides."

By that point, however, there was no solution coming from both sides. In the 1970s, if black people and white people couldn't have a constructive conversation about whose dog crapped on the lawn, they weren't going to hang out and write margarine commercials together, either. The younger black men coming up behind Eaton weren't content to leave their race at the door. They weren't willing to assimilate into the culture of the business, nor were they going to wait dutifully for the glass ceiling to magically open up on its own. So they did what every black group in America was doing. They organized, closed ranks.

In 1968, before the affirmative action wave came in, the blacks who were in the industry had formed their own trade association, the Group for Advertising Progress (GAP). Its initial focus was on recruiting, training, mentoring—integrating blacks into the business. But as ambition gave way to frustration, GAP became a forum and an outlet for protest; Madison Avenue had its own Freedom, Inc. The group began tracking discrimination complaints and EEOC violations. It went to management with complaints and issued demands. Some of the more outspoken members went public, airing the industry's dirty laundry at awards shows and conferences and in the press. "We jacked things up," one member would later boast.

"And that didn't help," Eaton says. "It created a resistance and a resentment on the part of the power structure. 'We've opened up a hornet's nest. We don't need this.' It did not encourage a continuation of hiring. It probably slowed it down. Closed it off entirely, as you can see now.

"Should they not have expressed their resentment?" he asks, pausing to consider his answer. "Of course they should have. But there was a price to pay."

....

The price they paid was the end of racial integration in advertising. Political activism and whistle-blowing, though noble, never got anyone the corner office. Blacks who were willing to go along, stayed. Some did well. But those who made too much noise were shunted to work on third-tier accounts. Left to stagnate, many just left.

What the political stalemate didn't kill, the recession finished off. In 1973, along with the rest of corporate America, Madison Avenue started handing out pink slips. "And the blacks go first," says Eaton. All the minority recruitment and training went, too, because why invest in the hiring pipeline when you're not actually hiring? After 1970, the employment data on blacks in advertising gets thin; no one was keeping track. Pressure from civil rights groups waned as the movement stuttered to a halt nationwide. The NYCCHR put the ad agencies on "voluntary" compliance, which of course meant no compliance at all. By the early 1980s, blacks were gone. The major agencies looked more or less much the same as they had back when Roy Eaton first wandered in by mistake.

Back in 1955, Eaton and Clarence Holte were pretty much the only two prominent blacks at major agencies. Despite what you'd think, the two were not close friends. "I didn't get to know Clarence Holte that well," Eaton says. "I knew him casually. There was a tension in the relationship because I was in general market. He was in blacks only. Creating that concept was in effect putting Jim Crow into the industry. I saw it as being done with negative intent. 'Okay, we've got to find a place for them. Let's put them there.' It was not done to benefit or expand opportunities for blacks."

But over at BBDO, Clarence Holte thought the opposite. Black business-men should embrace their role as racial emissaries, he felt, use it to speak up for black interests in the boardroom and to demand better goods and services for the black community, which was woefully underserved. Being "relegated" to the Negro market wasn't marginalizing. It was em-powering, a way to make black America stronger—and wealthier.

The frosty relationship between Eaton and Holte was, of course, noth-ing more than the latest chapter in the ongoing discussion between W. E. B. Du Bois and Booker T. Washington: fight for equal opportunity or build ethnic solidarity? In advertising, the agencies' brief experiment with integration had been such a disaster, and the taste it left was so bit-ter, that Booker T. Washington won by default. Defiant and proud, the Mad Black Men walked out, moved to the other side of Madison Avenue, and began building an advertising industry of their own.

[3]

A Whole New Bag

Byron Lewis and Roy Eaton started life on similar paths. Both grew up in New York, Eaton in Sugar Hill and Lewis in Queens. Both men were a part of the rising midcentury tide of black men able to go to college; while Eaton studied music, Lewis earned a degree in journalism at Long Island University. Both were drafted and served in Korea and returned home in 1955. When they reached Madison Avenue, however, their paths sharply diverged. The choices they made (and the ones they were forced to make) would come to define black America's place in the industry for the next fifty years.

Lewis didn't stumble onto Madison Avenue by accident. He started in newspapers, selling ads for the Harlem-based *New York Citizen-Call*. He wasn't terribly successful. White agencies controlled the purse strings for all the major advertising accounts, and very few media buyers saw the value in reaching black markets. (Cigarettes, liquor, and beauty-care brands were among the few products aggressively marketed to black consumers.) The *Citizen-Call* closed its doors in 1961 due to lack of advertising revenue. The same year, Lewis and several colleagues from the paper tried their hand at magazine publishing, launching *The Urbanite*. Featuring criticism and essays from the likes of James Baldwin and Langston Hughes, this *New Yorker*–esque publication aimed itself at the growing college-educated, middle-class black communities in the urban enclaves of the North.

In Harlem, Lewis had become part of a postwar generation of strivers. His entrepreneurial efforts had put him in the company of other ambitious black Americans, men like Reverend Adam Clayton Powell and Charles Rangel, who represented Harlem in Congress, and David Dinkins, who would go on to serve as New York's first black mayor. Unfortunately, being at the heart of Harlem's literary and political worlds meant little to the people who had the money. Langston Hughes doesn't sell Buicks, or so Madison Avenue felt at the time. Like the *Citizen-Call*, the *Urbanite* folded after just a few months. "I think it would have been quite successful," Lewis says of the venture, "had we understood more about advertising."

Few moments have had an impact on American history like Martin Luther King, Jr.'s "I Have a Dream" speech, yet when TV networks aired the 1963 March on Washington they had to air it commercial-free, because no sponsors would touch it; King got airtime only because the march was too big to ignore. Advertising is the thing that everybody loves to hate. But it's also the cornerstone of a free press, essential to the exercise of the First Amendment. Advertising pays, or doesn't pay, for investigative reporters to dig up the truth. Advertising pays for the news anchors and editors who shape the media narrative. Today, advertising pays for whole twenty-four-hour news channels. Control the ad dollars, and you control a great many things. Byron Lewis came away from his publishing failures with a firm conviction: if blacks were to have a real voice in American affairs, they had to assert greater control over not just the depiction of blacks in modern mass media, but also the corporate dollars that funded it. Shelving Aunt Jemima was just the start of it. This was about the money.

During the civil rights revolution of the 1960s, instead of marching the streets, Lewis sent himself to grad school. While taking business and public relations classes at NYU, he spent the next few years in and out of work and eventually landed a sales job in the classifieds department of the *New York Times*. It was not glamorous work, but every week it gave him an early preview of the help-wanted ads from advertising, marketing, and media companies—and a two-day head start in answering them. "The ads," Lewis says, "would typically read, 'College graduate wanted. Ivy League type. Own correspondence. Willingness to travel.' I was a college graduate, I did my own typing, and I was obviously willing to travel. So I would send letters to the P.O. boxes with my résumé. During the week after work and on lunch hours, I would call the people I got responses from."

He accumulated a large pile of rejection letters, but also a good number of interviews. He would go, the interviewers would be very polite, and then he'd never get called back. Lewis did this every week, he says, for four years—the same four years, it so happens, that Madison Avenue was inviting ALL BRIGHT YOUNG MEN AND WOMEN TO CONSIDER ADVERTISING AS A CAREER.

"Ignorance is bliss," Lewis says, "and I'm glad I was ignorant at that particular time. I just kept trying. Then one day I went for an interview, and the gentleman said, 'Mr. Lewis, have you been here before?'

"I had been to so many interviews, I couldn't remember. I said, 'I don't think so.'

"And he said, 'I think you have, because I remember you. And I kind of felt sorry.'

"He got up and he shut the door and he said, 'This conversation was never held, Mr. Lewis. Those ads that you responded to—"College graduate, Ivy League type"—did not mean blacks or Hispanics or even some other groups. That's what those ads mean; they're coded. In all other areas, you'd be an ideal candidate because you're willing and you're determined, and I only tell you this so you shouldn't waste your time.'"

Byron Lewis stopped wasting his time. He quit going on interviews, even quit his job at the *Times*, and turned to the resources he could trust in the black community to start his own company, UniWorld. Today, Lewis owns the oldest continuously operating black advertising agency in the country, and he's a millionaire many times over.

....

Before going into the ad game, Byron Lewis had spent considerable time as a social worker on New York's Lower East Side. His caseload included the early generations of European Jewish immigrants. From there he also witnessed the growth of Chinatown and the early arrival of African-American and Hispanic residents. The experience gave him a premonition of America's future, that each successive generation would be more culturally and racially diverse than the last—ethnic marketing was a growth industry. That idea became the basis on which he started his agency.

The odds were not in his favor. On the day he opened for business, a handful of other black agencies were jostling for the limited black advertising market as well, most of them run by people with far more experience than Byron Lewis. But within a few years, all of them, save UniWorld, would close. A successful black agency, it turns out, works pretty much the same way a successful white agency does. Lewis outlasted his competition because he knew a guy who knew a guy.

"I started based on relationships that I had developed in Harlem and when I was in sales," he says. "I was also part of a network that gave me real access to African Americans working in any capacity in communications—the black press, the people who were in marketing at major corporations on a national basis. If you were in a certain line of business, the black community was very small in terms of people who had 'made it.' It was really a network that extended through most of the African Americans who had gone to college. People like Percy Sutton, founder of the Inner City Broadcast Empire; Bruce Llewellyn, CEO of Philadelphia Coca-Cola Bottling Company; Earl Graves, the founder of *Black Enterprise* magazine. It also included people like the first black governor of Virginia, Douglas Wilder; Jesse Jackson; Jesse Owens. We had a remarkable kinship because it was like a family, which I'm very glad to have had—it is a relationship business."

The Madison Avenue network may have shut Lewis out, but through all his years of success and failure, he'd been building a network of his own. For UniWorld's first client, he approached Heublein, a food and liquor distributor with whom he had built a good rapport a few years before as a salesman. Based on their past working relationship, Heublein gave him the Smirnoff Vodka account for all black-targeted media.

UniWorld was now in business, but business was slow. During the early seventies, most of corporate America was reticent to invest in minority advertising. The cash crunch killed off most of the black agencies. UniWorld's viability would depend on other streams of revenue. While his competitors struggled, Lewis turned to his connections in the black political establishment, pitching his company to work on state and municipal campaigns for the emerging generation of black mayors and members of Congress. In 1970, UniWorld's political work helped elect Kenneth Gibson the first black mayor of Newark, New Jersey.

Years before, Lewis had also become friends with Al Bell, owner of the legendary Memphis R&B label Stax Records. Bell had recently approached MGM to adapt an action movie from a series of pulp crime novels by Ernest Tidyman about a detective working the mean streets of Harlem—a black private dick who's a sex machine with all the chicks. Bell's idea was that the movie would provide Stax with a vehicle to produce a sound track. He also leaned on MGM to hire a black ad agency to market the film. The studio agreed, and Bell recommended his pal Lewis.

"Shaft's his name. Shaft's his game."

Byron Lewis wrote the movie's catchy tagline, which was plastered on movie posters and used in commercials over Isaac Hayes's iconic, Oscar-winning score. With box office receipts of $15 million, *Shaft* was a huge hit, kicking off a host of sequels and the entire blaxploitation genre. UniWorld was in with black Hollywood on the ground floor. More work followed.

It's not just who you know, of course, but what you do with who you know. Lewis survived largely because he possessed the same qualities that any successful businessperson has. He was relentless, and he had good instincts. He also had a knack for turning adversity into opportunity—if conventional avenues were closed to him because of his race, he'd create new ones and make his money there. The single biggest obstacle in his path was structural. Ad agencies make their money as a commission on the volume of media dollars sold, and there just wasn't much black-targeted media space to sell. Local black-owned radio stations and newspapers were viable outlets. *Essence* and *Black Enterprise* had joined *Ebony* and *Jet* as national magazines aimed at black consumers. *Soul Train* had become a hit on syndicated television. But that was about all the territory a black adman had to work with. It wasn't enough. So Byron Lewis created his own.

In 1974, he took nearly all of his operating capital and used it to produce a daily syndicated soap opera for black radio, *Sounds of the City*, which gave him marquee programming to sell ads against. It was a huge risk, and it paid off. Quaker Oats signed on to sponsor the show. *Sounds of the City* gave UniWorld its first million in sales. Quaker remained a UniWorld client for decades. The company's portfolio expanded to include black-targeted work for Kodak, Ford Motors, AT&T, and Kraft. By 1975, Byron Lewis was clocking $5 million in annual billings, and he had the only black advertising agency left in New York City.

Lewis wouldn't be alone for long. UniWorld—along with other black agencies that were growing in Chicago, such as the Vince Cullers agency and Burrell Communications—had built a business model that worked, and other black entrepreneurs began moving in to compete for the space. Unlike Lewis, virtually all the people behind these new shops had cut their teeth in, and had left, the mainstream ad world. They were not the washouts or the political agitators, either; they were some of the most successful black creatives and executives ever to work on Madison Avenue.

As the head of the Miller Brewing account at McCann-Erickson, Frank Mingo had overseen the market introduction of Miller Lite. Its "Taste's Great, Less Filling" campaign would become one of the most successful product launches of all time. Mingo left McCann and joined forces with BBDO's Caroline Jones, the first black female vice president at a major agency. In 1977, they started Mingo-Jones, taking the black segment of accounts like KFC and the Walt Disney Company. That same year, thanks to one very memorable phrase—"Strong enough for a man, but made for a woman"—a young black copywriter named Carol Williams was named the first female vice president at the Leo Burnett agency in Chicago. In the early 1980s, she would leave and form her own company, too. Close to a dozen new black agencies emerged in those years. More would follow.

But even for a man of Byron Lewis's talents, the right instincts and the right relationships alone wouldn't have been sufficient to build a viable black-owned business in 1969. Capitalism requires, above all else, access to capital. Before Lewis's time, black entrepreneurs didn't have it. Major banks wouldn't lend to them, private equity saw little upside to investing in them, and corporate America had no interest in partnering with them. For black agencies just to get into the game, access to investment capital and corporate accounts had to be leveraged politically. "There would be nobody in these companies," Lewis says, "and we would not be having this conversation, without affirmative action."

And the man who gave them affirmative action was America's thirty-seventh president, Richard Milhous Nixon.

....

When assembling his new administration in the fall of 1968, President-elect Nixon appointed longtime confidant H. R. Haldeman to serve as his chief of staff. To staff up the West Wing, Haldeman and Nixon turned—where else?—to their old boys' network. Haldeman chose as his deputy a young man named Lawrence Higby. Dwight Chapin came on as special assistant to the president, responsible for appointments and television appearances. Ken Cole served as assistant to the president for domestic affairs. Most prominently, Ron Ziegler was tapped to serve as the administration's press secretary. Higby, Chapin, Cole, and Ziegler had all worked under H. R. Haldeman during the twenty years he'd spent as an account executive and vice president at the J. Walter Thompson advertising agency.

The Mad Men were running the White House. They'd also run Nixon's campaign, the messaging of which had been tailored perfectly for the Republican Party's new core demographic: the white suburban majority. Nixon didn't need black votes to get elected, but he still needed a solution to their problems. Implied in his pitch to suburban voters was the idea that "this Negro thing" could be managed without whites having to be bothered with it. And with the cities besieged by riots, something had to be done, as Nixon put it, "not to have the goddamned country blow up."

The country was blowing up because the one thing black people aspired to most was the one thing they hadn't gotten so far: results. To function in a capitalistic economy, owners need access to capital and workers need access to jobs. Nixon needed the country to function. So in April of 1968, with the country flailing in response to Martin Luther King's assassination, candidate Nixon rolled out the first of his new product pitches for black America. He took to the radio to lay out a comprehensive urban economic program. "Bridges to Human Dignity," his campaign called the address. In it, Nixon proposed a cornucopia of programs that spoke directly to the rising feelings of nationalist sentiment in the black community. He called for massive investments in depressed urban neighborhoods and schools, support for historically black colleges, job training that produced actual jobs. Nixon also outlined what would become known as his "black capitalism" initiative, government loans and incentives to foster "black ownership . . . black pride, black jobs, black opportunity, and, yes, black power, in the best, most constructive sense of that often misapplied term."

In a country where blacks were once owned, the idea of black ownership was a powerful one. Many black nationalists believed that a self-contained, self-determined black economy was the only way to escape exploitation at the hands of whites. That notion ran up against certain realities of the free market, but it still held considerable sway. Through the Booker T. Washington Business Association, conservative black leaders endeavored to build a strong entrepreneurial class. In the "Don't Buy Where You Can't Work" campaigns of the thirties and forties, black economic solidarity had played an important role in opening up what limited opportunities existed at the time. During the early sixties, Malcolm X more than anyone had championed the notion of "buying black," not letting whites own all the stores, keeping black dollars in black hands. The problem for black business was that even the most practical of these ideas had never delivered substantial, sustainable access to jobs and capital. It wasn't until 1966 that someone finally figured out how to use black pride to make the cash register ring.

During Martin Luther King's failed Chicago housing campaign, he'd established an economic development program called Operation Breadbasket, a grab bag of various tactics the movement had used in the past—boycotts, labor walkouts, selective-buying campaigns—all oriented toward wringing concessions out of white manufacturers and employers. In cities across the country, these tactics had produced minor, fitful gains. In Chicago, the program was run by a young, charismatic preacher named Jesse Jackson. Alternately described as a savior or a shakedown artist, Jackson took on corporate America with a savvy and a fearlessness that brought CEOs to the bargaining table. His first major victory, after a fourteen-week boycott against the A&P grocery store chain, yielded dozens of jobs, an agreement to stock products from black-owned companies on shelves, a guarantee to place ads in local black-owned media, and a contract to hire black-owned sanitation firms for the company's garbage collection.

Given the era, Jackson's success on the jobs front was bewildering. It was alchemy. In less than two years, Jackson's Operation Breadbasket had netted black Chicagoans more than three thousand jobs, increased their personal income by $22 million, and roped in $15 million in deposits for black-owned banks. Blacks rallied to Jackson's Sunday services by the thousands. Martin Luther King had inspired a generation with his sermons, but all his lofty talk of Promised Lands and mutual garments of destiny hadn't yet put bread on anyone's table. Jackson preached a gospel that resonated in the here and now: *"Say it loud! I'm black and I'm proud—and I buy Grove Fresh orange juice!"*

The product launch for Nixon's Bridge to Human Dignity was perfectly timed. Once in office, on the matter of protecting his white suburban voting base, the new president made little pretense about his intentions. In fact, his entire domestic agenda on integrationist civil rights policies can be neatly summed up in the instructions he gave his attorney general in selecting the administration's first Supreme Court nominee. The candidate had to be "a conservative Southerner" who was "against busing, and against forced housing integration in the suburbs." Beyond that, Nixon said, "he can do what he pleases."

Pivoting to the urban economic front, Nixon just as swiftly made good on his promise of results. Same as with school busing, real results demanded statistical proof of significant progress. Racial balance. Quotas. As hard as Johnson had pressed on racial balance in schools, jobs were a different matter. When the Civil Rights Act of 1964 was passed, it expressly forbade "preferential treatment to any individual or to any group" based on "race, color, religion, sex, or national origin." For Democrats, this was a stance made out of political necessity. Since most blacks were blue-collar wage earners, labor unions were the first groups to face the threat of racial preferences in hiring. Blacks were becoming a solid Democratic constituency, but Big Labor was still the backbone of the party; government procurement contracts were a fat, pork-laden pipeline for kickbacks and political patronage. Big Labor didn't want quotas, and whatever the Democrats' commitment to racial equality, they were going to let the plumbers and the electricians slide for as long as they could.

If Democrats opposed racial preferences out of self-serving pragmatism, civil rights leaders opposed them on ethical grounds. Martin Luther King had never ruled them out entirely, but felt it would be tragic if America reached a point where such a system were the only option left. Other black leaders agreed. When the subject of racial quotas was raised at the 1966 White House Conference on Civil Rights, one NAACP spokesman said flatly, "This is the very thing we have been fighting against." America's civil rights leaders still had their eyes on the prize: full civic, social, and economic inclusion in society. To come all this way and settle for a few thousand jobs here and there, they'd be taking the short money. They weren't in it for the short money—that is, until the money was actually on the table.

Affirmative action as we know it today was born out of a stalemate between civil rights leaders and labor unions in Philadelphia. As in most cities, black construction workers were consigned either to nonunion jobs or to the low-wage jobs of the unskilled labor unions. The skilled-labor unions—the ones with high-paying jobs and good pensions, such as the plumbers and electricians—excluded blacks almost entirely. At the time, construction was booming. Federal dollars were pouring into urban renewal and suburban housing and highway sprawl. The government should have had considerable authority to impose fair employment practices on the unions working those projects. It didn't.

The problem, again, was the old boys' network. Philadelphia's unions were controlled by an airtight network of family, church, and community. Forty percent of licensed plumbers in Philadelphia had sons who were also plumbers. In 1964, every apprentice accepted to the electricians' union had been either the son or nephew of a current member. The tile layers were Italian. Sheet metal workers were Scottish, Irish, or German. Every group had a lock on a particular union, and they all took care of their own. Between 1963 and 1967, pressure from the government and the NAACP had produced a total of thirty-four black construction jobs in Philadelphia.

To break the impasse, federal contract compliance regulators had tried to impose goals and timetables for hiring—the "Philadelphia Plan," this was called. But before it launched, Lyndon Johnson's comptroller general shut it down; the "goals and timetables" were really race-based quotas and therefore unconstitutional. However, President-elect Nixon and his domestic aides saw the plan as not only legal but potentially lifesaving. Republicans had no political stake in protecting Big Labor, black unemployment was at the root of the urban unrest, and good construction jobs were just the sort of results he'd promised to deliver to make the problem go away.

Nixon made the Philadelphia Plan a centerpiece of his very first address to Congress, calling it "historic and critical." By early 1970, the Philadelphia Plan was declared such a success that similar programs went into effect in nineteen cities across the country. Dozens more would follow. Affirmative action—meaning goals and timetables for hiring—was now in place.*

During its first nine months in office, the Nixon administration would fundamentally overhaul and redefine the relationship between race and the workplace. That spring, it amended the mandates President Johnson had established in government contracting. Before, the law had applied only to procurement contracts; now it was expanded to include any institution that received any federal funds of any kind, including universities, research institutions—everyone, almost, since so many institutions interact with the government on some level. In August, Nixon followed this up with Executive Order 11478, which called for swift and immedi-

....

*Nixon's people went to great pains in their PR efforts to insist that the program's "goals and timetables" weren't actually quotas. As soon as the plan was challenged in court, however, the unions were found guilty of not meeting the goals. The imposed penalty was that they had to meet the goals, which made them quotas. America is still trying to figure out the difference.

ate affirmative action in all government employment. Any idealistic notions about color blindness had gone out the window. Now the hiring, firing, promoting, and recruiting of minorities was all to be documented and detailed in every particular. The big racial accounting system we'd built to monitor our schools had expanded to cover nearly every corner of the workplace as well.

Nixon's signature civil rights initiative would be his "black capitalism" plan. Under the Johnson administration, blacks and other minorities had been eligible for special loans under the Small Business Administration's 8(a) program, but it was not a major legislative initiative. Nixon thrust it front and center, skipping congressional approval by putting his program under the wing of the executive branch. On March 5, 1969, Nixon signed an executive order establishing the Office of Minority Business Enterprise (OMBE) to much celebrity fanfare. Jackie Robinson (the actual Jackie Robinson) was a big booster of black-owned businesses, and he publicly endorsed the plan as precisely the kind of assistance the government should be offering. The OMBE set aside millions in federal dollars to fund black-owned businesses and Minority Enterprise Small Business Investment Corporations, venture capital funds run by private interests that would also invest in black business independently. These programs, Nixon promised, would give black America "not dependency" but "a piece of the action."

Nixon's sweeping affirmative action mandates had an immediate impact. By the end of 1970, 20 percent of all black workers were employed by government agencies—a number that included 72 percent of college-educated black women and 57 percent of college-educated black men. Between 1969 and 1972, total black income rose from $38.7 billion to $51.1 billion, and by 1973 deposits in minority-owned banks had gone from $400 million to $1 billion. Between 1970 and 1975, federal procurement from all minority-owned businesses rose from $9 million to $250 million. And on Madison Avenue, UniWorld and the business of black advertising finally had the foundation to start growing.

....

In the sixties, civil rights groups had demanded that Madison Avenue abandon its grotesque stereotypes of black America and create integrated, racially neutral advertisements. In the era of Black Power and black pride, black leaders and agencies now reversed course. They insisted on consumer messaging that spoke to blacks *as* blacks, in a visual and verbal language that only black agencies could understand and translate to the market. "Targeting for the black consumer is an anthropological consideration more than a marketing consideration," asserted Thomas Burrell, of Chicago's Burrell Communications. Vince Cullers, head of another black Chicago agency, developed a whole school of principles he called "soul marketing," complete with fully articulated instructions on how to use the terms "boss" and "jive."

In Washington, black leaders took affirmative action mandates and used them to secure black ownership of broadcast licenses for radio and television. On Madison Avenue, black agencies asserted their right to control the ad dollars that flowed to those outlets and the way blacks were portrayed on the airwaves, and affirmative action laws now mandated that some percentage of accounts be subcontracted their way. The pages of *Ebony* and *Jet* came alive with ads that declared "Black Is Beautiful." Swahili slogans pitched Afro Sheen shampoos to a fast-growing population of urban consumers. Black fathers shared tender moments with their sons and families. These were positive images that black America had never seen of itself in the national popular media. Where blackness had long been something to be ashamed of, now it could be aspirational, too.

"There was so little awareness of blacks as people," Byron Lewis says. "*Ebony* gave a view of successful people like Sidney Poitier, Lena Horne, Harry Belafonte. But we had no other national media that would give the African-American consumer a feeling of what we could accomplish in this society. I felt that anything that we did that would ultimately project a positive image of blacks would be a good thing. That little commercial we were able to do, given what was out there, helped give a lot of people hope that they could do things. And that's what I think we accomplished with UniWorld."

Undertaken with this noble intent, black advertising would still prove a difficult niche to work. Not every product we buy has a cultural component to it. In fact, a lot of them don't. An AC Delco car battery is an AC

Delco car battery. "Does it start my car?" is all people really want to know; there's only so much racial spin you can put on that. But if Uni-World wanted to get the AC Delco account, the first question it faced from the client wasn't "Why is this the best ad for our product?" but rather "What's black about it?" Everything had to be racialized, on some level, to justify winning the business—otherwise, why not simply go to a general-market agency?

The need to "blacken up" black advertising left black agencies trafficking in stereotypes of their own. Black America's cultural heritage is infinitely rich and varied; it ranges from the Afro-Caribbean music of New Orleans's Congo Square to the frontier stoicism of Wyoming's Buffalo Soldiers. But most of that got lost, dwarfed by fun-house caricatures of Black Power. In the late 1960s, studies showed that blacks smoked menthol cigarettes at a slightly higher average than whites, just enough that tobacco companies saw a market niche to exploit. The Lorillard To-bacco Company hired soul-marketing pioneer Vince Cullers to handle its Newport Menthols account. Cullers took the brand and made it synony-mous with Black Power. The print ads featured a stern, bearded black man with a righteous Afro in a bright blue dashiki, proudly introducing "BOLD, COLD NEWPORT . . . A WHOLE NEW BAG OF MENTHOL SMOKING." New-port's radio ads were broadcast "live" from Black Power rallies, calling on young black men to be "the boldest brothers in the country" by light-ing up a menthol.

The Brother in the Blue Dashiki was a hit—the Marlboro Man of Black Pride—and a textbook example of the power of aspirational advertising. Show people the world they want to live in, and let the product take them there. Soon, Kools and Merits were on the black bandwagon as well. Today, 75 percent of black smokers smoke menthols, as opposed to 23 percent of white smokers, and that's something all of us just "know." Same as we "know" that white people drive Volkswagens and drink chardonnay while wearing Dockers at our James Taylor concerts. The things we buy and the brands we use are just another way for us to pro-ject our preconceptions onto one another.

That type of bias had always existed, but instead of fighting it the black agencies embraced it, made it their raison d'être. After years of telling mainstream agencies that they had to market to black America, black agencies were now saying that mainstream agencies *couldn't* market to black America; only black agencies were qualified to do that. And in making their stand as experts on black culture, the black agencies only further cemented the institutional bias that had kept them out of the industry in the first place: if only black people can sell to black people, then surely only white people can sell to white people—and white people were the lion's share of the market. You take Boardwalk and Park Place; we'll keep Baltic and Mediterranean.

"What's the phrase?" Roy Eaton says. "'Hoist with their own petard?' The black agencies bought into the separation out of survival, but I resisted it. I could see its inequity." Still working at Benton & Bowles, Eaton watched as the best and brightest blacks in advertising left to stake their claim across the street, marginalizing themselves the moment they stepped out the door. If black agencies wanted "black" accounts, with few exceptions, that's what they'd get. When white executives leave companies, they generally take their big clients with them. Happens all the time. At McCann, Frank Mingo had overseen one of the biggest national product launches of the decade with Miller Lite; that should have given him the reputation to write his own ticket. But when he left to go on his own, he was offered only the black portion of Miller's business. The client's relationship wasn't with the black guy. It was with McCann, and that's where it stayed.

Worsening matters was the fact that the black accounts seldom stood on their own; they were subcontracted from the general-market agencies. Madison Avenue was still setting the overall creative message for the brands, and black agencies were left to adapt those general campaigns for black audiences. Rarely were they given the chance to do innovative, trendsetting work on their own. And even the work they got, they got under duress. Clients and general-market agencies didn't necessarily contract with black agencies because they wanted to, but because they had to. "They didn't really believe that there was critical mass in the African-American market," Byron Lewis says. "They thought that we were all poor, that we couldn't purchase national brands. And there was a total absence of minorities in the corporations and advertising agencies who could influence minority marketing decisions. If they did anything at all, they did it grudgingly."

Either general-market agencies didn't see the value in black consumers, and so didn't want to subcontract the work out, or they *did* see the value in black consumers, and so didn't want to subcontract the work out. Why not tap that market themselves? In 1972, Y&R tried to start an ethnic marketing division. The Group for Advertising Progress lobbied and had it shut down; Y&R was unfairly trying to muscle black agencies out of their rightful place. The law had redrawn the color line on Madison Avenue, dictating that black stuff was supposed to go here and white stuff was supposed to go there. But that line had to be constantly policed to ensure that the black stuff was going where it was supposed to go, a state of affairs that greatly enhanced the stature of Reverend Jesse Jackson.

By the early 1970s, Jackson had eclipsed the old civil rights establishment with his own black empowerment coalition, Operation PUSH (People United to Save Humanity). His success in imposing black demands on local Chicago grocery stores had since evolved into a multimillion-dollar enterprise rooted in policing the racial politics of corporate America. Companies involved in disputes—or fearful of becoming involved in one—began paying out settlements that were measured in commitments to minority hiring, subcontracting, and franchising.

Jackson's negotiations would always result in what he called a "covenant," in which the company would acknowledge its racial sins and outline its concessions. Through Operation PUSH, Ford Motors coughed up more than two hundred minority-owned dealerships. General Foods put $20 million into policies with black-owned insurance companies. Among companies that sold consumer goods, Jackson's settlements almost always included provisions for media buys to be made through black ad agencies. Avon cosmetics took its black account to UniWorld in 1975. Kentucky Fried Chicken's black account went to Mingo-Jones. In perhaps the biggest coup of all, Jackson negotiated for Burrell Communications to be named the agency of record for all of Coca-Cola's black accounts worldwide, including Africa, a piece of business worth over $7 million a year. Companies that didn't get a visit from Reverend Jackson didn't wait for one. They went into the minority-supplier business as a preemptive

PR move. Among themselves, the black agencies groused about the condescending nature of these transactions. They referred to the accounts as "get off my back" money. But they took it. They had to.

That was the catch-22 for the aspiring black businessperson in the 1970s. Byron Lewis offered a genuine service, real insight into a market that Madison Avenue was missing. In their bias, the white guys wouldn't take him seriously as an equal. Was there any way to overcome that bias short of government coercion and public shaming? In the short term, probably not. But if affirmative action and "get off my back" money helped make black agencies viable, the politics of it also stunted their growth. For the most part, Madison Avenue's racial transactions took place across a tenuous network of coerced, condescending, adversarial relationships—and that's no way to run a relationship business. As one black executive noted at the time, "On a long-range basis, you can't build a business model on white man's guilt."

....

Proponents of black self-determination loved to speak of black America's tremendous potential. If it were a separate country, they said, it would be the twenty-sixth largest in the world, have the fifteenth highest per capita income in the world, and a gross domestic product the size of Canada's. But black America was not a separate country. Though 11 percent of the total population in 1969, blacks earned only 6.5 percent of total personal income, represented 0.7 percent of the country's total wealth, and held 0.14 percent of the nation's stock market investments. Relative to America as a whole, one prominent black economist pointed out, those numbers were "distressingly feeble." Romantic ideas about black capitalism were "dangerous nonsense," and to encourage them was "to perpetuate a cruel hoax" on the black community.

Affirmative action was sold as a mechanism to lift black America up and in, but the people who sold it knew it was anything but. Within a few weeks of calling the Philadelphia Plan "historic and critical" in Congress, Nixon jotted a note to a domestic aide calling the program "an almost hopeless holding action at best" and saying, "Let's limit our public action and $—to the least we can get away with."

The goals and timetables of the Philadelphia Plan proved that quotas can create jobs, but they also proved that once you turn race into a numbers game, you're inviting people to game the numbers. Labor unions produced paper compliance through practices known as "motorcycling" (moving a handful of blacks from one site to another to meet the quota on each site) and "checkerboarding" (putting all the black guys on the one government-financed project and ignoring the issue elsewhere). By 1973, all the "Philadelphia Plans" implemented in cities nationwide had produced only 3,243 jobs.

Black capitalism also produced mixed results. Only five days after signing the executive order to create the Office of Minority Business Enterprise, Nixon sent a memo to the head of the initiative, observing that the average small business has a 75 percent chance of failing, but that "minority small business has a 90 percent chance of failing—good luck!" Affirmative action for minority-owned business did create a number of successful, wealthy black entrepreneurs, but it also became a way for companies to subcontract their racial problems out the door. Back in Kansas City, the black-owned Buick dealership on Troost Avenue serves as a perfect example. Forced to hand over minority dealerships and franchises, companies gave black owners the downtown locations and transferred white owners out to the newer, more profitable suburban branches. Ten years later, the guy on Troost was out of business.

The immediate dividends paid by affirmative action were sorely needed; realistically speaking, there was no more direct way to transfer that much money into that many black wallets that quickly. In that sense, affirmative action produced results and was necessary. Black America was long overdue for satisfaction. But Nixon wasn't selling satisfaction. He was selling instant gratification—that's what a good ad man does. Many people in Nixon's camp had genuine faith in affirmative action. It wasn't *designed* to fail, but it wasn't exactly designed to succeed, either; the intent behind it was not rooted in a desire to help black people attain equal standing in society. It was riot insurance. It was to provide a financial incentive for blacks to stay in their own communities and out of the suburbs. It was also a way to dilute the strain on the corporate human resources department. With the majority of college-educated blacks working for the government and with the brightest entrepreneurial talents siphoned off into black-owned business, there were fewer white-collar black hires left for the Fortune 500 to deal with. Affirmative action in government hiring and subcontracting ensured that the corporate glass ceiling would rarely be challenged. Unsurprisingly, the earliest supporters of affirmative action were the corporate- and suburban-friendly Republicans. The *Wall Street Journal* called black capitalism "promising." In Congress, the Republican Policy Committee backed it, too.* Preferences and quotas were an easy answer; they took racial justice and turned it into a line item, an annual allotment for good PR. It was a minor cost, easily absorbed. And as long as the riots didn't come back, it was money well spent. All corporate CEOs had to do to meet their minimal affirmative action mandates was hire a few tokens for the social responsibility department and delegate some work to the minority franchise across town. Then you paid your annual tithe to Jesse Jackson and you were out of it.

When the Madison Avenue Project launched in 2009, its primary complaint wasn't about entry-level hiring. It was about promotions in the upper ranks. "Where are all the mid- and senior-level black executives?" the NAACP asked. The short answer is that they had left. The most successful blacks to emerge in the 1970s—the ones who stood a chance of breaking the glass ceiling, or at least cracking it for the next generation— all took the minority-incentive dollars to go out on their own. The old boys don't respect you, you can make a better living across the street *and* have your name on the door? Who wouldn't take that deal?

"They did it because all the perks of success would be available to them in a separate situation," Roy Eaton explains. "There is that ingrained presumption: 'If it's open to me, I'll exploit it.' Simple as that."

Which is precisely why so many black leaders were against minority business set-asides from the get-go; they were a diversion, a financial incentive to self-segregate. Once the black advertising niche had become profitable, many of the blacks who were left at major agencies quickly defected; the black agencies offered a comfortable atmosphere, no glass

....

*So did the granddaddy conservative of them all, California governor Ronald Reagan, who wrote a personal letter to the head of the OMBE praising "bootstrap" programs for minorities. Reagan was for minority set-asides before he was against them.

ceiling, decent money, and the chance to do important work for the community—an easy sell over suffocating WASPiness. With no pressure to replace those black hires, agencies didn't. When the EEOC checked back in on black hiring in the industry in the mid-1980s, the percentage had fallen from a high of 3.5 percent in 1970 to a new low of 1.7 percent— both of those numbers including custodial and clerical positions. Madison Avenue just forgot about black people. The old boys were free to go right back to selling margarine, snorting cocaine, and banging their secretaries. "The basic power structure of the industry," Eaton says, "was not impacted at all."

In the pages of *Ebony* and *Black Enterprise*, the UniWorlds and Mingo-Joneses were lauded and celebrated. They were "a force to be reckoned with" and "serious contenders for big-budget accounts." Yet they weren't. As the years went by, black agencies did begin to forge meaningful partnerships with genuinely invested partners that produced good work. With brands like Burger King and 3 Musketeers, UniWorld's portfolio would sometimes go beyond minority quotas and extend into the general-market arena. Black agencies did begin to amass annual billings in the hundreds of millions. But Madison Avenue's balance sheet runs in the hundreds of billions. In 2000, *Black Enterprise* published its annual list of the top twenty black-owned advertising agencies. After three decades of minority business incentives, all twenty agencies combined accounted for 0.5 percent of the industry's total revenues.

All the power stayed in the corporate boardrooms of the Fortune 500. If Black Power didn't exert power there, it had no real power at all. The idea of a self-determined, "buy black" economy was a fantasy. Nowhere is this illustrated more tragically than with the Marlboro Man of Black Pride himself, the Brother in the Blue Dashiki. Lighting up a bold, cold Newport, he sold a whole new bag of menthol smoking—the profits of which all went to Lorillard Tobacco, a subsidiary of the American Tobacco Company, which grew out of the tobacco plantations of the Carolinas. Lorillard would later be named in a 2005 lawsuit as being a beneficiary of "assets acquired through the forced and uncompensated labors of enslaved African-Americans."

The Brother was shilling for The Man.

Thirty years after Madison Avenue's color line was broken, the industry had reverted all the way back to major league and Negro league. By the time the split was finished, even Jackie Robinson was asked to leave the field. In 1980, Roy Eaton found himself in a disagreeable spot with the woman brought in to run the division above his. They clashed, he refused to cede control of his team, and she froze him out, cutting his budget to the point where the agency couldn't afford to keep him. It was a personal vendetta, he insists, and not race. But if his color didn't get him fired, his rarefied status offered him no protection, either. "Before that," Eaton says, "any personal difficulties I'd had were insignificant because of the status I had built. But the self-satisfaction of 'been there, done that' with the blacks meant all bets were off. It enabled them to, in effect, fire me without fear of consequence."

Eaton left Benton & Bowles and set up his own music production shop, hoping for big things. "You would think that my reputation over the years would have opened doors to all the agencies. It didn't." White clients didn't come beating down his door. Despite his philosophical differences with the black agencies, he wound up very happy to have them, as he relied on them more and more for commissions. The only work Roy Eaton got from the general-market agencies came not because of his credentials, he says, but through his friends.

[4]

The Inescapable Network

The idea that only blacks could advertise to blacks—and by extension whites to whites—chugged along smoothly and largely unexamined until December of 1983. With *Thriller* on its way to becoming the bestselling album of all time, pop superstar Michael Jackson landed a $5 million endorsement deal from Pepsi. It was the biggest celebrity endorsement deal in history. It would hold that record until Jackson reupped it for $15 million two years later.

Pretty soon, Bill Cosby had the number one TV show in the country, and Eddie Murphy was one of the biggest box office draws in the world. Run-DMC came out of Hollis, Queens, and brought hip-hop into the mainstream. It became painfully clear what Roy Eaton had known all along: culture doesn't have a color line. Groups may have a different vernacular, their art may be rooted in certain ethnic traditions, but once a great idea gets out into the ether it doesn't respect any boundaries. You can't take a business of ideas and mandate where black stuff and white stuff is supposed to go. "The division had nothing to do with talent," Roy Eaton says, "or even profitability. It was just based on racial assumptions."

Eaton had started selling Beefaroni to white people in 1955, and even then the only reason blacks "couldn't" sell to whites was because they were rarely given the chance. The only reason whites "couldn't" sell to

blacks wasn't because they were white, but because they were stone ignorant. But after Michael Jackson, Madison Avenue started to reconsider its
assumptions. In Portland, Oregon, a bunch of white guys at a firm called
Wieden + Kennedy took Nike's Air Jordan and made it one of the iconic
brands of urban America; Air Jordan grossed $130 million in sales in its
first year alone.

Sorting white talent and black talent on opposite sides of the street
officially became a terrible idea in 1992. MC Hammer became the first
rapper to land a major endorsement deal for commercial television.
Young & Rubicam hired him to be the spokesman for Kentucky Fried
Chicken. In a now infamous commercial, MC Hammer rolls into a small-
town KFC while on tour, and no one behind the counter can believe
that he's really *the* MC Hammer. So Hammer does his flashy Hammer
dance . . . and then they give him some fried chicken. Every black person
in America looked up at the TV set and said, "Really? Black man dancing
for chicken?"

Byron Lewis had called it: America was becoming an increasingly
multicultural marketplace, but Madison Avenue didn't have the vocabu-
lary to communicate with its own customers. Regardless, there was no
going back. No matter how the advertising industry was structured,
the Great American Mix Tape kept on mixing. White kids started buying
De La Soul albums in their baggy jeans, and black kids were hitting the
courts with little alligators on their tennis togs. Ever true to its nature,
corporate America followed the money. General-market agencies started
big-footing black agencies, muscling in on their turf—and kept making
horrible MC Hammer–grade mistakes in the process.

Madison Avenue needed black people. Only when agencies looked
around the recruiting pipeline to find them, they weren't there. Most aspiring black professionals were following their peers into other fields;
they never thought to consider a career in advertising because there
weren't any black people in advertising to tell them about all the wonderful opportunities for black people in advertising. In 1968, urban riots had
finally given Madison Avenue a financial incentive to bring minority talent in. One year later, Richard Nixon and Jesse Jackson flipped the script,

giving ad agencies every incentive to pay the diversity dollars out—they would get in trouble, in fact, if they didn't pay the diversity dollars out. And black agencies had every incentive to take the money and stay on the other side of the street. Then everybody spent a couple decades not talking to one another. All through the eighties and early nineties, for appearances' sake, most of the major agencies kept up halfhearted minority recruitment policies, but nothing was done to mentor or groom those young people to become players in the industry. Very few stuck around and broke through. Few enough that they're real easy to find. "As far as black creative directors out there who are doing really interesting work," one said to me, "in my personal opinion, there are seven of us. And that's being generous. Maybe eight? It's a problem."

....

Vann Graves wound up in advertising because he was a big fan of *Bewitched*, the kitschy 1960s sitcom about a suburban witch/housewife and her put-upon husband, Darrin. "I wish it were a more dramatic story," Vann tells me. "But I watched that show all the time when I was a kid. Darrin was in advertising, and I thought, 'Wow, what a cool thing. He's got a nice house and a nice-looking wife.' That was my introduction to the business."

Born in 1968 in Richmond, Virginia, onetime capital of the Confederacy, Vann Graves was part of that singular generation of black Americans, the Children of the Dream, vested with the hopes of all their parents had fought for in the civil rights era. Vann's father had been on the front lines of that battle, going to jail in 1960 for desegregating the downtown lunch counters with a group of students known as the Richmond 34. By the time Vann came along, his father worked for a juvenile detention home—worked two jobs sometimes—and his mother worked at the department of motor vehicles. In 1969, they were one of the first black families to move into what was then the all-white neighborhood of Ginter Park so that Vann and his older brother could attend the public schools there. "Growing up with parents who were active during the civil rights movement," Vann says, "their expectation was, 'Now that we've done our part and built the foundation, you can be a doctor or a lawyer.' So when I started talking about advertising, they were like, 'What are you talking about?' I may as well have said I wanted to be the Tooth Fairy. Advertising wasn't seen as a real career path."

In high school, Vann had been told by one of his white teachers that he would never go to college, that he wasn't even equipped to graduate from high school. Today, Vann has one master's degree completed and is working on his second, from Harvard. "The racism started early," he says, and he wouldn't have gotten past it but for his family behind him, pushing him. But in applying to college, other than vague thoughts about advertising, all Vann really knew was that he wanted to see the world outside Richmond. This was not the world he'd seen on *Bewitched*, but one that came into his living room every Thursday night on NBC.

Had W. E. B. Du Bois been a television critic, he might have written about the "twoness" of *The Cosby Show*. What the Children of White Flight took from *Cosby*—certainly what I took from it—was that black people were Just Like Us. Black doctor and black lawyer in a nice big house. Nothing not normal about that. Several hundred miles away in Richmond, Vann was watching a completely different program than I was. What the Children of the Dream took from *Cosby* was to honor their cultural forebears, stay true to their black identity, follow that, and *that* would bring them the American Dream.

When it first aired, *Cosby* was often criticized for showing only the comfortable, middle-class life of a black doctor and attorney, for avoiding the problems of race. But in its own way, *Cosby* was all about race. The painting that hung in Cliff and Claire Huxtable's living room was a seminal work from Harlem Renaissance artist Ellis Wilson. When Cliff goes to a school charity auction, he gets caught up bidding on a vintage LP of Dizzy Gillespie's "A Night in Tunisia." The defiant stance of black identity made by the Brother in the Blue Dashiki had been framed all too often as a rejection of whatever was white, but the quiet revolution of *Cosby* was to celebrate black accomplishment in and of itself. Being black wasn't predicated on rejecting anything; it was entirely consonant with mainstream American success.

One thing the Huxtables were proudest of was that Mom and Dad had met and courted at the historically black Hillman College, a lightly fictionalized stand-in for Howard University in Washington, D.C., itself sometimes known as the "black Harvard" or simply "the Mecca." Wanting to carry on that tradition, when the show's third season began in the fall of 1986, Denise Huxtable goes off to school at Hillman. For all of Vann's senior year in high school, Denise was on TV calling home every Thursday night, loving black college life. The very next fall, the story of her sophomore year was picked up in the *Cosby* spin-off, *A Different World*. When it did, Vann was watching from his dorm room at Howard. "There was this new resurgence of black pride brought on by the world of *Cosby*," he says. "There was pride in historically black colleges and things that stemmed from the African-American culture. Why wouldn't you want to be a part of that? I remember watching the very first episode of *A Different World* and hearing the Whitley Gilbert character saying, 'Richmond was so hot you could fry an egg on a Jaguar.' As goofy as it may sound, I saw that someone from *my* hometown had made it. It wasn't far from reality. A black kid from Richmond *can* go to college, can go beyond Richmond. A lot of the kids that went to Howard then, if you ask them what pushed them as far as seeing what was possible, at some point they're going to reference back to *The Cosby Show*."

The year after Denise Huxtable went off to Hillman, applications to America's historically black colleges and universities, or HBCUs, spiked by 14 percent nationwide. They had been on the rise, in fact, since the early 1980s. In 1983, America's majority-white colleges reported their first overall dip in black student attendance since the civil-rights era. That same year, Howard's enrollment spiked by 25 percent, many of them transfers from those same white schools. Black college presidents boasted of a cultural homecoming. Their students had "gotten over" the assimilationist notions that white schools were inherently better. In December of '83, *Ebony* reported a "dramatic comeback" in the growth and vitality of black fraternities and sororities, on both black and white campuses alike. So many applications that "we just can't accommodate all of them," said the president of Alpha Phi Alpha, the historic fraternity that boasted alumni ranging from Martin Luther King, Jr., to Supreme Court Justice Thurgood Marshall to the Olympian Jesse Owens. It was a generational shift. The Children of the Dream were coming of age and going off to college, and, like all college students, many were rebelling against the mantle that others had tried to put on them. "Part of the reason a lot of African Americans went to HBCUs at that time," Vann says "was because our parents had sent us to white high schools to give us opportunity or we'd been bused to a white high school, but many of us felt isolated and cut off. We were the Children of the Dream, but we also wanted to have some kind of shared experience in the African-American culture."

Being at Howard during the *Cosby* renaissance, Vann enjoyed his shared experience in the culture. He joined his classmates in reviving the spirit of the sixties, occupying the campus administration building to protest the appointment of Republican Lee Atwater to Howard's board. A fellow classmate, Sean "Puffy/Puff Daddy/P. Diddy" Combs, was lighting up the campus with epic dance parties, landmark events in the emerging hip-hop scene that would soon come to dominate the country's cultural landscape. An exciting time, all in all, even if he had to work three part-time jobs and take a few semesters off to save enough to pay his way through. Graduating in the Class of '93 with a bachelor's degree in marketing, Vann took his diploma to look for work on lily-white Madison Avenue, and there he quickly realized the one thing his historically black college had not given him.

"It's all who you know," he says, "and I didn't know anyone."

....

Given the way black high schools in the South were shattered under court-ordered integration, black America's attachment to its own colleges is tenacious. Still today over 20 percent of all bachelor's degrees awarded to blacks are earned at HBCUs. According to the United Negro College Fund, black colleges produce 70 percent of all black dentists, 50 percent of black attorneys, 50 percent of black engineers, and, consistently, more than half of all black PhDs in the last twenty years. If you look closely, however, you'll see that those are all credentialed professions. It's no coincidence that Cliff and Clair Huxtable found success as a doctor and a lawyer, respectively. Pass your medical boards or the bar exam, and you get called up to the show. Unfortunately, like advertising, a sizable chunk of the American economy doesn't offer professional credentialing of any kind. Qualifications are softer, more vague, and more susceptible to racial bias. I've yet to come across the figures boasting of black colleges' success in social and cultural industries like media and publishing; I suspect those figures don't exist.

Another fact often touted by HBCUs is that they produce half of all black students who go on to earn a graduate degree. An impressive stat, until you flip it over. Oftentimes, when you come out of an HBCU, you *have* to go to grad school because you've put yourself in the wrong pipeline. After Howard, already swimming in student loans, Vann Graves moved to New York and enrolled in the master's program at Brooklyn's Pratt Institute. Pratt is an art and design school with a strong feeder program for the advertising industry; Vann had to backtrack his way into the business. From Pratt, he landed a summer internship at BBDO through the 4A's Minority Advertising Intern Program. Vann got the chance to do some work on the Pepsi account. He thought that would be the thing to get him noticed, but his big break wound up being something entirely unexpected. "Phil Dusenberry was one of the original Mad Men," Vann says. "He ran all of BBDO. He called me to his office one day, and he said, 'I need you to help work on a special project, a Christmas card.'

"A Christmas card? Then he clarified. It wasn't his Christmas card. It was his *dog's* Christmas card—a senior art director was working on his. But I said, 'You know what? I'm gonna bust my ass on this.' Fa la la la la, bow wow, meow, and the rest is history. I had to go back to finish my degree, but Phil called me twice and said, 'When you're done with school, I want you back at the agency.'" In 1993, Vann joined BBDO as a permanent, part-time assistant art director. He was one of three black creatives in the entire agency, out of about two hundred fifty.

Two years before Vann arrived at Pratt to start his master's, Geoff Edwards had already left with his bachelor's, headed to take a job at Chiat/Day/Mojo. Geoff had come to New York for college by way of Detroit. Where Vann had been inspired by the Cosby kids, Geoff was a Cosby kid. He'd gone to one of the best private high schools in the country, University of Detroit Jesuit High School and Academy. His father, a doctor, had emigrated from Guyana in South America to go to medical school. His mother, Motown born and raised, was a chemistry teacher in the city school system.

"Advertising is one of those callings that you don't choose," Edwards says. "It chooses you. Your unique perspective and creativity come from things you see and experience in life, and advertising is a career that no one is exposed to early on; I certainly wasn't. I just knew that I wanted to be an artist. I grew up drawing. Anything creative I could get my hands on, I did. At Pratt, you had to declare a major sophomore year. My dad said, 'What are you going to do?' I told him I wanted to be a painter. He said, 'Okay, what do you want to do for a *living*?'

"This is my father, who grew up without shoes in a house of eight brothers and sisters in South America, came to the United States, and became a doctor. So to hear his son say 'I want to go paint on canvases' wasn't something he thought was great. So that pushed me to things like graphic design, industrial design. Finally, someone mentioned advertising. It was a unique combination of all the things that I love—photography, motion picture, storytelling. The more I got into it, the more I liked it.

"At the time, Chiat/Day was the best advertising agency in America. They were like the Yankees. When I graduated, I told my teacher that's where I wanted to go. She said, 'You should have a second choice. They don't take a lot of people.'

"I said, 'That's why I want to go there.'"

And he went, first as an intern and then moving up to art director. "I was the only chocolate chip in the cookie," he says. "I had no idea it was going to be that abrupt. Fortunately my name was not a barrier, spelled the way it is—Geoffrey Taylor Edwards. With that on my résumé, I don't think anyone ever expected me to show up."

Vann Graves and Geoff Edwards were both Children of the Dream. Both came out of the same school and started out in the same job at around the same time. Both were at major agencies renowned for producing some of the best work in the industry. And both were almost totally alone in a vast ocean of white dudes, neither of them given a whole lot of guidance to help show the way. One of them had an easier time of it than the other.

....

Much like Hollywood pats itself on the back every year with the Oscars and the Golden Globes, advertising agencies celebrate their own annual achievements with awards shows like the One Show, the Clios, the Cannes Lions, and through institutions like the American Advertising Federation Hall of Fame. Big-name creative directors submit their work to be judged, and other big-name creative directors do the judging. Then the following year they all switch places.

The lawyers from the NAACP say they want the industry to institute a credentialing process and uniform standards for promotion, metrics for a racial accounting system. But there's no rational standard for assessing the value of a commercial. You either like the creepy ETrade baby or you don't. Some commercials are inspired ideas that in the end sell no products. The ads that sell the most products—discount coupons—require no thought or talent at all. There is no metric. Which is why the most sophisticated performance evaluation system the industry has ever developed is to have a bunch of dudes get together in a hotel ballroom, drink way too much, and then sit around telling each other that they're awesome. You earn promotions in advertising by "getting your name out there." You show up at events with the right look, shake hands, win awards, and generally create the impression that "you're the guy."

"It's all about street cred," Vann Graves says. "There's enough talented people out there to sell soap or shoes. It's how you package that. It's letting your client know that, good or bad, you've got their back. 'You need me to make you look good.' It's how you approach the game, and a lot of it is a game. Some agencies spend more on producing the entries to awards shows than it cost to create the work that they're submitting. There are people who hire their own PR firms just to keep their names out front. You get opportunity based on reputation, but no one is giving you the opportunity to work on the big campaigns that give you that reputation if you don't already have it. So either you've got street cred, a little nepotism helping you out, or both."

When he started at BBDO, Vann had neither.

Vann showed up at the tail end of the Mad Men era. Three-martini lunches. People smoking in their offices. Having come in through a minority internship program, he was probably the only guy in the building who wasn't there because of a school or family connection. He got along well enough, but he didn't really fit in, and he wasn't getting ahead.

Growing up in Richmond, Vann's parents had moved across town to get him across the color line. There were barely enough black people at his high school to have a black cafeteria table, and Vann had made white friends with no problems. His parents raised him to sit anywhere in the cafeteria he wanted. "Almost to the day he died," Vann says, "my father would say, 'You have to run faster, work harder, and aim higher just to be considered average. You can't make everything about race, even if it is.'" But then Vann went to Howard, which made him doubly conscious of his race. That would be both a blessing and a burden.

"I was empowered by going to an HBCU," he says. "The benefit of going somewhere like Howard was understanding the history of race and discrimination. They equipped me for that. I became a much more aware individual. But coming out of that environment and going into corporate America, there was also a level of defensiveness on my part. I had my back up, always thinking that racism was what kept me from succeeding, the reason people weren't giving me opportunities. The hardest thing as a minority is to step back and say, 'Are they being racist, or is this the process?'"

Advertising is a shitty business for black people. It's also just a shitty, frustrating business. The rock stars get to handle all the cool projects, and until you're one of them you might spend five years in a cubicle thinking up new ways to peddle sugared cereal to fat kids and hating yourself for it. When your big break finally comes, you show your boss thirty great ideas and maybe one makes it to the final presentation. Then, the night before the big meeting, your one idea gets scrapped and left behind. Then you start all over again. Black people aren't the only ones who quit.

In a department of two hundred and fifty white guys—and we are talking mostly guys—there was no shortage of slights and affronts for Vann to be offended by. Never any overt hostility directed at him, he says, but more of a deep-seated lack of awareness and cultural understanding. And given the era, with white agencies fumbling awkwardly to cash in on this new hip-hop thing, he found himself designated "the black guy." He was thrust into the middle of a lot of meetings where MC Hammer–grade train wrecks were waiting to happen, a lot of black men dancing for chicken and soda and four-door sedans. Vann didn't know how to pick his battles, when to speak up and when to let something go. He picked a couple of the wrong battles early on. He might have flamed out completely if it hadn't been for one person who cared enough to reach out and help. "The creative manager, June Baloutine, a great friend and mentor. She pulled me into her office one day and said, 'I'm not going to let you ruin this for yourself. Once you've established yourself and earned some authority, *then* you can challenge the way things are done around here, but not before.'

"Then she told me to open my eyes and said, 'Look around. They're hard on everybody.' And it was true. There was a white guy right next to me, she pointed out, an incredibly talented illustrator and artist; he'd been there longer than I had but hadn't gotten as far as I had. Was there some racist stuff going on? Sure. Did my color hurt? Sometimes. Did it help? Sometimes. But I realized that they messed with everyone. Everybody had to be pledged, and there were white guys who got pledged just like me. The way agencies worked back then, if you were there you probably knew someone, because you weren't just rolling up into BBDO. So while I came in as a MAIP intern, I also just came in with all the other guys. As far as my department knew, I wasn't the black intern. I was just another pair of hands like all the rest of them. I was given the same chances to screw up that everyone else got."

Vann also came to realize something else. As offensive as the lack of cultural awareness in the office was, part of that deficit was his own. They didn't understand him, but he didn't understand them, either. "I used to walk into the office dressed to the nines," he says, "top to bottom, because that's what Howard taught me. 'This is what you do. This is professional.' Then I realized, Huh, everyone here, including the senior management, is in casual clothes. I was making myself separate from them. I wasn't a part of the culture.

"So I said to myself, 'I need to step up and learn what these people do. I need to understand not how *I* think they should play the game, but how the game is played.' I toned down my clothes and my attitude, and I did more listening than talking. I learned it's not a hard adjustment to make if you're willing to make it. And that doesn't mean you're giving up your blackness. It doesn't mean giving up anything. It's not assimilating, it's learning. It's creating opportunities for yourself."

According to the NAACP's employment figures, the average black employee washes out of advertising in less than seven years. Vann stayed at BBDO for fifteen, building a portfolio of award-winning work on accounts like Gillette, AT&T, Motorola, Snickers, and Visa. He was promoted to vice president and creative director in 2004.

Across town at Chiat/Day, Geoff Edwards was learning to play the same game as Vann. "It's impossible for you not to feel race in advertising in America," Geoff says. "You name the meeting, I'm the only guy who looks like me at every meeting of the last nineteen years of my career. I struggled with it a bit. There were a few occasions where I was asked not to be in a client meeting, or a pitch; that's where, for me, it was a little bit of an eye-opener."

The difference between Vann and Geoff, regardless of their respective talents, was that Geoff walked in the door with the tool kit to work around the problems he encountered. "Maybe it's just the way I grew up," he says, "but my experience has always been a healthy one in terms of my parents raising me to not see color as much as possible. My dad went to Indiana University in the 1950s; it's pretty easy to find him in the yearbook. He experienced a great deal of racism. But he also came from a country where there were all sorts of people—black, Indian, Asian— who all considered themselves Guyanese. He didn't raise us to think that we were any less or any different than anyone else. I had a mom who told me I could be anything I wanted. When I first went to school, it was just never an issue. I had friends who were white and I had friends who were black. So once I was in advertising I was always able to network at a very high level with people who weren't black."

Consistently able to network one level up from himself, Geoff got his ideas in front of the people who mattered. His talents were quickly recognized. He jumped around to a few different agencies, landing at DDB in 1994. Soon, he was networking at the highest levels imaginable, on both sides of the color line. Looking for a director to helm a television spot for Budweiser, Edwards cold-called one of his idols, filmmaker Spike Lee.

Lee signed on to do the piece, and they worked on it together. "We went to dinner one night," Geoff says, "and he told me, 'I'm gonna let you in on a secret. I've always kind of wanted to be in advertising. Remember the work I did as Mars Blackmon with Nike? Ever since then, I've wanted to be in this business. I love it. I think more of us should be in it.'

"So I said, 'Why don't I talk to some higher-ups at DDB and try and make this happen?' At the time, neither of us really knew what that meant. But I got Spike on a conference call, and before you know it, we're crafting a deal to launch an agency together."

In December of 1996, Spike/DDB launched as a joint partnership, with Lee taking a 51 percent controlling interest. Edwards and his writing partner went with Lee to head up his newly minted creative division. Only five years in the business, not even thirty years old, and Edwards was already founding an agency with the most famous black filmmaker in America while the Mad Men wrote checks to cover the overhead. After DDB, Geoff leapfrogged to Foote, Cone & Belding in Chicago, then back to Chiat/Day in Los Angeles, and finally to T.A.G. in San Francisco. In 2006, he was named Top Art Director in the Country by *Boards* magazine and a Creative All-Star by *AdWeek*, and his client Adidas was named Advertiser of the Year at the Cannes Lions International Advertising Festival. "What's amazing about this business," Geoff says, "is that it's a business of ideas, and ideas have no color. Once you're in, it really is about the work. It really is about talent."

....

In the past decade, the Congressional Black Caucus, the New York City Commission on Human Rights, and now the NAACP have made a lot of noise about tearing down the walls of the old boys' network, but none of them has made a whole lot of progress. In part, perhaps, because they seem to have fundamentally misdiagnosed the problem. Madison Avenue doesn't have an old boys' network. It has two of them.

"A few months ago, I went and signed up for LinkedIn," Vann Graves says. With over one hundred million members, LinkedIn has become the primary online networking site for business professionals; in an industry that's all about street cred, most people at least keep a presence on it to help get their names out there. "I was looking for folks to work for me and work with me. So I signed up, joined LinkedIn Plus and the whole package, and I started looking through my business connections, and then through my connections' connections, and I was like 'Wow. This is weird. There are no black folks on LinkedIn.'

"But I kept adding people and then I started getting through to those fifth and sixth degrees of separation, and I was like, 'Oh, wait. There's a *lot* of black people on LinkedIn.' It was just that their professional networks were all several degrees away from mine."

Vann Graves and Geoff Edwards work in advertising. Most black people don't work in advertising. They work in black advertising. Or "multi-cultural marketing," as it's now often called, lumped in with Hispanic advertising and Asian advertising. Advertising and multicultural marketing are not the same thing. They're two separate industries built on separate business networks—and separate social networks, because in a relationship business there's no difference between the two. Nowhere is this more apparent than on LinkedIn and on Facebook. LinkedIn is strictly for business, and Facebook is allegedly social, but to look at them side by side proves what everyone knows to be true. Your friends are often your business contacts, and your best business contacts generally become friends, because you like doing business together. That was true in 1955 when Roy Eaton and Charlie Feldman bonded over being ethnic outsiders in a world of WASPs. It was true in 1971, when Byron Lewis and his friend Al Bell collaborated on the hit marketing campaign for *Shaft*. And it's true for Vann Graves and Geoff Edwards today.

"My AT&T client?" Geoff says. "We'll close a deal over Facebook. It's basically a business tool in that way. I just joined LinkedIn recently, and I actually think that Facebook is a better business tool *because* it's social. People see you. They see what you're up to. They see your status updates. They comment on them. What's interesting about Facebook and LinkedIn is that, given the two, people want to see who you are. If there's a choice of looking at someone's résumé and seeing how they interact and how they live and what they're about? You'd be surprised how much that factors in."

Advertising is making friends. Not contacts, friends. Which, for the most part, means making white friends. Vann has 395 LinkedIn connections and 587 Facebook friends. Having just joined LinkedIn, Geoff's only up to 162 connections there, but his business partner calls him "the Mayor of Facebook"; with 783 friends, he's on it all the time. Roughly speaking, Vann's Facebook network is about 30 percent black, 60 percent white, and 10 percent other. Geoff's network is closer to 20 percent black, 65 percent white, and 15 percent other. (And I say "roughly speaking" because not everyone's ethnicity is readily apparent from his or her profile photo, and also because I'm using a pretty broad definition of "white." Is the Turkish guy white? How about the half-Brazilian/half-Moroccan girl who totally looks Jewish? The boundary between "white" and "other" is pretty hard to nail down. For that matter, the boundary between "black" and "other" is getting pretty hazy, too.)

Today, Vann and Geoff lead lives that are wholly integrated, not just with white people but with everyone. Not surprisingly, I found the exact same thing to be the case for every black person working successfully in advertising that I've met in the last three years. They're not black Anglo-Saxons. It's not 1969 anymore. You can be authentically black and still be assimilated; these things aren't mutually exclusive, as Vann discovered. If you take an online stroll through the social universe of blacks on Madison Avenue, the numbers may vary this way or that, but it's always a broad mix of blacks, whites, Jews, Iranians, Koreans, Panamanians, Croatians—whatever. They're a part of the general, Middle-American population. They're in the melting pot. And while I can't say that this is universally true, I can say I've yet to encounter anyone in the business for whom it is not true.

So, do these people have a lot of white friends because they work in advertising, or do they work in advertising because they have a lot of white friends? Are ad agencies unfairly biased in favor of whites and assimilated minorities, or is assimilation just a prerequisite for the job, like knowing Microsoft Word? To judge by the letter of current civil rights law, it's possible to pick apart the numbers and say that, yes, these agencies are unfairly biased and are therefore engaged in illegal hiring practices. But to judge from Facebook and LinkedIn, the laws of social interaction carry far more weight than anything coming out of Washington, D.C.

You can take any of a number of entry points into the black advertising network. You can start at the profile pages of the larger black agencies, like UniWorld and Burrell Communications. There's also a host of networking groups for black media professionals, like Black Creatives or the National Association of Multicultural Media Executives. And once you start clicking and scrolling through the profiles of black people in those networks, you've effectively left the white working world behind. You've entered the world of diversity suppliers and minority-targeted media and urban radio and black PR firms. It's a separate system. To eyeball it, it's 80 to 90 to 99 percent black most every page you click. Not always, but generally. And a lot of the white faces you do see belong to human resources people and supply-chain managers and "inclusion specialists" (i.e., the intermediaries appointed to manage the color line and show that companies Care About Diversity). And once you're two or three degrees into the black advertising and media networks, you then find yourself moving out into the social ecosystem that feeds it: the alumni networks for HBCUs, black fraternities and sororities, and other affinity groups. You can click and scroll for days and days, seeing only the odd white face here and there. This is among four-year college graduates. In a country that's only 13 percent black.

Ever since the Madison Avenue Project launched, every industry convention has been packed with diversity seminars and multicultural mixers and even a new multicultural awards show, AdColor. But when you look at the Facebook photo albums posted up from these events and see who's commenting on them and who's commenting back, it's the same black people going to the same events over and over again. Follow the daisy chain of job recommendations black people are posting for each other on LinkedIn, and the vast majority of the activity is black people recommending black people to other black people. It's a closed loop.

White people's social networks are no better. They're just as lopsided. But then so is corporate America. We're out there looking for jobs, too, and the people we need to be networking with look a lot like us; that's the unfair advantage we have. The rationale behind all the diversity mixers, allegedly, is to help close that gap. But the atmosphere at those things—having attended a couple dozen of them—is artificial, transactional. The events are 90 percent black, and, again, most of the white people you'll meet there are the intermediaries, the appointed diversity outreach specialists. You don't get anywhere networking with those people. You build a career by networking with your peers, the people who are going to move up and take you with them. But rank-and-file white people don't come to diversity events, because white people don't work in diversity. White people work in advertising. They go to advertising events.

"One of the mantras they taught us at Howard was 'networking,'" Vann Graves says. "But networking alone gets you where? You've got to have leverage. In this business, only networking with other African Americans is like me networking with myself. The problem is, we're paying that forward. The younger folks come in and get into the system, and they're pissed off because 'I'm black, and I can't get a break.' So they keep going to these multicultural mixers, not realizing that part of it is a self-fulfilling prophecy. It's the same people rolling around in the same circles. It all feeds on itself."

"I've lost friends to black agencies," Geoff Edwards says with a heavy sigh. Leaving the black cafeteria table always comes at a cost. For a very brief spell in the 1990s, Geoff did a turn at a black agency in New York, the Mingo Group, and very quickly realized he had to get out. "There are people that I went to college with at Pratt," he says, "people who are extremely talented and could be in no different a position than I am, but the difference is they felt that calling to go and be in the black agencies. It hurt their careers.

"In this business, you are what you eat. If you have a great reel, you're going to go to a great place and you're going to continue to go to great places. That's how the fraternity works, right? People at my level, you look at their records and you see the great agencies. You see Weiden + Kennedy, Chiat/Day, Goodby. But once you go to one of the multicultural agencies, it's very hard to make the jump back. Some people do it, but it's difficult. People get trapped. Maybe you have a career that's lucrative in terms of financial success, but in terms of just being a part of the cultural vernacular of advertising or being around the people who are associated with award-winning work? You're done. You're cooked."

When you're stuck on the outside of a social network, it seems impenetrable, like an exclusive country club that won't grant you membership. But once you break in, however you break in, what you learn is that the network doesn't really run on exclusivity. It runs on reciprocity. Do your boss's dog's Christmas card and get a part-time job. Put your boss in a meeting with Spike Lee and get your own agency—with Spike Lee. You spend years building up personal credits, large and small, and then you cash in those IOUs to move up. That's what Vann calls street cred. And over the last four decades, black advertising and media professionals have been coming out of college and investing their time and talent and street cred in a parallel pipeline, one with almost no money and very few jobs, leaving them with precious little social currency to spend in the larger economy and very little leverage to help the generation behind. So everybody's still back at square one, scrambling and inviting ALL BRIGHT YOUNG MEN AND WOMEN TO CONSIDER ADVERTISING AS A CAREER. In the meantime, how many mid- to senior-level black creatives will you find on Madison Avenue? There are seven of them. Maybe eight. It's a problem.

....

In 1999, the Civil Rights Project at Harvard University published a now landmark report titled "Resegregation in American Schools." It showed that the country made steady progress toward a healthy racial balance up until the late 1980s. Since then, due to a number of factors, primarily the hostility of conservative federal courts opposed to race-based desegregation, the trend toward diversity and racial balance has reversed precipitously. In the 1996–1997 school year, ratios of black to white students in public schools fell below the levels achieved in 1972. As of 2006–2007, 73 percent of America's black children attended schools with at least 50 percent minority enrollment, and 38.5 percent attended schools with at least a 90 percent minority enrollment.

In the decade since, left-leaning activists and academics have been increasingly up in arms about the dangers of "resegregation," which is the latest buzzword people use in policymaking circles when discussing the problems of race. Resegregation is a "perilous" trend, they say. Except, like most trends, it isn't actually a trend. To say that America's schools are resegregating is to misstate the facts. They can't resegregate. They've never integrated. The absence of artificial transfer programs to shuffle kids around just means we're seeing the country for what it has been all along, what it never stopped being.

Starting in the late 1960s, America hurled its public schools headlong into a hugely disruptive, shot-in-the-dark experiment. We spent billions of dollars, all of it just to corral the Children of White Flight and the Children of the Dream and put them under the same roof. Given that historic opportunity, we all came together and . . . we sat on opposite sides of the cafeteria. Then we went and hung out at different clubs and fraternities at opposite ends of college campuses, or at completely separate colleges altogether. Ever since *Brown v. Board*, there's been a steady chorus of academics and politicians pronouncing all the wonderful things that integration is supposed to do for America. Integrated schools will produce better educational outcomes. Diversity programs will give us integrated workplaces that offer competitive advantages in a multicultural world. Etc. It's all a lot of crap. Integration doesn't *do* anything. It's something that is done, by people, and only by mutual choice. It's certainly true that too many avenues of integration were impeded by socioeconomic inequality or shut down entirely by racist and discriminatory actions. But it is equally true that among those who were given the opportunity to integrate, most of us chose not to.

When people say "It's all who you know," strictly with regard to the workplace, it connotes some buddy-buddy, scratch-my-back system that won't give the outside guy a break. Sometimes it is that. At its worst, it really is a restricted country club of cronyism where high-end real estate developers collude with the federal government to line their pockets with millions in taxpayer subsidies. But down here on the ground, down here where the normal people live, "It's all who you know" is simply a statement of fact. You are the sum total of the people you meet and interact with in the world. Whether it's your family, peers, or coworkers, the opportunities you have and the things that you learn all come through doors that other people open for you.

"It's all who you know" is, in fact, the whole reason we had to have a civil rights movement in the first place. "I cannot reach fulfillment without thou," Martin Luther King said. "All life is interrelated. All men are caught in an inescapable network of mutuality, tied in a single garment of destiny." After a century of Jim Crow, we hated and feared each other because we didn't know each other. Knowing each other—"sustained intergroup, interpersonal doing," King called it—was the only way to undo the damage of not knowing each other. When cast against the harsh reality of racism at the time, what King was saying seemed impossible. It might still seem impossible. But that doesn't mean that it's wrong.

Even in the 1960s, King saw where Facebook and LinkedIn would take the inescapable network. "Through our scientific genius we have made of this world a neighborhood," he said, "now through our moral and spiritual development we must make of it a brotherhood." We didn't. We gave up on King. Quite famously, by the time he got to Memphis in April of 1968, King himself had almost given up on seeing the dream fulfilled. The final, undelivered sermon he was supposed to give that next Sunday was simply titled "Why America May Still Go to Hell." White hostility was fueling black anger and frustration, destroying what remaining hope the country had for reconciliation. After King was murdered, for a while, everything really did go to hell. But some people, some black parents, didn't give up on King. They didn't give up on white people, really, despite all the available evidence that they should.

When the post–civil rights era began, certain types of affirmative action were absolutely critical. Those programs provided access to jobs and education, allowing blacks to move up at a time when, socially, they couldn't move in. But however you do it, you still have to move in. Which is why some parents made the deliberate choice to push their kids away from the black cafeteria table. They took the modest gains that affirmative action offered, and they invested it. Not in education, but in integration. Whether it was Vann Graves's father carrying two working class jobs just to get him across Richmond's color line, or Geoff Edwards's father sending him to the finest prep school in Michigan, the idea was the same. Those families bought white social capital for their children, because they had a hunch that, in America, white social capital would be the thing that paid dividends. It did.

In the 1990s, my friends and I had the dumb luck to walk out of college right into the biggest economic revolution since the invention of the steam engine, and the Children of the Dream were nowhere in sight. The Internet boom took off, and it was all who you knew because it was moving too fast to be anything else. Whether you were in interactive advertising in New York or at some dot-com start-up in San Francisco, it was lily white and Asian as far as the eye could see; you could count all the black faces on one hand. It wasn't just that we had better access to computers. It's that we had access to the people who knew what computers were going to do.

Whatever the next big thing is, whether it's environmental technology or farming hydroponic tomatoes on the moon, right now that thing is just two guys in a garage with an idea. And if you don't know the guys who know those guys, then you just don't know them. By the time their idea is big enough for the lawyers to show up and build the diversity pipeline, the real money and the real opportunities will be gone. So if we're not talking about why black people and white people don't hang out and play Scrabble together, we're not talking about the problem.

What's Black About It?

On September 11, 2001, two planes hit the Twin Towers of the World Trade Center in lower Manhattan. Less than an hour after the second tower fell, Vann Graves walked down to the U.S. Army Recruiting office on 125th Street in Harlem and enlisted in the Army Reserves. You hear about people doing that, but you never actually meet them. Not in advertising, anyway.

"My colleagues at BBDO thought I'd gone mad," he says. "But I was a creative director at a major advertising agency, a little soft around the middle, living the American Dream, and the only reason I could do that was because someone else fought for *my* rights. At a certain point, you have to give something back."

Vann deployed to Iraq in 2005 and served as a public affairs officer with the 101st Airborne and the 11th Armored Cavalry Regiment, escorting embedded reporters into forward combat zones. During his tour, he was promoted to captain, received a Combat Action Badge, and was inducted into the Order of the Spur for outstanding efforts while being actively engaged by anti-U.S. forces. After his Striker ran aground on one of Iraq's roadside IEDs, he was awarded a Purple Heart. It was a little disorienting to come home and start writing Snickers commercials again. "I went back to work," he says, "and they had basically sealed off my office.

Everything was right where I'd left it, and nothing had changed. But I had changed. Nothing seemed the same to me anymore.

"I had been at BBDO for fifteen years. When I started, there were three African Americans in the creative department. When I left, there were three African Americans in the creative department. The world was evolving, especially in a time with a black president, clearly moving in a different direction. I wanted my work to be a part of that change that was happening."

The change that's happening, of course, is in the fabric of America. All the demographic indicators now point to the year 2042, when America will become a "majority minority" country—all the black, brown, and yellow people will tip over 50 percent of the population, and the white cultural hegemony, we're told, will be in retreat.

Byron Lewis at UniWorld is especially bullish on the next decade. "You're really talking about a marketing opportunity that is now very apparent to everyone," he says. "I'm passionate about it. I believe in the validity of what we represent. Consumers of color represent most of the best known, most visible, and most influential folks in the domestic and global culture, in music, sports, entertainment, and street fashion. Why shouldn't multicultural agencies be the lead agencies on major accounts? My attitude is that I feel totally capable of competing in a space where I think there's equal opportunity. I don't want to work on pieces of accounts. I think the road for us is to follow the trend of the population. It's not time to divorce it; it's time to elevate it."

So in 2008, UniWorld reached out and hired Vann Graves to serve as its new chief creative officer, to bring his corporate agency experience to the multicultural ad space and help make a new paradigm for the shifting population: the ethnic market as the general market, and vice versa. For Byron Lewis it was a chance to move beyond the political limitations of his company's past. For Vann, it seemed an opportunity to make a stake in something he felt was relevant to the country's new direction. It was an opportunity to bridge the gap and bring black agencies into the big game. But the missionary zeal of the census watchers and the aspirations of UniWorld—the whole business of racially targeted media, in fact—has run into one very significant obstacle: the Internet doesn't care if you're black.

....

In 1996, some web-savvy entrepreneurs launched a dot-com start-up named DoubleClick. The company positioned itself as a new kind of media buyer for the web, purchasing ad space on websites for all those banners and pop-ups. Shortly thereafter, a black-owned media company in New York launched the AdHere Network—"the black DoubleClick"— to execute the same media-buying functions across the growing number of black-oriented websites. While my friends and I were working on the Internet, it turns out, the Children of the Dream were off working on what might be called the black Internet.

In 2007, Google bought DoubleClick for $3.1 billion in cash. The Ad-Here Network, along with a large chunk of the black Internet, was already long gone. "The whole thing failed," says Neal Arthur, managing director for the New York office of Wieden + Kennedy.

Arthur, who is black, started out at W+K as the company's director of strategic planning, responsible for analyzing cultural demographics to map out where and how ad dollars are most effectively spent. His job is to know what every kid in America is going to eat for breakfast tomorrow, how many hours they spend on Facebook, and how much their parents are going to spend on back-to-school clothes this year. In the early 2000s, Arthur was watching closely to understand how, and why, black Internet companies stumbled so quickly.

"There used to be a top-down pipeline for black culture," he tells me. "We created BET instead of thinking you could have black content on MTV. Then people tried to do that with the web. They were thinking, 'Oh, we'll give black people this pipeline, and that's all they'll consume.' But the Internet is a consumer-driven medium, and they underestimated black people's interests—*that's* what's so fascinating. Black people had underestimated themselves for so long that the web was like a slap in the face. 'Oh, wait, black people like sushi? I had no idea. I'd been selling them Kentucky Fried Chicken for so long.' The Internet has made it clear that black people like a lot of shit you didn't know about. That pipe has blown wide open."

It has, but black companies are still out there trying to duct tape it to-gether. Rushmore Drive—"the black Google"—launched in 2008, offering to push black content to the front of the line based on users' searches. That same year saw the launch of Blackbird—"the black browser"—which likewise purported to filter and present the web through the lens of black interests. The list goes on and on: a black MySpace (OurSpace .com), a black LinkedIn (BlackBusinessNetwork.com), and even a black YouTube (quite original: TheBlackYouTube.com). No policy of discrimina-tion exists to keep blacks off the mainstream iterations of those sites. There is no Troost Avenue on the Internet. Yet here black America was building its own. Even as black Americans streamed online in massive numbers—68 percent, and 90 percent of teens, are now online—the black Internet stalled. Rushmore Drive went under in fourteen months. The black browser? You won't find too many people using it.

The Internet has offered black writers, artists, and journalists more freedom of expression than ever before. But it's precisely the breadth of that opportunity that has hobbled the primacy of the black-centric busi-ness model. Among the most successful black-owned media enterprises on the web is Interactive One, the online subsidiary of urban radio power-house Radio One. It includes several properties like The Urban Daily and the social networking site Black Planet. The company bills itself as *the* destination for the online black community, drawing 9 million unique visitors a month. But 28 million black Americans are now online. Nobody can claim anymore that only they can speak to the black consumer—and that scares the hell out of the people who for decades have made their liv-ing claiming just that. The door between black and white America has been fiercely guarded by its self-appointed gatekeepers: black politicians, Jesse Jackson, black media owners, and black ad agencies. The reason their legitimacy is on shaky ground is because it's never been based on the consent of the black masses, but mostly on the ignorance, guilt, and anxiety of white people. "They're the ones who are violating the system," Arthur says of the gatekeepers, "because you gotta make that dollar. The easiest thing for me to do is to make you insecure as a white marketer and say, 'Look, we know how this shit rolls, and you don't. We know the music, et cetera.' It just feeds on that white insecurity."

It's testimony to just how ignorant and insecure white people are that this game keeps getting played. Corporate America keeps pouring billions into all these propositions that sell the white man on the fact that he needs an intermediary just to talk to black people, even as the demographics of black America call for it less and less. "You used to be able to buy a 'black' media plan," Arthur says. "*Essence* and *Ebony*, BET and ESPN. That was how you reached black people. Now, when you think about your audience, you have to be much more sophisticated. The Internet is democratizing the urban experience. What's fascinating is how quickly and how broadly the cultural references travel. What black kids are sampling is incredibly wide. Now the question is what *type* of African American are we going after? I do focus groups for Jordan all the time. I was in a group the other night, and there was this black kid from Houston who was like, 'Yeah, my style is mainly Japanese.' Really? Okay. It's become quite cool to push the boundaries of what the African-American experience is."

Black-owned media grew out as a necessary alternative to America's white cultural hegemony, but it became a cultural hegemony of its own, monolithic in its orthodoxy and its point of view. Ditto the black advertising that supported it. "You look at black advertising from the seventies," Arthur says, "it was blaxploitation. All that Billy Dee Williams shit? You talk about perpetuating the problem—we created that. And we still suffer from it. Back then, just having black people in ads was a breakthrough, so much so that it provided disproportionate power to those brands. The beauty of now is that that's not enough. You have to say more."

Today, a lot of black advertising has become a watered-down version of a formerly Afrocentric self: bourgie black yuppies gettin' *down* with their Big Macs to an R&B-tinged "I'm Lovin' It." Some of it's difficult to watch. The black political and business establishment protects its interests by insisting that blacks have to be marketed to as blacks through black media. Black consumers, on the other hand, are decidedly split on the matter; some find it pandering. The biggest sea change of the digital age is not that companies can go around the gatekeepers; it's that black people can go around them, too. The Internet is changing everything because it cares only about what you *want*, how you behave. What are your "likes"? Google's search engine is just a mathematical algorithm driven by user choices. The web is just ones and zeros flying through a series of tubes. The tubes don't care whose are which. If you're on YouTube watching a JayZ video or a Phil Collins video, the computer serving you an ad isn't concerned with what color you are. The computer only cares that you like JayZ or Phil Collins (or both), and it will serve you an ad based on something else it thinks you might like. A nice JayZ/Phil Collins mash-up, perhaps. Targeted media has gone light-years past targeting your race; it targets you.

Advertising is aspirational. It takes what people want to believe about themselves and then sells it back to them in the form of a car or a house or an iPod. At the end of the day, people don't *really* aspire to whiteness, or to blackness. Back in Kansas City, J. C. Nichols wasn't selling segregated housing. He was selling status. The Brother in the Blue Dashiki wasn't really selling black pride, either. He was selling a salve for wounded male egos. The veneer of an ad may be racial, but the sell is always personal. If you're a person who understands people, you can sell anybody anything.

Ethnic marketing will always have its niche; it's critical when there's a genuine cultural or linguistic barrier to overcome. But it's a small niche. The gold standard for any brand is to achieve a global status that transcends those barriers, that needs no translation. Nike. Apple. BMW. They're not black. They're not white. They're just cool. That's the brand that makes money. And the only way to be that brand is by connecting with each individual personally while still having a message that resonates universally. Which is why good advertising is really hard to do, and why most of it sucks.

....

When the NAACP announced its Madison Avenue Project in 2009, it did so in a state of mild self-delusion. While insisting that major agencies integrate their staffs from top to bottom, the civil rights group is simultaneously insisting that black advertising agencies be allowed to maintain their politically protected status. "In doing this project," says the NAACP's general counsel, "we don't want to dilute what the African-American advertising firms have created." But if Madison Avenue were racially integrated top to bottom, as the NAACP says it should be, the major agencies would be fully capable of giving clients the whole spectrum of ethnic sensibilities, including white people, under one roof and at considerable economies of scale. If that happens, the entire rationale for black agencies evaporates.

The emotional attachment to the black agencies is understandably strong: they've played an important role in black America's cultural history. Like Vann Graves, at one point or another, nearly every black creative in the business has wanted to be the one to bring black agencies into the game, or at the very least save them from obsolescence. Geoff Edwards gave it a try when he joined the Mingo Group in the 1990s. "I just didn't believe that black advertising had to be bad," he says. "I fundamentally *did not* believe that you had to dance for chicken, that you had to do the Running Man to sell burgers. Between blacks and Hispanics, you're talking about buying power of over two trillion dollars. Amazing potential. So I went there to change the world. I failed. I heard some things in my one and a half years there that I've completely deleted from my memory bank, because I couldn't believe those kinds of things were being talked about in the mid-nineties—sitting in meetings where white clients would say, 'I don't think it's black enough.' It's *un*believable."

As nauseating as the ignorant white people were, the thing that ultimately put Edwards off was the attitude of the older black managers above him, the fact that they had acquiesced to their second-tier status in the industry. "That was what hurt the most," Geoff says. "The system that's created in a lot of those shops isn't conducive to doing big ideas, because at the end of the day they're responsible for coming up with an insight that's 'black.' My partner and I would come up with great ideas. Then we would go to our creative director, and he would say, 'Okay, this is good, but what's black about it?' I actually had someone sit me down and say to me, 'You understand that if we do work like general-market agencies, then there's no need for us.' And that was the last thing I needed to hear before I started to get my résumé on the street."

Soon after taking the job as chief creative officer at UniWorld, Vann Graves realized he didn't have the stomach for it, either. And Vann survived a convoy bombing in Iraq. "When I came here," he says, "Mr. Lewis felt like, 'Okay, it's time I really invest in making my agency not only a good agency but a great agency, to elevate ourselves in the public eye, to show that we can do great creative.' That's really what my focus was." But when the new chief creative took his team and tried to forge that new path, he found himself sitting in a lot of the same meetings that had made Geoff so queasy. "In every pitch," Vann says, "the first question always seemed to be 'What's black about it?' What do you mean, 'What's black about it?' Every person who's worked on this is African American. It comes from their personal insight. It's fully thought out, it's planned, it's executed, and just because it isn't some stereotype, you're asking me what's black about it?"

That's the racial assumption this industry was built on: white people don't understand black people, so they shouldn't even try. And whenever they do want to try, they should go to the gatekeepers, and the gatekeepers will tell them how that shit rolls—this is the highly scientific process through which billions of media dollars are allocated in America every year.

Vann Graves and Byron Lewis thought they'd had a meeting of the minds. They didn't. They had a generation gap. Graves wanted to build a general-market agency that had multicultural assets seamlessly woven in. Lewis, along with the other census watchers, was banking on the general market coming around to the multicultural mind-set, continuing to treat each ethnic segment as unique. But that's not the way the market is going. As minorities become the majority, minority consumers are more important than ever. Which means the real opportunity for minorities is across the street in assimilating with the majority. The melting pot is running away with it.

The Internet has fundamentally questioned the balkanized, racialized business model of Madison Avenue. Whiteness alone doesn't cut it anymore, but neither does blackness. It has to be both working together. Advertising simply has to be culturally competent across the board. To get there, integrating the white hierarchy of the big agencies is going to take years. In the meantime, black agencies are still asserting ownership of black consumers, but their seventies-era, race-based business model isn't any better suited to the new media universe than the white guys'. Which is precisely where the NAACP's Madison Avenue Project runs into major problems. Do black people want to be in the game, or do they want to be on the other side of the street? It can't be both. The reality is that it isn't really a choice. "The only way that I see black agencies surviving," Neal Arthur says, "is by legislation."

That's exactly where they're turning. The more marginalized black agencies feel, the more they're turning back to the same affirmative action playbook. In 2000, President Clinton's executive order on diversity in government advertising set an ambitious target: that 23 percent of all government media dollars should go to minority-owned businesses. As determined by a congressional audit in 2006, however, minorities were still getting just 4.7 percent. So a group of black agencies formed a new trade association to lobby Congress to fight the "persistent bias" of white companies that had kept Clinton's order from being followed. Yet the government's audit found that efforts made by the federal media buyers were "consistent" with the rules outlined in Clinton's directive. The law was followed. It just didn't work. Because it never has.

According to the U.S. Census Bureau, in 1997 black-owned businesses made up 4 percent of all U.S. firms, yet accounted for only 0.7 percent of employment and 0.4 percent of revenue. Five years later, at the end of the dot-com boom, the number of black-owned businesses had increased to 5.2 percent of all U.S. firms—yet accounted for only 0.7 percent of employment and 0.4 percent of revenue. A quota is a quota. It's a ceiling, and it's fixed, no matter how many minorities are clamoring for a piece of it. Today, black agencies and Hispanic agencies are fighting with each other for a share of the diversity supplier business—and the black agencies are losing, because the language factor gives Hispanics the justification to take a bigger slice. The minority agencies are squabbling over loose change, and at the same time demanding that the government ramp up enforcement of the policy that keeps them squabbling over loose change. "At some point that legal credit becomes an issue," Geoff Edwards says. "It becomes a barrier between doing great work and being able to say, 'We're supporting diversity' or 'We're working with black vendors.' It was a model that was established when I was a baby, and it hasn't changed. But if those agencies are going to survive, they *have* to evolve. Otherwise they'll disappear."

As of right now, it's hard to tell how much the black agencies want to evolve, or if they even can, given their history. Earlier this year, KFC ran some horribly misbegotten ad in Australia in which a white guy makes friends with a bunch of dancing Aborigines at a cricket match by giving them a bucket of fried chicken. Black men dancing for chicken. Again. The standard uproar ensued. Jesse Jackson appeared on cue and demanded that KFC spend 10 percent of all its national media dollars targeting blacks through minority-owned advertising agencies, increase its minority-owned franchises to 33 percent, up its managerial-level hiring to 25 percent, and hire a diversity director to carry out all of the above. KFC agreed to all of it, and at the 2010 Rainbow PUSH convention, the company president trotted his ass out to the podium and did the White Man Apology Dance: "At KFC, we are very proud of our diversity track record and the progress we've made over the years, but we realize there's a lot more we can do."

"It's regressing back to the 1970s," Vann Graves says.

Byron Lewis was right. While the Madison Avenue boys were up on the forty-second floor writing margarine commercials to air on *The Brady Bunch*, Lewis saw the teeming, multiethnic throngs on the Lower East Side and knew that they would be a big part of America's future. Madison Avenue told him to stop wasting his time, but what he and the other black agencies did in proving the value of minority consumers paved the way for Madison Avenue to take Nike and Michael Jordan and go to the moon. Now, the more successful Lewis's original vision is, the less necessary his own business becomes. "UniWorld is Byron Lewis," Graves says. "He's an O.G., and I respect him immensely for what he's done. He stood on that pedestal and said, 'I'm going to do this.' And it worked. And it was needed. But the world has changed."

The world's not changing. It's reverting, going back to its natural state.

In 1890, when the Separate Car Act was put to a vote in Louisiana, before it went on to be sanctioned by the Supreme Court in *Plessy v. Ferguson*, some of the law's loudest critics were the railroad companies. If the coach car on the five o'clock train was only half full, and only three colored passengers had bought tickets, why should they haul a separate railcar for a handful of people? With the extra fuel and freight, they'd lose money. It didn't make sense. Segregation never made sense. Which is why, as far as the market is concerned, separate will never be equal—if I have to install two water fountains where I only need one, I'm not going to spend a whole lot of money on the second.

The black-for-black's-sake business model never really worked in the ad business, and the constant complaint is that racism is to blame for that. But what if that's not the only reason? What if the market is just telling us it doesn't want separate railcars anymore, because it never wanted them in the first place? And what if that's a good thing? The Internet has given black media a whole new playing field, but it has also obliterated the idea that black-owned businesses can exist inside their own politically supported ecosystem. Wherever our new information economy is taking us, it's too fluid and too fast moving for a system that says black stuff goes here and white stuff goes there. The Internet doesn't want to haul separate railcars. In fact, it won't haul them for very much longer, and you've got to make the jump from one to the other if you want to stay on the ride.

In October of 2009, after just eighteen months at UniWorld, Vann left to take a job as group creative director at McCann-Erickson.

....

When critics of advertising say that the industry is racist, that it does not practice discrimination but that it is discriminatory in its nature, they're absolutely right. A liquid will always take the shape of the container you pour it in. In much the same way, a relationship business will always take on the qualities of the social environment that surrounds it.

At the diversity events that agencies put on, people always get up and go on about how we need to make this industry "look like America." But that's just it. Madison Avenue does look like America. White people with all the best-paying jobs on one side, black people struggling with limited opportunities on the other, and a bunch of lawyers and consultants negotiating the demilitarized zone in between. That's America, and that's the problem. In a relationship business in a country that's majority white,

and where white people have the majority of the money, whites and assimilated minorities will always move much further, much faster than
unassimilated minorities. Is that unfair? Yes. Is it illegal? Maybe. Is it
prosecutable? Not on any level that means anything.

The NAACP has done and continues to do many important things.
Thus far, threatening to sue the advertising industry wouldn't appear to
be one of them. A social network is not an institution to be attacked. It's
a maze to be navigated, a puzzle to be solved, and the black political establishment hasn't shown much aptitude for solving it. As I write this,
lawyers for the Madison Avenue Project have collected what they say are
concrete claims of discrimination against all four major holding companies, and they have filed those claims with the EEOC. Now everyone
gets to sit and wait while the wheels of justice grind forward. Whatever
kind of settlement is in the works, lawyers being lawyers, no one is really
saying. But it's now been three years since the Madison Avenue Project
was launched. It's been seven years since the New York City Commission on Human Rights opened hearings on the industry's hiring practices, twelve years since President Clinton ordered up more blacks in
advertising from the Oval Office, and thirteen years since the Congressional Black Caucus started banging heads with Ogilvy & Mather over
those anti-drug commercials that don't actually get kids off drugs. In
that time, the first Internet revolution has come and gone, the second one
is already well under way, and another generation of young black people has come of age and not gone into advertising.

While the NAACP has been busy railing on about the old boys' network, other people have been solving it, rewiring it, putting it to better
ends. In 2009, just as Vann Graves was headed back to the major-agency
world, Geoff Edwards was walking out. He quit. He was tired of playing
the game the way it was being played. His feet felt heavy going to work.
"This industry is supposed to be about breaking rules," Geoff says.
"We talk to our clients all the time about taking chances and doing things
differently, but we don't take our own advice."

Geoff and his creative partner, Mauro Alencar, left their jobs, holed up
at a San Francisco coffee shop, mapped out a five-year plan, and in December of 2009 launched DOJO, a boutique agency specializing in what

they call "tradigital," work that transcends the old media silos of print, TV, and Internet. It's all seamlessly integrated—like the people who created it.

"On paper," Edwards says, "technically we're a minority-owned company, but it's impossible to say this is a black agency, because the culture is made up of several different cultures. The management team is an African American and a Brazilian. We kind of laugh a bit. If this were a model for all the agencies, the industry would be there already. In our first year we had fifteen employees who represented seven different countries. And it's not like it was picked that way. It's just talented people who showed up with great work and fit our culture. We had a common dream, and we had people that we knew who shared that dream and who helped us bring it to life." One important person they knew was Nizan Guanaes, the head of Grupo ABC, a Brazilian conglomerate and one of the twenty largest media companies in the world. Many years before, Guanaes had hired and mentored Geoff's partner Mauro. Once plans for DOJO were finalized, they went to Guanaes, made their pitch, and Grupo ABC agreed to bankroll the new shop, writing them a substantial check to get started. "It was definitely through a relationship," Geoff says. "I don't really believe in the old boys' network, so let's just say it *was* an old boys' network but not the way it's typically been done. The old boys' network is being reinvented."

Since 2008, the current recession has cost the advertising industry over 200,000 jobs. During that same recession, DOJO has more than doubled in size, growing from fifteen to forty full-time employees. It recently expanded to a second floor in its San Francisco headquarters and opened satellite offices in Rio de Janeiro and São Paulo, Brazil, and in New York City—right on Madison Avenue. In August of 2011, the agency was awarded the global launch campaign for GoogleTV.

A year after taking his position at McCann-Erickson, Vann Graves was promoted to oversee the agency's global account for Coca-Cola. And in September of 2011, he was promoted to executive vice president and executive creative director, making him the highest ranking black creative in the history of the agency. And so the next kid coming up behind him won't have to backtrack as much as he did, Vann established the

R. Vann Graves Endowed Scholarship for students at Howard University seeking a career in advertising.

"What I have learned," Vann says, "is that advertising is a blood sport. It's business savvy, and it's politics. It hasn't been easy, by no means. I've taken my lumps, and I'm sure I'll take a lot more. But I'd rather take my lumps because I stayed in the game. I know I cannot walk around my agency saying it's the white man's fault I didn't sell a piece of work, or that I didn't get an 'A' because Tanner got an 'A.' It doesn't work anymore.

"I wish I could say that I was some magically talented guy, but the truth is just that I had a handful of people who *wanted* me to succeed. If people like Phil Dusenberry and June Baloutine hadn't reached out to me, I wouldn't be in this industry. I was lucky that people saw me and said, 'Hey, Vann's someone who can make us look good beyond his race. But he's black, so that helps us, too—and he doesn't scare us.'

"Advertising is still about what goes on in the room, me selling you something. And for me to get inside that room, I have to speak your language. I have to make you feel comfortable with my being black. I have that extra piece of real estate to carry. The minute you're uncomfortable with my race, my forward motion stops, which kills it for the next black person coming behind me, too. Once you're not walking around on eggshells, *then* I have a chance. That's the whole premise of the old boys' club. 'This guy's got my back.' But I have to work extra hard to show you that I got your back. That's really what it comes down to. That's the only way to do it."

....

In 1986, Roy Eaton returned to classical concert performance at Lincoln Center's Alice Tully Hall. From there he toured Europe, South America, Asia, and Russia, and produced four albums, one an international bestseller. In January of 2010, he was inducted into the American Advertising Federation Hall of Fame. In his acceptance speech, Eaton recounted the time Y&R's Charlie Feldman flew out to Utah to help him recover from a coma after his wife had died, suggesting that perhaps what the industry really needs is more friends like Charlie Feldman. Eaton then capped off the evening with a performance of Frédéric Chopin's *Fantaisie-Impromptu*. When he finished, nobody asked him what was black about it.

"Ultimately," Eaton says, "the solution has to come from the level—the only level—that is of any significance, and that is the consciousness with which we view this world. It goes beyond these surface things of a white agency or a black agency, integrated or not. These things are just flotsam and jetsam, coming from a root-level malaise in the value system of the nation. That is where the change has to occur."

$$\left[\text{PART 4} \right]$$

CANAAN

[1]

The Race That Prays Together

In the early spring of 1964, on a quiet Sunday morning during Lent, Wallace Belson went to church. Belson, a black man, lived in the town of Grand Coteau, which sits just west of the Atchafalaya Swamp in the heart of Acadiana—southern Louisiana's Cajun Country. Like many of the quaint farming towns you'll find tucked away in the wetlands of the Mississippi River Delta, Grand Coteau could have been pulled straight from the sketchbook of a Hollywood set designer: weathered old wooden buildings with high-pitched tin roofs nestled under sagging canopies of live oak. The name Grand Coteau translates from the original French as "big ridge." The town sits atop what, around here, qualifies as high ground, fifty-six feet above sea level. But in spite of its big name, this town is actually very small. Its population, then as now, hovers just above a thousand full-time residents, most of whom profess the same Roman Catholic faith. In 1964, Grand Coteau wasn't even big enough to support a single traffic light, yet it was home to two separate and distinct Catholic parishes.

The first of these was the Church of the Sacred Heart. First incorporated in 1819 under the name St. Charles Borromeo, it was the seventeenth Catholic parish established in the state of Louisiana. In 1879, the parish replaced its original, modest building with a new one, one that its congregants hoped to be "worthy of Almighty God." Plans for the new church—drawn up by a prominent New Orleans architect and blessed by the pope himself—laid out a stately, whitewashed, wood-frame building in the Greek Revival style. Adorning its roof was an elegant belfry of a type not commonly seen in North American churches. Inside, ornate frescoes, stained glass, and intricate woodwork gave it an atmosphere more like the classical churches of Europe than what you'd expect to see in a small Southern town. The church itself was set at the end of a picturesque alley of oak trees draped in Spanish moss. Today, it is listed on the National Register of Historic Places.

The other parish, Christ the King, was incorporated in 1931, and its main church was built in 1942. Unlike its stately neighbor a mere three hundred yards away, Christ the King was a simple, redbrick box. It did not sit at the end of a grand oak alley, but on a circular drive just off the road. It had no architectural pedigree, nor any slot on any national registers, yet it was historically important in its own right. The black citizens of Grand Coteau had built it with their own hands, laid every brick, cut and sanded every pew. It was the sanctuary they made for themselves in a time that offered them no other. Even their own faith refused to welcome them just up the road.

Blacks were not allowed at Sacred Heart. Wallace Belson was about to get a very harsh reminder of this, because on that quiet Sunday morning in 1964, he went to the wrong church. He walked down the long oak alley, up the front steps, opened the door to the white church, and went inside. Upon seeing a black man enter, two white men left their pews, went over, and confronted him in the vestibule. Then they started beating him. Right there in church. Dropped him to the floor, kicked him in the head, the back, again and again, then threw him out the door and down the steps into the parking lot below.

All of this took place while the other congregants sat in their pews and looked on, saying and doing nothing.

....

It was Martin Luther King, Jr.'s constant lament that Sunday morning at eleven o'clock was the most segregated hour in the country, but it's hard to imagine how our divided country could have kept holy the Sabbath any other way. Given the pivotal role Christianity played in sanctioning and promoting slavery, it seems a wonder that black Americans would subscribe to it at all. But God's Holy Bible is a funny thing. For a supposedly sacred, infallible text, it reads a lot like a Choose Your Own Adventure novel. Just flip through and pick whichever story line suits your needs. While the slaveholders built their economy on Leviticus, the slaves found hope in Exodus. "I have indeed seen the misery of my people in Egypt," said the Lord. "I have heard them crying out because of their slave drivers. . . . So I have come down to rescue them from the hand of the Egyptians and to bring them up out of that land into a good and spacious land, a land flowing with milk and honey—the land of the Canaanites. . . ."

Through faith in God, the slaves would be delivered from bondage, through the wilderness, and into the Promised Land. This was a Christianity they could get behind, and one they sorely needed. The native religious traditions of Africa had been deliberately destroyed by Southern slave society; tribes and families were torn apart by white masters in order to sever the common bonds of language and culture and folklore that might help the slaves unite. Fragments of those traditions survived, however, and synthesized with the Christianity of the New World. Protestant hymns met African rhythms and became Negro spirituals, laying the foundation for a style of worship totally distinct from that of the white European church.

In the North and in larger cities, free blacks began forming their own Baptist and Methodist congregations as early as the 1790s. In 1816 in Philadelphia, blacks broke from the main Methodist hierarchy and organized the African Methodist Episcopal (AME) Church, America's first fully independent black denomination. In the antebellum South, both Catholic and Protestant slaveholders were encouraged to Christianize their slaves. Many did, but feared (quite rightly) that religion would give slaves the means and the motive to rebel. Southern states passed strict laws compelling slaves to meet and worship only under the watchful gaze of white ministers. But the hunger for physical and spiritual freedom would not be so easily contained. Slave religion went underground, becoming "the invisible church." Away from the plantation house, under cover of darkness, slaves met in secret, learning to read from the Bible, passing on tales of Moses and the Promised Land and plotting their escape.

When the Civil War finally brought America to a reckoning, the country broke in half. The Protestant Church shattered into a million little pieces. Sect after sect, it fractured along the fault lines of geography and race. The Southern Baptists seceded from the American Baptists. The Methodists, Episcopalians, Presbyterians, and Lutherans all established Confederate franchises as well. After Reconstruction, those Southern offshoots fiercely embraced the turnabout to segregationist theology that laid the foundation for Jim Crow: where God had once ordained slavery because blacks were naturally submissive, he now ordained apartheid because blacks were inherently dangerous.

After the war, the emancipation of 4.6 million slaves presented what one Catholic bishop bluntly described as "a golden opportunity for reaping a harvest of souls." Northern Protestant missionaries, black and white, flooded south to build churches and schools. But because white ministers had been deployed to constrain blacks before, given the choice, the freedmen instinctively flocked to their own. The invisible church became visible. The AME denomination added fifty thousand new adherents in less than a year. Baptist churches, being independent from any centralized authority, sprouted up anywhere a preacher chose to hang out his shingle. Hundreds of them grew out of the Southern grassroots, eventually organizing under the National Baptist Convention in 1895, which would go on to become the largest black religious institution in the country. A sprawling constellation of other black Protestant denominations would soon emerge as well, in the way that Protestant denominations always do. Despite this golden opportunity for reaping a harvest, however, the number of former slaves who ran for the embrace of the Roman Catholic Church would turn out to be practically zero.

....

The Catholics might have done better for themselves. They were, after all, one of the first major Christian denominations to categorically reverse their stance on slavery, having done so in 1839. The Church of Rome was also the only major religion that didn't break along sectional lines during the Civil War. Technically, it couldn't. It's one church—the One True

Church, if you believe the marketing brochure. This idea stems from the principle of the Mystical Body of Christ, which holds that the Holy Roman Catholic Church is the physical manifestation of the body of Christ on earth, with Jesus as its head in heaven.* The dictionary definition of "catholic" is "universal in reach; involving all."

While the church did look upon blacks with a paternalistic noblesse oblige, it was rare that Catholic priests actually used their pulpits to promulgate a segregationist theology—a segregated Catholicism is a contradiction in terms. Being true to its principles, the Catholic Church should have offered blacks a refuge from Jim Crow at the start. But Catholics had a problem of their own: Protestants. Anti-Catholic prejudice among America's Protestants was pervasive; in the South, Catholics were routinely vilified and threatened by the Ku Klux Klan. And so as Jim Crow began to take root, Catholic priests and bishops mostly remained silent. To do otherwise would have invited unwelcome attention. Segregation was a political matter, the church decided. But in accommodating the Protestant power structure of the South, the Catholic Church would have to conform to it, mimic it, and ultimately become indistinguishable from it. Where Southern Protestant churches actively evangelized a segregationist doctrine, the Catholic Church tacitly condoned and camouflaged itself in that doctrine, fully knowing that this violated its core beliefs.

In Maryland (a Catholic colony) and in Louisiana (formerly under French and Spanish—i.e., Catholic—rule), the church had built and nurtured a significant black following. But to send priests into the Deep South after the war would have been to send them into hostile, possibly deadly territory. And converting a nation of black Catholics would saddle them with the problem of having to integrate black Catholics and white Catholics into the One True Church. The solution to this was simple: don't convert any more black Catholics.

As Protestant missionaries raced into the former Confederacy, the papists stayed home. Twice, in 1866 and in 1884, the Vatican ordered

....
*"We were all baptized by one Spirit *into one body*," 1 Corinthians 12:13; Christ "is the head of *the body, the church*," Colossians 1:18.

American bishops to come up with a plan to bring the former slaves into the Catholic fold. On both occasions, the bishops convened a national council, talked, and voted to sit on their hands. An invitation was extended to European missionaries to come and work in the South if they wanted to. Some did. But the only major initiative undertaken by the American church was to pass the hat: once a year on the first Sunday of Lent, a collection was to be taken up to support a special commission on Indians and Negroes. That the church would file the Negro in the same drawer as the Indian tells you exactly how much of a priority they were. By the time the Catholics even thought to do something about expanding their black ministry, the Methodists and the Baptists had already run the board. Today, fewer than 2 percent of black Americans are Roman Catholic.

Though the church's negligence is in large part to blame for this, outside of those areas where blacks were already steeped in the Roman tradition, it's debatable how much success Catholic missionaries would have had among the freedmen. Since white clergy had been used to suppress black spirituality under slavery, the top-down, white-run, authoritarian orthodoxy of Catholicism held little appeal for many of the newly emancipated. The Do It Yourself ethos of Protestantism, on the other hand, would prove to be an ideal fit for the century to come.

Under Jim Crow, America made it abundantly clear that blacks would be categorically barred from nearly every civic and social institution in the country, from schools to hospitals to the Rotary Club. The black church would step in to fill virtually all of those roles. In many black communities, the church house was also the schoolhouse, the meetinghouse, and the music hall. Social clubs, death and burial societies, fraternal organizations, black-owned banks and insurance companies, historically black colleges—like spokes on a wheel, they all radiated out from Sunday morning at eleven o'clock.

The church would become the single greatest source of black America's strength, but that would also make it the deepest and most enduring root of its separateness. Though Martin Luther King obviously advocated for the black church, he openly struggled with the paradox it represented, calling it the "so-called" Negro church because "ideally there can be no Negro or white church." Their separation was an accident of history, a crime first perpetrated by whites and now perpetuated by vested interests on both sides.

In all the newsreel footage of gospel-singing freedom marches, one sees the black church as the most righteous and upright institution in the cause of integration and civil rights. It was and it wasn't. There was the ugly side of it, too. As King's crusade gathered momentum, the president of the National Baptist Convention was one Reverend J. H. Jackson of Chicago's Olivet Baptist Church—"the Negro Pope," he was called, for his tenure and his grip on power were that absolute. Jackson always gets left out of the feel-good Black History Month highlight reels, because from the pulpit of the largest, most powerful black religious institution in the country, he denounced the civil rights crusaders as "hoodlums" and "criminals." They threatened to usurp the system on which his power was predicated.

At the National Baptist Convention's annual conference in Kansas City, Missouri, in 1961, King attempted to dethrone Jackson's presidency by gathering a pro–civil rights coalition to back an opposition candidate, Reverend Gardner Taylor of New York. When King's insurgent delegation tried to challenge Jackson's loyalists on the convention floor, a riot broke out among the twenty-five hundred clergymen there in the meeting hall. One preacher was trampled to death. Jackson called in the police to suppress the insurrection, saw to it that King's delegation was removed from the convention, and then had himself reelected through an uncontested and illegitimate ballot. His position secured, Jackson stripped King of his office and title in the National Baptist Convention and publicly accused the civil rights leader of being responsible for the death of the preacher who'd been killed. King and his pro–civil rights allies were excommunicated, and had to form their own splinter group, the Progressive National Baptist Convention. Under J. H. Jackson's continued rule, the nation's largest black religious organization spent the rest of the 1960s publicly and spitefully opposed to any and all endeavors of Martin Luther King, Jr.

....

It was during the Lenten season of 1963 that Martin Luther King brought his civil rights campaign to Birmingham, Alabama. His reasoning was more secular than spiritual: an organized boycott of the department stores during the Easter shopping season would have the greatest financial impact. Still, it wasn't long before religion became a flash point of the confrontation. The stores being picketed were owned by Jewish businessmen, dismayed to find themselves directly in the line of fire. One Jewish community leader was prompted to write that their businesses should be left out of the whole affair. This civil rights issue wasn't really a black and white problem, he said. It was a Christian problem. He wasn't entirely wrong.

It is certainly no coincidence that the most segregated city in America is where all of America's Christian problems came crashing into one another. Birmingham is where Protestant nativists exploited anti-Catholic hatred to drive George Ward from power in 1917, paving the way for an increasingly repressive system of Jim Crow. It's where Martin Luther King had to contend not just with segregationist preachers, but also with those local black leaders who resented his intrusion, called him an outsider, and lobbied to put the brakes on his boycott, lest it disrupt the cozy and lucrative niche they'd built by accommodating the white power structure. And as the 1963 confrontation approached, while black demonstrators were organizing and praying at Sixteenth Street Baptist, the Ku Klux Klan was plotting its bloody retribution in the basement of Highlands United Methodist.

On the day the demonstrations were to commence, the leaders of Alabama's white churches issued an open letter to Birmingham's black community. Entitled "A Call for Unity," the letter urged blacks to stay home, not make trouble, and wait for the issue of segregation to be settled in the courts. "A Call for Unity" was published on April 12, Good Friday. Which, apparently, is not the proper occasion for Christians to make a sacrifice in the name of justice.

But the protesters marched on Good Friday nonetheless, and Martin Luther King was arrested and jailed that same morning. Just four days later, on April 16, King released his now famous "Letter from a Birmingham Jail." Mostly remembered as a general treatise on nonviolent civil disobedience, the letter was in fact written as a direct response to the eight ministers responsible for "A Call for Unity," politely but firmly calling them out for their cowardice. Instead of setting the moral standard that society should follow, King argued, the church had been content to accommodate the immoral status quo. Too many religious leaders had "remained silent behind the anesthetizing security of stained-glass windows." In the midst of injustice, white preachers stood "on the sideline" mouthing "pious irrelevancies" and "sanctimonious trivialities." In the great moral crisis of its time, the white church had done nothing.

In Grand Coteau, to Wallace Belson, the white church had done far worse than that.

[2]

The Strange Career of Jesus Christ

The story of how Jim Crow came to America and the story of how Jim Crow came to the Catholic Church are one and the same. They both start in Louisiana. So did I. Before I moved to Birmingham, I grew up in the city of Lafayette, the largest of Acadiana's small towns. The social life we had as kids grew almost entirely out of the families we met at St. Mary's Church, and everyone we met at St. Mary's was white. Lafayette's black Catholics were over at Immaculate Heart on the north side of town, separated from us by a big set of train tracks and a hundred years of bad ideas.

As much as we talk about the importance of "diversity" in our schools and workplaces, the notion of integrating the church is the last thing anyone, black or white, seems willing to put on the table. So much as broach the topic, and a chorus of voices will rise up to tell you it cannot be done. It's impossible. But if you want to talk about how and where relationships are made, if you want to change the way the social fabric is stitched together—particularly in a small town, and especially in the South—you have to start with the man on the cross.

The tragedy of Louisiana is that, in an alternate universe, this is where the interracial ideal of the One True Church *might* have found its greatest expression. The Franco-Anglo-Afro-Iberian-Caribbean melting pot that exists there brewed a very different ethnic stew than you'll find anywhere else in America. You had the landowning, slave-owning whites, but you also had the swamp-dwelling, French-speaking Cajuns, who weren't considered white at all. You had black slaves, free blacks who were Caribbean born, free blacks who were European born, a large mixed-race Creole population—which didn't consider itself black—and on top of that you had people with every shade of skin tone in between, many of whom passed themselves off as any or none of the above.

Before the Civil War, New Orleans was home to more than eleven thousand free people of color. In 1869, the state established the only integrated public school system in the South. The following year, it legalized interracial marriage. By the end of Reconstruction, Louisiana's black and Creole populations had produced a number of successful businessmen, not to mention thirty-two state senators, ninety-five state representatives, two parish judges, four mayors, and three lieutenant governors—one of whom served briefly as acting governor.

On top of which: *everyone* in southern Louisiana is Catholic. It's like a humid Ireland with better food. Acadiana in particular is one of the most populous Catholic regions in the country. Today, there are more than 331,000 of the faithful, making up nearly 60 percent of the total population. Within that, Acadiana has the highest proportional representation of black Catholics anywhere in America, over one in five. Given those demographics, and given an *alleged* commitment to the Mystical Body of Christ, all those fine, churchgoing folk ought to be joined together as one, united in an unbreakable covenant ordained by Heaven above.

And yet, Wallace Belson.

The fact that Wallace Belson was assaulted in Grand Coteau's "white" church is especially curious when you consider that black and white Catholics in Louisiana had for many years gone to church together. In New Orleans, records dating back to the 1720s show free people of color getting married at otherwise "white" parishes; blacks sat in and among the main congregation and joined integrated choirs, too. Outside of New Orleans things were not quite as cosmopolitan. In rural parishes, colored parishioners typically sat in separate pews at the rear or on the side of the church. They also had to go to communion last, after whites. And in no parish were people of color allowed to participate in the liturgy; they could not become priests or hold any meaningful position in the church hierarchy.

By 1890, thirteen years after the end of Reconstruction, blacks' relatively higher standing in Louisiana had begun to deteriorate. That summer, two major questions came before the state legislature. The more divisive issue was whether to renew the license of the Louisiana Lottery Company, which for twenty-five years had operated a statewide gambling lottery. Up at the statehouse, leading the antilottery faction was senate president Murphy Foster. He was determined to see gambling outlawed, only he lacked a voting majority. The prolottery faction was expected to carry the day; included in that group were all of Louisiana's black senators, as the game was a popular entertainment among their constituents.

Far *less* important was the Separate Car Act, which intended to mandate separate railcars for colored passengers. Similar ordinances were already in place in Tennessee and Mississippi, but their passage in Louisiana was not yet guaranteed. The act had passed in the house, but when it came to the senate it just sat, deliberately bottled up in committee. Many senators hoped it would die there. As was true across the South, some whites saw Jim Crow laws as unnecessary, no matter their personal feelings about blacks. One white senator objected to the Separate Car Act on the grounds that if we were going to start cordoning each other off by race, the proposed legislation did nothing to insulate him from white trash and Chinese—"both more obnoxious than many colored persons."

Then, the senate voted to extend the license of the Louisiana Lottery Company; it was an embarrassing loss for the antigambling faction. A vindictive Senate President Foster pulled the Separate Car Act out of committee and put it on the floor for a vote—for the sole purpose of using it as leverage to change the votes of the prolottery blacks. It didn't work. On July 8, the senate voted down the Separate Car Act. It was all but dead. Forty-eight hours later, however, the antigambling coalition had exercised every last legislative option to try to ban the lottery. They had come up empty, and angry. And so, one antigambling senator, who himself had initially voted *against* the Separate Car Act, brought it back to the floor again, changing his vote to yea. And by the time the antigambling whites put the screws to all the undecideds, they had a majority. On July 10, 1890, the Separate Car Act passed and was signed into law—not because of overwhelming popular demand, but mostly as a petty getback against a handful of black politicians over some stuff that didn't have anything to do with anything.

In New Orleans, Homer Plessy and the Comité des Citoyens mounted a legal challenge to the law, took that challenge to the Supreme Court, and lost. Now protected by the Constitution, Jim Crow's slow creep across the South began to accelerate. Louisiana's multihued melting pot began sorting itself into ever stricter definitions of "black" and "white." Antimiscegenation laws overturned two decades of interracial marriage. Literacy and property requirements cut the number of enfranchised blacks from 130,344 to 5,320 in a single year. And by the mid-1890s, having snuck into the railcar, the bedroom, and the voting booth, Jim Crow finally came knocking at the door of the One True Church.

....

Before the Separate Car Act had passed, the Archdiocese of New Orleans* had no desire to expunge people of color from its existing integrated churches. Local priests were particularly opposed to the idea. They knew well what was true then and is true now: blacks put more in the collection plate than whites. Louisiana's people of color were dedicated and valuable parishioners—unlike white Europeans who, as one priest put it, "are as stingy here as they are in their own country." And at the time, the Archdiocese needed all the Sunday offerings it could get; a string of bad property investments in the 1870s had left it teetering on bankruptcy. The church's position was clear. "Separate and distinct parishes are not advisable," it said in a statement in 1888.

Then, in 1889, Francis Jaansens, a Dutchman, was named archbishop of New Orleans. Jaansens brought with him a sharp mind for fiscal

....

*At the time, the Archdiocese of New Orleans encompassed all of Louisiana and Mississippi. Since then, as populations have grown, the region has been subdivided several times. The Diocese of Lafayette, comprising the core of Acadiana, was established in 1918.

matters, and he very capably pulled the church back from financial collapse. On the emerging question of Jim Crow, however, he proved far less adept. Unlike most of his contemporaries, who looked upon blacks in a condescending, paternalistic way, Jaansens was a genuine advocate for racial equality in the church; he openly lobbied for more colored priests to join the seminary, for example, and was instrumental in seeing several ordained. In this, his motivations were genuine. Also, since emancipation, black Catholics had been pushing to participate more fully in the liturgy and the community life of their parishes, and Jaansens was eager to oblige them—if blacks could not fully join in the Catholic faith, they would go across the street and join the Protestants, and there would be no getting them back.

Despite his good intentions, Jaansens was also a foreigner, unschooled in the racial politics of the South, and his concern for blacks was being overtaken by fear of his fellow whites. As the 1890s progressed, Jim Crow laws had a disturbing effect on the national mood. Whites began to accept, and then to insist, that separation from blacks in all public areas was natural and right. White Catholics began to ask, "If we don't share restaurants and railcars, why should we go to church together?" (Even though they had always gone to church together.) In rural areas, away from the church's authority, white parishioners began making violent threats against their own pastors for holding integrated masses. One priest in southwest Louisiana was so scared of his own congregation that he took to saying mass with a loaded pistol under his vestments. So how was the diocese to give blacks a greater role in the Catholic faith at a time when more and more whites simply wanted them out? Jaansens thought he had the answer.

The basic unit of the Catholic Church's hierarchy is the territorial parish. As its name suggests, a territorial parish is defined by its geographical boundaries; it is designed to be the anchor of the community that surrounds it. "As a general rule, a parish should be territorial, i.e., it should embrace all the Christian faithful within a certain territory." So says the church's law books. The exceptions to this rule are called "nonterritorial" or "national" parishes, and they take a different approach to "forming a community." They're defined not by geography but by language or ethnicity. If, for example, thousands of Vietnamese Catholic refugees emigrated to Minneapolis tomorrow, the local diocese might establish a "National Vietnamese Parish," giving mass in the Vietnamese language and offering social services tailored to that group's specific needs. For the German, Polish, and Italian immigrants who flooded into America during the nineteenth century, national parishes had often served as necessary way stations on the road to assimilation. After the Civil War, the church's official position was that, in light of America's "peculiar situation," local bishops had the discretion to decide whether an integrated territorial parish was even feasible, or if an ethnic or national parish would be better suited "for the profit and salvation of the Negroes."

Jaansens began to entertain the idea of a "National Negro Parish," a place where a colored congregation alone could enjoy fuller autonomy without troubling the waters of the diocese. Except that blacks in southern Louisiana weren't immigrants. They were not a separate nationality. They were very much Americans. They spoke the language, had lived here for centuries, and already belonged to established churches in the territorial parishes where they resided. For them, a National Negro Parish would not be a step toward assimilation, but a step back.

The archbishop went back and forth on the plan. He wrote his fellow clergy for counsel, and they wrote back with advice along the lines of "What a terrible idea" and "Don't do it." Similar protests were voiced by the Comité des Citoyens. Having failed to halt the institution of separate railcars, the group now put all its chips on stopping Jaansens's Negro parish. The Comité publicly challenged the diocese, saying the plan would put God's stamp of approval on the injustice of segregation. "If men are divided by, or in, the Church," they wrote in a newspaper editorial, "where can they be united in the bonds of faith and love of truth and justice?" The archbishop had his own reservations, too, readily admitting that "a church for colored people alone may deepen ill feeling and separate still more the two races. . . ." Still, after mulling it over, Jaansens made his decision.

On May 19, 1895, with great fanfare, the Archdiocese of New Orleans opened the doors of St. Katherine's, New Orleans's first Negro parish. The church itself was a hand-me-down, the old home of a majority-white parish that had moved to fancier digs up the street. At St. Katherine's inaugural mass, Jaansens spent the whole of his sermon justifying the church's creation, denying that it was in any way a step down, or back. The church was optional, he stressed, repeatedly. It was a place for blacks to come only "if they prefer" or "if they want" or "if they desire."

But the Comité des Citoyens called it for what it was: a Jim Crow church. Defiant, they called on all people of color to boycott St. Katherine's. Most did. The new parish was not a huge success. It drew enough congregants to remain open, but baptismal records of the time show that the majority of blacks stayed in their territorial parishes. Plans for a second Negro church in New Orleans were scuttled following a great deal of protest from both blacks and the local clergy. When Jaansens died in 1897, the drive for Negro parishes died with him; no more would be seen for a decade.

That decade, however, was one of the worst in America's already miserable racial history. Restrictive housing covenants made their debut. Lynching, a common practice since the end of the Civil War, reached epidemic levels, the highest the nation had ever seen. In 1909, Hubert Blenk was named the new archbishop of New Orleans, and by that time the racial climate in the city had become toxic. Blenk eyed a solution in Jaansens's national parish experiment. But what Jaansens saw as optional, the new archbishop saw as essential, mandatory—the only measure that would keep peace between the races. Starting in 1911, he carved up the territorial parish boundaries in the city of New Orleans, erecting six more Negro churches in less than a decade, and adding several more in the small towns surrounding the city. Blacks were now strongly encouraged to attend them.

As bad as things were in New Orleans, it was in Lafayette that Jim Crow Catholicism took its most dramatic turn. In 1912, Monsignor William Teurlings was overseeing the construction of Lafayette's new cathedral, St. John's. Teurlings called a meeting with his black parishioners to inquire as to where they wanted their separate pews to be located in the new church—on the side or in the back. During the debate, an older woman abruptly spoke up and told Teurlings he didn't need to worry himself about the separate pews. Just give us our own church, she said. We want out.

Fifteen years earlier, Louisiana's black Catholics had met the opening of a Negro parish with outrage. Now they demanded one. Teurlings consented. Upon hearing of the blacks' desire for a separate church, the white Catholics of Lafayette gave a joyous prayer of thanks—so moved were they by the Holy Spirit that they even offered to pay for it. Blacks refused, insisting on raising the money themselves. This belonged to them. Lafayette's first Negro parish, St. Paul's, opened in 1912. The church was embraced and celebrated by its parishioners, for it gave them what they had never had before, a spiritual community of their own.

In the years that followed, the Diocese of Lafayette started incorporating Negro parishes throughout Acadiana. Most of the congregations were simply cleaved off from existing mixed-race ones, and this time there was nothing optional about it; baptismal records show a complete exodus of blacks from their original churches. Ultimately, thirty-five Negro churches would be established in Lafayette and in the surrounding towns of the diocese. The last opened its doors in 1962, eight years after *Brown v. Board*. Louisiana's One True Church had split in two.

....

The "National Negro Parish" established at St. Katherine's had been based on an exception to the rule. But across southern Louisiana, the exception became the rule, bending it to the point where it was essentially broken. Most of the little Cajun towns around here are so small that the black parish and the white parish overlap each other geographically, both covering what should be the same territorial parish, but splitting the resident community along racial lines, thus contradicting the very definition of what a parish ought to be. In fact, there is only one place on the entire surface of planet Earth where it has ever been the consistent, deliberate policy of the Catholic Church to physically break apart territorial parishes based on the color of a man's skin, and that is the place where I grew up.

So back to my childhood home I've come. It's the first Saturday in January—the worst of Louisiana's drizzly, lukewarm winter—and I'm headed out through the back roads and bayous of Acadiana to see if Jim

Crow and Jesus Christ are still getting along. My first stop is the town of Breaux Bridge, and there they are, right as you drive up North Main Street at the center of town. First you pass St. Bernard's (white), and just a half mile up the road is St. Francis (black). Next up is St. Martinville, with St. Martin de Tours (white) and Notre Dame (black). The town of Maurice has St. Alphonsus (white) and St. Joseph's (black). In Carencro you'll find St. Peter's (white) and Our Lady of the Assumption (you get the idea). By late afternoon, I've driven through at least a dozen small towns, and they're all the same. Sometimes these churches are across the tracks from one another. Sometimes they're across the street. Sometimes they share a parking lot.

And how do you tell which is the white church and which is the black? Doesn't take long to figure out. Some of the black churches are quite nice, but they're always proportionally *less* nice than the neighboring white one. If the white church is gilded and ornate, the black church is boxy and plain. If the white church is boxy and plain, the black church is some prefab aluminum deal. And so on. To see them side by side, you can't help but think of all those old pictures from the history books: the fancy white water fountain next to the dilapidated colored one. Only this isn't history. It's now.

As the sun fades, I wind my way down some back roads to the small town of Duson, right off Interstate 10. On the outskirts, I drive past St. Benedict the Moor (black, obviously), and head across the tracks to the nicer, newer St. Theresa's, situated in the heart of Duson proper. I'd plotted my day's itinerary to arrive here just in time for the Saturday vigil mass, attending both churches back to back, just to see. Duson had jumped out at me from the parish listings for one reason: St. Benedict's and St. Theresa's share the same pastor. Different buildings, opposite sides of town, but one priest? It seemed the height of absurdity.

It is. This weekend, the first after New Year's, is the Feast of the Epiphany, and the Gospel reading from the book of Matthew tells the story of the three wise men—kings from exotic, foreign lands who brought gifts of gold, frankincense, and myrrh to the newborn Christ. After the Gospel reading, the priest delivers his homily. Like most homilies, this one illustrates the message of the Gospel with a little story. The priest tells us about a sculpture he once saw in a museum. The artist had molded these gaunt stick figures and arranged them all walking around in different directions. "And when you look at these figures," the priest says, "you realize their paths are going to cross but they're never actually going to meet. This man's art symbolizes our inability to make contact with one another and to really be a part of one another's lives." Then the priest goes on, telling the story of the Magi and the paths they traveled and how people of all races and cultures must come together and learn to love each other through Christ. He delivers this sermon at the white church. Then, half an hour later, he drives 0.7 miles across the tracks and delivers *the exact same sermon* at the black church . . . thus symbolizing our inability to make contact with one another and to really be a part of one another's lives.

At St. Benedict's, two middle-aged white ladies are there for the black service. Curious, I follow them out to the parking lot, introduce myself, and politely inquire as to what brings them across the tracks. Hectic schedules, it turns out. They belong to St. Theresa's, but they missed the four o'clock so they're here to catch the five thirty. Blacks will drop in at the white church now and then for the same reason, and that's all fine. But the bingo nights and the Bible study—the things that actually make a church a church—those are all separate, the women say.

"But does the church ever do anything to try to bring the two communities together?" I ask.

They look at me like I'm crazy. Then it starts to rain.

Driving home, and in the weeks and months following, I tried to put myself in a bit of an 1890s frame of mind, to understand the motivations of Archbishop Jaansens, and of that first black woman in Lafayette who'd stood up and said just give us our own. I could certainly empathize with how and why they made the decisions they made. Still, I had a hard time squaring their intentions with what I'd seen of Louisiana that day. Because what I'd seen, in town after town, had gone against all common sense, basic notions of equality, sound principles of bureaucratic organization, fiscal sanity, energy efficiency, the fundamentals of church law, the foundations of Catholic theology, the Gospel of Matthew, and the true meaning of Christmas.

....

In January of 1963, the Catholic Church convened the Conference on Religion and Race at Chicago's Edgewater Beach Hotel, an interfaith gathering of nearly a thousand clergymen from every major church in the United States. This was Catholicism's belated attempt to bring its principles and its practice into some sort of alignment.

A steady stream of religious leaders ascended to the dais and offered up lukewarm platitudes about fostering dialogue and understanding. Then an Episcopalian theologian by the name of William Stringfellow got up to the podium and launched into a real stem-winder—if you can imagine an Episcopalian stem-winder—in which he savaged Catholics and Protestants alike for lending four hundred years of moral sanction to slavery and segregation. He pointed his finger at every last preacher in the room, including himself. They were to blame—*they* had done this. He derided the efforts of the conference as being "too little, too late, and too lily white." Stringfellow's solution? He didn't have one. "The most practical thing to do now," he said, "is weep."

In 2002, the director of Black Catholic Services for the Diocese of Lafayette conducted a survey of 155 black and white church leaders from across Acadiana. The results more than justify Stringfellow's pessimism. While everyone gave a hearty endorsement to the idea of church unity, most every response came back loaded with caveats and conditions. The racial parishes were "still necessary." They made people "more comfortable." The cost of change was "too great." This is not to say that nothing has gotten better. Population shifts have closed down some parishes and opened up new ones with less rigid ethnic identities. Hispanic and Vietnamese Catholics have moved into the diocese in increasing numbers, mixing up the whole equation. And today the diocese has six black priests (up from zero), one of whom was recently named pastor at St. John's Cathedral downtown—a first. But these changes, while significant, are happening here and there, around the margins. In town after town, separate churches are still the norm, rooted deep in the culture and permanently fixed in brick and mortar and prefab aluminum.

The Bible is pretty clear about whether you should build your church on rock or on sand. But what are you supposed to do when you've built your church on a mistake? Is weeping really your only practical option? Probably. But there is also the impractical option to consider as well. The impossible is always waiting for anyone who wants to give it a try.

[3]

The Miracle of Grand Coteau

Father Charlie Thibodeaux doesn't look like the kind of guy who'd start a revolution. In a crowded room, you'd probably walk right by him without stopping. Slight of frame and unassuming, he has a quiet, gentle demeanor. Now in his eighties, Thibodeaux speaks softly, almost haltingly. Like my grandfather and other Cajuns from that generation, English was not Thibodeaux's first language. He grew up speaking the local French patois, learning to talk American formally in school.

In 1964, Charlie Thibodeaux was a young Jesuit priest serving as an associate pastor at the Sacred Heart church in Grand Coteau. Both of the town's churches, white and black, were run by Jesuits, members of the Society of Jesus established by St. Ignatius Loyola in 1534. The Jesuits are an elite body of clergymen, sometimes referred to as "God's Marines." Their order was founded with a unique mission to serve in higher education and work for social justice for the poor. Their aim is to improve people's lot in this life, not just prepare their souls for the next one.

America's Jesuits were fully complicit in condoning slavery. The order's Maryland province owned slaves up until 1837, when the practice was formally renounced. Though some of those slaves were freed, many were actually sold to plantations, leaving a moral stain on what otherwise might have been a wholly noble reversal of conscience. Since then, however, judged on a relative scale, the order has been far more forward leaning than other religious bodies in the cause of racial equality. At Loyola University in New Orleans, Jesuit clergy were instrumental in organizing integrated student groups as early as the 1940s; Loyola also hosted the first integrated college sporting events in the state of Louisiana. In his "Letter from a Birmingham Jail," Dr. King cited only a handful of positive actions taken by the white church, one of them being the integration of the Jesuits' Spring Hill College in Mobile, Alabama, which admitted black students peacefully and without incident prior to *Brown v. Board*. It is also no accident that St. Francis Xavier, the parish at the heart of 49/63 in Kansas City, is run by Jesuits as well.

In 1962, the Roman Catholic Church convened the Second Vatican Council, an effort to bring the church's doctrine more in line with modernity. Of the many reforms that were made, one was a directive to engage the laity directly in working to implement Christ's teachings for the poor and underprivileged—like the Jesuits, laboring for social justice as opposed to giving to charity. Just as the church was reaching out into the outside world, it also asked parishes to bring the outside world into the church. Vatican II encouraged local congregations to take the standard Roman liturgy and, where appropriate, embroider it with cultural folkways and traditions—whether African, European, or Cajun—making the churchgoing experience more accessible and meaningful to people of different nationalities. As a result, many young priests who came out of seminary in this era were steeped in the ideology of social change. While the old bishops were trying to stall Martin Luther King in Birmingham, the new kids were out marching with him in Selma. They may have been men of the cloth, but they were still the children of the sixties.

Charlie Thibodeaux wasn't in church the day Wallace Belson was assaulted. He heard about it from the police shortly thereafter. But he went straight to his superiors and threatened to quit if measures weren't taken. "Either they go, or I go," he said. That same week, Thibodeaux visited the homes of the men who'd committed the assault, demanding an apology before they would be allowed back at mass. Both men were visibly nervous and ashamed—though most of their guilt stemmed from knowing they'd disrespected the church, rather than any sudden stirrings of racial tolerance. Both men quickly admitted to being in the wrong, but tried to rationalize their actions just the same.

"They said he was drunk," Thibodeaux says.

Belson was known in Grand Coteau as a man who enjoyed his drink; his struggles with the bottle were no secret. One of the assailants, perversely, tried to claim that he got on well with Belson, was friendly with him. On a recent winter night, the man said, he'd come across Belson lying in the road, inebriated and half frozen, and had helped carry him home to safety. But for a black man to enter the white church? In that kind of state? That was something else. Whether or not Belson had actually been drinking that morning no one can say with any certainty. "But even if he was drunk," Thibodeaux points out, "that's no reason to jump him."

After the beating of Wallace Belson, Thibodeaux decided that healing the town's racial divide was the mission to which God had called him. Two Sundays later, he took to the pulpit at Sacred Heart and gave what would be the first of many spirited sermons on the matter. "I laid a little Matthew 25 on 'em," Thibodeaux says. "'Whatsoever you do to the least of these, my brothers, you do to me.' I told them if Christ came into this church, and Christ was black, you'd be rejecting him, rejecting Christ." The image of Jesus Christ as a black man didn't exactly go over with the all-white congregation. "By the time I was done," Thibodeaux says, "you could have heard a pin drop."

Charlie Thibodeaux grew up as "the least of these" himself. Poor, one of nine children on a small family farm in nearby Carencro, he was out in the fields at the age of four, picking cotton side by side with the day-laboring blacks who came to work the farm. They were always welcome in his family's home, he recalls. Those who knew him say he was more at ease among blacks than he ever was around the more sophisticated, well-heeled whites at Sacred Heart. When I first spoke to Thibodeaux, it was via a spotty phone connection from the San Ignacio mission in Asunción, Paraguay, where he has lived and worked among the poor for the last thirty years.

From the spring of 1964 onward, the young priest kept up his crusade. He preached and preached, week after week. He even waded into local politics, openly campaigning against the formation of a local White Citizens' Council. For a long time, the only measurable effect of Charlie Thibodeaux's actions was a net increase in the hatred of Charlie Thibodeaux. Whenever he said mass, pictures of monkeys and racist cartoons were passed up in the collection plate. The cars outside church were leafleted with flyers from white supremacy groups. Eventually, the parish had to call the town marshal to stand guard in the parking lot during services. Reports began to circulate that the young priest would be beaten himself, or killed. Phone calls came to the rectory late at night with empty, ominous silence on the other end. Finally, a group of white parishioners tried to hit the church where it had always been vulnerable in the past: withholding their weekly tithe from the collection plate. Thibodeaux dismissed the threat out of hand. "This isn't a club," he told them. For six years, the priest did not let up, but nothing really changed, either. One or two black parishioners would attend mass at Sacred Heart here and there, and there was no more violence. But the root problem remained: Grand Coteau had two churches where there should have been only one.

....

Your average Catholic will throw an unholy temper tantrum if the priest moves the ten o'clock mass to ten thirty, never mind use the entire church as a racial experiment. So as much as Father Thibodeaux argued for acceptance of blacks in the white church, the one thing he never proposed was to make the black church and the white church into one church. Because who would be crazy enough to suggest something like that? Churches aren't water fountains. You can't just tear them down. Sacred Heart was the gilded trophy of the white community. Christ the King was the humble heart of the black community. To reconcile that division and make them whole would require a miracle. Fortunately, this was Grand Coteau, and Grand Coteau is the kind of place where miracles can happen.

Literally. If you believe in that sort of thing.

In 1821, the Sisters of the Sacred Heart arrived here to build a convent and to establish what would become one of the finest all-girls Catholic preparatory schools in the region. In October of 1866, a young postulant (think Maria in *The Sound of Music*) arrived at the convent and soon fell terribly ill. For weeks she suffered. Unable to eat, she wasted away to nothing. Her skin became purple with bruises. She was eventually given last rites and holy communion, during which she convulsed violently and then collapsed lifeless on the bed. The nuns left her body in repose to await burial. Then, inexplicably, just an hour later, she was awake and walking about, every trace of her illness gone. The Miracle of Grand Coteau, as it came to be known, was the first documented, authenticated miracle ever to take place in the United States of America.

It would be disingenuous to depict Grand Coteau as some little ol' Southern town where white folks and black folks had a chat with Jesus and then tried to patch things up. It's not. It's a company town. The Miracle of Grand Coteau made it a Catholic pilgrimage site; thousands travel here every year for spiritual retreats. Soon after the Sacred Heart sisters came, the Jesuits founded a neighboring men's school, St. Charles College, and took over pastoral duties at the St. Charles Borromeo parish, which would later have its name changed to the Church of the Sacred Heart. Today there's also St. John Berchmans school for boys, the Our Lady of the Oaks retreat center, and a Jesuit novitiate, training young men for the priesthood.

Some years ago, a local priest was asked what the main industry of Grand Coteau was. He replied, "The main industry of Grand Coteau is religion." Sitting just a stone's throw from the Chevron station and the Popeyes chicken on Interstate 49, the Catholic campus at the heart of town feels as if it belongs to another world and time, with languid live oak trees that hang over crumbling gothic cemeteries. It's easy to see where the town gets its nickname: people call it the Holy Land of South Louisiana.

All of which is to say that the Catholic Church holds an extra bit of sway in this town. And because the parish here is run by the Jesuits, it has a certain autonomy from the local diocese and from local politics. With that autonomy, the Jesuits decided to do something. Six years of Charlie Thibodeaux's sermonizing had accomplished nothing. In the summer of 1970, the priests of Grand Coteau finally arrived at the obvious: so long as the church itself maintained separate and unequal parishes, its moral authority to condemn racial prejudice was hollow. The Word had to be made flesh. The two churches had to become one.

....

In selecting a priest to oversee the parish unification, Father Thibodeaux was passed over. He was too young, and had stirred up too much ill will. The Jesuit provincial felt that an outsider was necessary to bring an objective, neutral presence to the endeavor. Father David Knight was an up-and-coming Jesuit with big ideas about changing the world. Ordained in 1961, he'd spent three years as a missionary among the Ngama tribe in Chad, after which he enrolled in a doctoral program at Catholic University in Washington, D.C. That's where he was, wrapping up his dissertation, when he got the call from Grand Coteau.

Father Knight was not the first choice for the job, either. Fourteen different priests had been offered the position. All had turned it down. Knight just happened to be next on the list. "The provincial called me up," Knight says, "and he told me they wanted to integrate these two parishes because it was getting to be a disgrace—those weren't his words, but that's what he meant." Father Knight's demeanor was as brash and forthright as Thibodeaux's was quiet and unassuming. Knight is the kind of man who actually calls a disgrace a disgrace, when everyone down South knows you're supposed to call it a delicate situation. "I felt that integration was a big priority for the church," he says of his reason for taking the job nobody wanted. "And I'd just gotten out of college. What else was I going to do?"

In August of 1970, Knight joined Thibodeaux and two other priests in a group ministry that would serve both congregations at Sacred Heart and Christ the King, with the ultimate aim of bringing them together. The first step, the team felt, should be a symbolic one. That November, they wrote to Lafayette bishop Maurice Schexnayder, asking him to dissolve the existing black and white parishes and unify them, canonically, into one. The act of physically integrating the congregations would follow, but this would serve as a signal that change was coming and it was real. The bishop wrote back that their request would be granted. While the paperwork was going through, they should proceed as if it were a done deal.

Most everyone knows the biblical story of King Solomon. Two women came to him, each claiming to be the rightful mother of an infant. In his wisdom, Solomon told them simply to cut the baby in half, knowing that the true mother would reveal herself by agreeing to forfeit the child rather than see it chopped in two. It was in this spirit of Solomonic compromise that Knight's ministry moved forward. At the outset, the Sunday congregations themselves weren't called on to do anything. The pastors moved slowly with small, deliberate gestures. The first thing to integrate was the church bulletin; instead of wasting paper printing two, all the weekly news was condensed into one. A few weeks later, the ministers shut off the separate rectory phone numbers and replaced them with a single extension that rang to a central parish office.

Next came the church letterhead, which would seem to be an item of minor consequence, but it forced the priests to decide on a new name for this amalgamated parish while it waited to be officially unified. They had the Church of the Sacred Heart of Jesus on the one hand, and Christ the King on the other. Since "Jesus" and "Christ" were handily interchangeable, the Church of the Sacred Heart of Jesus and Christ the King now became the Church of the Sacred Heart of Christ the King. Cumbersome, but guaranteed not to leave anyone out. By the end of 1970, an integrated bingo night had started up as well. Confessions and baptisms were held at Sacred Heart one week and at Christ the King the next. One for me, one for you.

Emboldened by the changes of the era, both in Grand Coteau and out in the larger world, younger black parishioners began asserting their right to be at "the big church." Julia Richard was a high school senior in the fall of 1970. Once the doors of Sacred Heart were open, she started going to regular Sunday mass there, just to show that she could. "I marched right up to the front," she says. "I wasn't going to sit in the back."

When she marched in, however, many whites blocked the entrance to their pews, or simply got up and left. If they allowed her to sit, they'd refuse to shake her hand when offered the sign of peace. That kind of hostility was common. Many of the older blacks chose not to go at all. If they did, they sat in the back or in the side chapel that had been the designated colored section back before blacks had their own church. Richard's grandmother, for one, wouldn't sit in any pew in the white church at all. "She would just stand in the back for the whole mass," Richard says, "even with empty seats."

Knight and his team followed their administrative changes by putting a new mass on the schedule: the Global Village Mass. It would be a voluntary service for those parishioners in favor of integration, a place where no one would walk out or refuse to shake your hand. In true Solomonic spirit, it was held at both churches on alternating Sundays. "That was the best, and best attended, mass of the week," Knight recalls. "Everyone was there because they wanted to be there. And there were lots of white people who came, too. The singing was wonderful. It worked."

Through the winter months, integration moved slowly, haltingly forward. On March 14, 1971, ninety-seven children, almost evenly split between black and white, received their first communion together—the first time such a thing had ever been done. The congregation was "a little stiff at the beginning," Knight observed at the time, "but by the end of mass the atmosphere was one of relaxation and joy." He called it "a sign of progress and a symbol of the future."

The future arrived five days later, when Bishop Schexnayder issued an open letter to the people of Grand Coteau formally dissolving the twin parishes of Sacred Heart and Christ the King and declaring them to be "one parish in the eyes of God and of His Holy Church." Giving a nod to Louisiana's checkered history, the bishop wrote that "the adoption of separate churches for whites and blacks proved practical if not genuinely Catholic. [But] for more generations than we had hoped, this procedure continued unchanged. In the light of a greater awareness of the teachings of Christ, we see not only the advisability but the necessity of correcting a system which can no longer endure."

No opposition to the bishop's decree was voiced by either congregation, black or white, a stark contrast to Charlie Thibodeaux's efforts of just a few years prior. "The whites showed a respect for the bishop that I frankly hadn't expected," Knight says. Within a matter of weeks, the two parish councils had merged—six black members and six white. Together they began to hammer out the nuts and bolts of forging a single, integrated community: pooling the parish finances, setting a new mass schedule, and, most important, deciding on a permanent name. The Church of the Sacred Heart of Christ the King didn't exactly roll off the tongue.

After some deliberation, it was decided that the new name should be the old name: St. Charles Borromeo, as the parish had originally been called in 1819. Charles Borromeo had served as the bishop of Milan during the Counter-Reformation of the 1500s, a period in which the Church of Rome attempted to right itself from the corruption and decadence that had sparked the Protestant Reformation. It was Borromeo's reforms, in large part, that brought corruption under control and helped lift the church out of the Dark Ages—an apt symbol for a community trying to begin anew.

With the bishop's decree and the adoption of the new name, Knight and his fellow pastors had only one final obstacle to face: the impossible one. Where Grand Coteau once had two churches in two parishes, it now had two churches in one parish, a problem that would stump Solomon himself. This was not a single baby to be cut in half. Here you had two babies, each one near and dear to the hearts of those who claimed it, and one of them simply had to go.

If churches *were* water fountains, there wouldn't be any argument over which one to keep: you keep the better one. Sacred Heart, by almost every measure, was better. Better constructed, better facilities, bigger parking lot, and so on. And Christ the King, with two-thirds the seating capacity, could never under any scenario accommodate both congregations. Objectively, there was no choice to be made. But objectivity has a hard time trumping sentimentality. If anything, the "lesser" black church possessed greater spiritual value; it had been the only community its congregants had ever known. Once it became clear that the smaller church was going to come out on the losing end, many black parishioners were suddenly more reluctant than the whites. Christ the King was theirs. Having already lost so much, why should they be the ones to give something up?

Knight took counsel and testimony from both sides and then wrote a letter to the parish council, attempting to negotiate a middle path. Whites, he ventured, were opposed to integration *in theory*, their fears driven largely by false and imaginary preconceptions of blacks. Once integration proved those preconceptions wrong, white opposition would fade over time. Blacks, however, were opposed to integration *in reality*. Their fears were all too real: the fear of being assaulted, of being denigrated. Integration had always come with painful costs, like the loss of historically black schools. Therefore, Knight reasoned, the blacks' attachment to their building wasn't really about the building. "What they are concerned about," he wrote, "is their position in the new community that is about to be formed. Are they being asked to 'give up' their building as a sign that they are also giving up the sense of identity, leadership, and parish life that they have found in Christ the King? If so, they will not give up their building."

If the white church were the only workable option, a gesture was necessary to prove that blacks would not enter this new parish as second-class citizens, and so Knight proposed a compromise. At the time, Sacred Heart happened to be in need of a paint job and extensive repairs. Knight proposed that they take the opportunity to remodel the interior and make it into a shared space. The side chapel that had once served as the colored section was separated from the main congregation by a separate altar and pulpit. They would tear out that altar and pulpit and move the side pews to join the main congregation—they would lop off the back of the bus, and no one would ever have to sit there again. "Let us make it a new church for a new parish," Knight said, "a church that will be what it is by the labor of black and white alike."

Knight's proposal was enough for the black council members to go along, despite their reservations. On November 8, 1971, in a show of unity, a black council member made the motion to accept the white church as their new, permanent home. Another black parishioner seconded the motion. The entire council, white and black, voted unanimously for its passage. Then they announced the plans to the rest of parish.

"And that's when everything broke loose," Charlie Thibodeaux says.

....

If Catholics get upset when mass gets moved by half an hour, that goes double for moving the furniture. The reactionary faction of the white congregation met the renovation plan with outrage. Nobody had told them that they'd actually have to, you know, make some sacrifices from their end to move this along. Share a phone line and a bingo night? Fine. Some Global Village thing once a week for the hippies? Sure. But make changes to their own church and help pay for it besides?

Hell, no.

Father Knight found his plan stymied at every turn. He was black-balled by every contractor in the phone book. "There wasn't a single carpenter in town who would touch that church," Knight says. "So I finally told everyone that if they wouldn't renovate it, I'd do it myself. I said, 'I'll go in there Monday morning with a hammer and a crowbar and I'll tear out that woodwork! I'll destroy it! Then you'll have no excuse.'"

But Knight never got the chance to do any demolition. Just as the dispute was coming to a head, his mother fell ill; he took leave that December to be with her. Which was just as well. Several dozen families, black and white, had already left the parish. More were poised to follow. Going after the altar with a crowbar probably wouldn't have helped. "They got me out of there at just the right time," he admits with hindsight. "I'm not always very bright." After his mother's funeral, Knight was transferred to a parish in New Orleans. He never went back to St. Charles Borromeo.

After Knight's departure, Charlie Thibodeaux assumed the responsibilities of pastor. In March of 1972, after consulting with an architect on the steps needed to do the remodeling, the parish council voted, again, to move forward. And then the backlash got nasty. Digging through the parish archives, I found more letters about the proposed 1972 renovation than I did pertaining to any other subject in the parish's 190-year history. White parishioners flooded the bishop's office with petitions. Removing the side altar was "a tragedy" and "a desecration." It left the churchgoers "sick" and "depressed." The renovation was being done "out of spite." It was "revenge" and "retribution" against the whites. Never mind that the black council members had just voted to forfeit their own church *in its entirety*, these whites were being asked to give up three, maybe four pieces of eighty-year-old cabinetry, and that kind of injustice was simply not going to stand.

Given the progress the parish had made in just two years, it almost seems like a bad joke that the whole thing would fall apart over a plan to move around a few wooden benches. But that's what happened. Knight's compromise was sound in theory, but in execution it fell victim to one of integration's classic blunders. It gave white people their out. It made the argument about something other than race, something that whites could whine about. You can't move our pews. I don't want my kid to ride the bus. In the dozens of letters fired off to the bishop, most of them make no mention of race at all. Insofar as they do, most of them have "no problem" with blacks, and "support" integration. They just oppose the one thing that would actually allow integration to take place.

Putting cabinetry on a higher moral plane than the unity of God's children was foolishness, but the whole episode laid bare the crux of the integration dilemma. Even if you're on the right side of history, how far can you push people before you're doing more harm than good? The whites were willing to go to war over the woodwork, and in doing so destroy what progress had been made. The two parishes had become one, in a way. The biracial council worked well together. A few dozen blacks attended weekend mass at the white church and were received, if not with open arms, at least with civility. A handful of whites also went without complaint to weekday services at the black church. Grand Coteau had traveled a great distance since Wallace Belson, and perhaps that was enough for now.

Charlie Thibodeaux decided that it was. The bishop had replied to the deluge of letters with a terse statement saying that the renovations were minimal and everyone should get over it. But Thibodeaux had a better feel for what the parish was thinking and how much more it would take. He shelved the renovation plan. "Charlie was an extraordinary man," Father Knight says of his successor. "I honestly believe he was a saint. He kept it from becoming violent. If I'd pushed for that renovation, if I'd gone in there and touched that church, we might have had violence. Or who knows what. It would have been stupid of me. But he had the prudence and the gentleness that I lacked."

Thibodeaux served as pastor for a short while longer. Then he wound his way south of the border to work at his mission in Paraguay under the brutal dictatorship of strongman Alfredo Stroessner, where, presumably, the political climate was easier on his nerves. He has been there ever since. Father Knight left the Jesuits some years later and now works as a diocesan priest in Memphis, Tennessee. The failure of the whites to make any meaningful compromise was proof to the reticent black congregants that they had been right all along. Unifying the churches was a losing proposition. So the whites held on to their cabinetry and the blacks held on to their building. Both retreated into their own churches, and that's where they stayed.

From that day forward, St. Charles Borromeo was integrated in much the same way that America was integrated—on paper. This odd duck, this single parish with two congregations, became the new status quo. To differentiate between them, officially, what had been Sacred Heart became known as "the church" and what had been Christ the King was now called "the chapel." In casual conversation, however, you were more likely to hear them called by their unambiguous possessives: *their* church and *our* church. The phones all rang to one office. The business was all done on the same stationery. The collection plates all went into the same kitty. But socially and spiritually, Sunday morning at eleven o'clock was still the most segregated hour of the week, and it would re- main that way for some time. As one parishioner put it, "You have to go through Good Friday to get to Easter, and we went through an awful lot of Good Fridays."

[4]

In the Wilderness

Nearly every time I sit down to talk with someone in Grand Coteau about the history of the parish, he or she will eventually, inevitably, lean forward to say, "Well, you know, there was a black man tried to go to the white church back in '64 . . ."

Wallace Belson casts a long shadow over the town's conscience, but the man himself is no longer here. He passed in the mid-1990s. The closest living source to the incident is his son, Wallace Belson, Jr., now in his late sixties. When I finally reach the younger Belson by telephone to ask about the integration of the churches, he's fairly candid about his feelings on the matter.

"I ain't swallowed it right yet," he says.

Still, he's happy to talk and invites me over to his home, a modest brick ranch house just a few blocks from the church. Belson's mother has passed on, too, and his wife. But he has two daughters, one a nurse and one a teacher. Today, he works as the head of Grand Coteau's volunteer fire department, but he spent many years as a cook over at the Jesuit novitiate. He's got a stocky build, solid for a man of his age, but his shoulders are stooped a bit, and one of his eyelids hangs slightly lower than the other. Even when he's smiling he comes across as a bit weary. Overall he gives the impression of a man who's been struggling against gravity his whole life, which he has.

Like Charlie Thibodeaux, Belson was driven to act by what was done to his father, but Matthew 25 was the last thing on his mind. "When they beat him in the church," Belson says, "the pastor, he looked the other way. Just a nigger got whipped. That was it. I'll be honest with you—and I'm not proud to say this—after they did that to my daddy, two Sundays straight I went over to that church for mass. I was ready. I *wanted* them to do it to me. I wanted them to beat me, whip me, kick me, spit on me."

"So they'd give you the excuse to fight back?" I ask.

"Oh, no," he says. "I wasn't gonna fight. I was gonna do something worse than that, you know what I'm sayin'? There wasn't gonna be no fightin', no sir. And I know God's gonna punish me for going into church like that. I went there thinkin' the same way those white men were thinkin', with hate. I went there like an animal."

....

No one ever assaulted Wallace Belson, Jr., and he never assaulted anyone in return. But when the drive for integration stalled in 1972, Belson became—and would remain—a vocal part of the faction that was glad to see it die.

By 1977, it had. That was the year that Darrell Burleigh started working at St. Charles Borromeo as parish manager. Burleigh looks like the kind of old-time Cajun you'd see in a tourism commercial, a full head of white hair, his face heavily creased with age, his thick Louisiana accent peppered with colloquial French. Thanks to a bad back, today he's propped up on a pillow in a creaky, old wooden chair, sitting at his paper-strewn desk in the rectory office. Perched at this same desk for the last thirty-plus years, he's spent a lifetime on the color line, negotiating all the business between their church and our church.

"In the earlier years," Burleigh says, "it was civil. But don't bring up anything pertaining to the chapel versus the church. *Phew!* Everything would blow up. From the get-go, it was my dream that we could just have one St. Charles Parish, but every time a new pastor would come, he'd say, 'We need to bring that chapel over here. That's the only way we'll make integration work.'

"Then word would get around and people would start gettin' all riled up. One time, somebody came to me. Down he sits and says, 'The pastor talks like that, he better have his bags packed.'

"I say, 'Packed for what?'

"He says, 'Anybody tries to close that chapel, he won't be here a week.'

"Then the next pastor would come along, then the next one, and then the next one."

All told, beginning with Father Knight, thirteen pastors would come and go before the black and white parishioners of Grand Coteau sat together as one. In the 1980s, one priest suffered a nervous breakdown over the matter. As the years went by, tensions did begin to ease up. Younger black families had started coming more and more to services at the white church, but it was still a "white" church—Anglo-European in tone with lots of blue-eyed, blond-haired dead people on the walls. The chapel up the road, meanwhile, had grown only more entrenched in its separateness. It was in the winter of 1993 that Pastor No. 9, Father William Rimes (now deceased) and his associate, Father Warren Broussard, decided it was time for the work of integration to be completed.

"When I got to St. Charles," Father Broussard says, "all of the liturgies were fairly well integrated at the main church. The four p.m. vigil mass was the least integrated because it was mostly older people, but the family masses were almost fifty-fifty black and white. To me, that part of it was going pretty well. Most of the white community, and probably a good percentage of the African-American community, felt that it was pointless to continue the separation, but the group in the chapel had become even more removed. I tried to be sensitive to their feelings, but at the same time it seemed so unhealthy—separate but equal, only it wasn't equal."

Lent was approaching. Since the parishioners would be rededicating their faith to the church, the pastors felt it made sense to have them also rededicate their efforts to unification. Rimes and Broussard wrote to Bishop Harry Flynn, proposing to close the chapel during the seven Sundays of the Lent and Easter season. If all went well, they would do it again during Advent and Christmas. "Worship together during the major liturgical seasons," the priests wrote, "will stand as symbol and example of the better union of minds and hearts which we all should seek." As a practical note, they added, the cost of mounting separate seasonal celebrations at both churches was proving to be a significant strain on parish resources; consolidating the observances would save a good deal of money. The bishop agreed.

For seven Sundays that Lent, the chapel was closed and the black and white congregations worshiped together, completely together, for the first time in decades. The first Sunday after Easter, however, the black congregation went straight to the pastors to make sure the chapel would be reopened. Come December, everyone worshipped together for Advent and Christmas. Again, the chapel was back open before you could say Happy New Year. When the 1994 Lenten season came around, the priests went to proceed with what they hoped would become an annual tradition and a prelude to unification. Only this Lent, instead of Wallace Belson trying to get into the white church, Wallace Belson was trying to get out.

If a church had done to my father what Sacred Heart did to Wallace Belson's father, I can't say I'd ever set foot in that church, or any church, ever again. And if a white man had been assaulted at the black church in 1964? Forget it. That church would have been burned to the ground. Yet Belson remains a devout Catholic. He's one of Grand Coteau's most dedicated and active parishioners. He considered leaving. He was wooed by his Protestant friends, took some literature from the Nation of Islam, but in the end he came back home. "I'm not gonna change my religion because of somebody else," he says. "I'm a Catholic, and I'll die a Catholic. All the money I spent giving my daughters a Catholic education, if I had it today you know where I'd be? In the Bahamas, every summer." Belson's devotion to the parish, however, has been almost entirely in service of the chapel alone. As an officer in the Knights of Peter Claver,* for decades he's volunteered hours and hours each week to keep Grand Coteau's black congregation thriving and to keep it separate.

....

*Because blacks were excluded from the Knights of Columbus, the Catholic Church's principal fraternal service organization, in 1909 black Catholics formed their own, the Knights of Peter Claver, named for a Jesuit priest who ministered to slaves in the seventeenth century. Much like the black and white parishes of Acadiana, both organizations still exist serving similar roles in separate communities.

....

After Martin Luther King died, his civil rights gospel of passive, peaceful reconciliation no longer held the universal appeal it once did. Black Christian leaders had to refute claims like those Malcolm X had made, that they were peddling "the white man's religion." The black church needed a new narrative—it needed a new *brand*, one with an aspirational marketing strategy for a newly assertive and Afrocentric generation.

Black liberation theology was born out of this era, marrying the militance of Black Power with the Gospel teachings of Jesus. God's only son was a fervent partisan for the oppressed and the poor, and because the oppressed and the poor in America were black, it followed that Christ himself was black—literally or metaphorically, depending on whom you ask. This was not the Jesus who turned the other cheek, but the one who cast the money changers out of the temple. Like the Israelites of old, in the American paradigm, blacks were God's Chosen People. It was their divinely appointed task to emancipate Christianity from the white supremacist ideology that had corrupted it, and in doing so, liberate themselves as well. In the church, as in politics and in business, the path to the Promised Land lay in ethnic solidarity and self-sufficiency, challenging the white power structure from a position of strength rather than accommodating it from a position of weakness.

Though mostly rooted in certain Protestant denominations, black liberation theology would make its influence felt even within the rigid, top-down orthodoxy of Roman Catholicism, where it would be recast through a uniquely Catholic lens: the One True Church would be a universal church for humankind (i.e., would truly be *catholic*) only when it accepted its black members in a full and equal embrace. The black clergy and the black Catholic laity began organizing, making demands straight out of the Black Power playbook: that more black parishes be established to serve black communities, that only black priests be assigned to those parishes, and that they be given direct authority over the affairs of black congregations.

The Catholic hierarchy did what it could to meet many of these demands—and not simply due to political pressure. For the first time in America's history, the church began making a sincere effort to give black

Catholics their due. Most every diocese with a significant black representation opened a dedicated office for black Catholic affairs. (Lafayette established its office of Black Catholic Ministries in 1973.) In the 1980s, a national African-American Catholic Youth Conference was formed. More black clergy were recruited and promoted to positions of real authority; Atlanta would welcome the country's first black archbishop in 1988.

The mass began changing, too. Following the acculturation directives of Vatican II, black parishes began incorporating more traditional African and black American customs into their liturgy. By the late 1980s, it wasn't unusual to walk into a black Catholic church and see a gospel choir decked out in Kente cloth robes and hear the call-and-response of "Amen, brother" coming up from the pews. By creating and supporting a "black Catholic" experience, these programs succeeded in retaining many black congregants and in bringing earlier defectors back to the faith. There was only one problem: the church had already tried this tactic once before, in New Orleans in 1895.

Separatism begets separatism. First you adjust to it, then you come to prefer it, then you can't live without it. Even as segregation heaped insult and injury on black America, it also created a sanctuary, a separate world with its own institutions and traditions. Slavery was evil in every dimension, but segregation offered a balm for the very wounds that it inflicted. Which is why Jim Crow was so insidious. Black teachers in the South tried to maintain separate schools for fear of losing their jobs. Black politicians fought to keep black neighborhoods intact because that was the root of their strength. Black businessmen had a profit motive to fight for the same. But the black church has the strongest gravitational pull of all, because church provides something far more important than jobs or money or even power.

Even as the congregation at Grand Coteau's main church grew more diverse—perhaps because it had grown more diverse, thus threatening the chapel's relevance—the holdouts had drifted further and further away, keeping the rest of the parish at arm's length, insisting that their institutions, cultural traditions, and styles of worship were worthy of being preserved. Which they were, and still are. But as David Knight had noted during the first go-round, the real source of black resistance stemmed from something else. It wasn't about the building. It wasn't really about cultural traditions and styles of worship, either. And it had absolutely nothing to do with the theological implications of whatever color Jesus used to be.

"The only thing the blacks wanted was a little respect," Wallace Belson says, "and we didn't get it. I don't want to be around somebody who ain't comfortable around me and I'm not comfortable around him. If I'm sitting by you in church and Father says to shake one another's hand, and you look the other way and I look the other way, we're not going to church to worship the Lord—we're going to church with hatred. And that's not the way it's supposed to be."

Church is a place of acceptance, of belonging. No matter who you are in the world, every Sunday morning you can go someplace and with a simple profession of faith you get to be a member of the club—a member of *the* club, the one going to heaven. At the chapel, Wallace Belson was an important parishioner, and he more than anyone had every legitimate reason to believe that the white church wouldn't give him the same respect he enjoyed right where he was. So as the Lenten season of 1994 approached and integration threatened once again, Belson and several other members of the Knights of Peter Claver took it upon themselves to be the last-line defenders of the chapel. For weeks, they petitioned Bishop Flynn to step in. They wrote letter after letter, each one more plaintive and insistent than the last, demanding that the diocese keep the chapel open "to preserve the dignity, respect, and needs of our black Catholic community."

On February 10, Flynn intervened, directing Father Rimes not to suspend the Sunday chapel mass. Rimes wrote back, requesting that the bishop reconsider, lest he halt the first progress made toward integration in some twenty years. But Flynn would hear no debate on the matter. He simply ordered that the chapel stay open, period, and gave no reason why. The bishop then went one step further. He went over the parish priests' heads and issued a letter directly to the chapel's congregation. In it, he offered his personal guarantee that their church would never be closed again at any time for any reason. When the letter was read aloud at the Sunday morning mass, a joyous celebration was had—anybody who tried to close that chapel wouldn't be here a week. Shortly thereafter, Pastor No. 9 packed his bags.

"Father Rimes was pretty pissed off," Warren Broussard recalls. "The way the bishop handled it was very disrespectful of his position. It also didn't take into account the larger experience of the African-American congregation here. The bishop didn't solicit any information from anyone except the people who were complaining, and not everyone in the black community thinks the same way."

....

Charles James was born and raised in Sunset, another small country town just across Interstate 49 from Grand Coteau. Growing up in the fifties and sixties, he attended the black parish at Christ the King from baptism to first communion to confirmation. His family left for Houston in 1970, came back in 1973, and he's been here ever since, working for Exxon Mobil as a maintenance crew chief on the company's coastal oil pipeline. He's served on St. Charles's parish council for a total of twenty-three years, with five different stints as council president.

In that time, James has been a leading voice for that part of the black community very much in favor of integration. Tall and barrel-chested, his dark complexion offset only by a few streaks of gray hair, he's the kind of guy whose presence really fills a room. As council president, James had little use for the timid politics of the bishop. "We got a lot of crap from the diocese," he says. "'Hold down the fuss' is what they wanted us to do. But the fuss was gonna be had, because God ordained the fuss."

Despite the council's biracial membership, James found that it had become more an instrument of division than of unity, as originally intended. "When I came on the council," he says, "every policy, every action was to keep things like they were, to maintain that separation. The white members of the council felt the black church really wasn't their concern. Their feeling was that they contributed the majority of the money to the parish, therefore they ought to be able to get what they want. With the blacks, it was always something like, 'We spent this much money on the main church, so how much will be spent on our church?' If the subject of coming together was ever brought up, the whites would go to the white side and the blacks would go to the black side. And if you were standing in the middle, you had problems. But fortunately for this parish some folks were standing in the middle, black people and white people, folks who heard God's call and understood where we needed to be."

Charles James chose to stand with the people in the middle, he says, because he refused to put his race above his Catholic faith in man's common humanity. "I always felt that society should reflect the church, rather than the church reflecting society. That was the basis of our problem— we had brought segregation and that foolishness into the church, rather than being present to God and taking that out into the world. And since I was council president, I felt I had to make a point to talk about that. Well . . . I didn't know what I was doing. I was right, you understand. *It* was right. But at the same time, I didn't realize how challenging it was going to be."

Unaware of just what he was starting, in the mid-1990s, James began pressing the issue at the weekly council meetings. "I would say, 'Folks, listen. We're here for a reason. God ordained us to be here to do *something*. If we don't grow as individuals spiritually, then we're all wasting our time. We need to understand what has to happen, and what has to happen is that we need to combine these two churches, literally. These churches have to become one to make *us* one, as God intended. And we need the courage to do that.'"

Eventually, the council came to a tentative agreement on the best course of action: open the discussion to a public meeting and then put it to a parish-wide vote. "Everyone agreed that putting it before the congregation was the right thing to do," James says. "So I said to them, 'Okay, I need a motion from someone and a second so we can vote on this thing.' And all I got was dead silence. Not one person raised his hand."

In 1972, a black board member had courageously made the motion to accept the white church as everyone's new home, and the whole council had backed him unanimously. Twenty years later, no one, black or white, would step forward even to sponsor the move to put it up for discussion. "People's mentality got stuck," James says. "The priests spent more time *talking* about race than anything else. But when you just stand up and you talk about racism, whites feel that you're talking about them, which in turn translates into 'I'm not a good person.' So they pull back. And the blacks are sitting there, and we're all puffed up and smiling, because we say, 'Hey, we ain't got to make no effort. We're the victims here. We don't have to meet these people halfway.' So everything just lingered."

With the bishop's injunction on one side and a deadlocked parish council on the other, closing the chapel was not an option. After Rimes's departure, Warren Broussard had been promoted to serve as Pastor No. 10. Together, he and Charles James tried to make improvements where they could. One priority was dialing down the whiteness of the white church to make it feel like everyone's church, the very thing the 1972 renovations had tried to do and failed. Rather than take a hammer and crowbar to St. Charles's historic interior, Broussard decided on a less invasive approach. He took some of the dead white Europeans down off the walls and replaced them with works by local artists that depicted Christ ministering to children of all races. "It was a way to begin to create a more welcoming atmosphere," he says.

To match the changes in the church's physical landscape, they decided to change the liturgical one as well. Like any halfway decent Catholic, I can breeze through Sunday mass on autopilot. During the first service I attended at St. Charles, I was zipping right along through the Apostle's Creed. "*We believe in God, the Father Almighty . . . was crucified under Pontius Pilate . . . the life everlasting. Amen.*" And there I stopped, like you're supposed to. But everyone around me kept going. So I stood there like an idiot while the rest of the congregation recited in unison:

We of St. Charles Parish desire:

To be one family in service to God and to each other.

To be one people through worship, reconciliation, and renewal who are present to the needs of all God's people.

To be a community that in faith welcomes all to be one with us in the Love of God.

To be in union with Jesus, inspired by the Holy Spirit to proclaim the word of God.

To hold sacred the celebration of the Sacrament of the church.

To see our parish as the body of Christ carrying forward the work of Christ on earth.

"It was a parish mission statement," Broussard explains. "The pastors came up with it together with Charles James and the council. We began reading it at all of our masses. We felt that if we started praying it, together, every week, people would stop to think about what they were saying."

He was right. In adding the new prayer, Father Broussard forced his congregation to get out of rote habit and see things from a different angle. Standing in a mixed-race congregation, saying that prayer, one can't help but be conscious of what it means. Changing the liturgy and the artwork were not insignificant steps, but in five long years, they were the only ones Broussard was able to make. In the fall of 1999, he packed his bags.

....

As Pastor No. 10 moved out, Pastor No. 11 settled in. Father Dave Andrus arrived at a transitional moment in both the diocese and in the parish. Bishop Flynn had retired, taking with him his protectorship of the chapel. The chapel itself was almost sixty years old and needed major structural renovations; the air-conditioning and electrical systems all had to be gutted and replaced. The Jesuits felt that the parish couldn't afford to spend thousands of dollars refurbishing a building that was used only one hour a week by less than half of the church's population. So as the new millennium got under way, Pastor No. 11 was given one primary task by his superiors: close the chapel and integrate the congregations.

A quiet, soft-spoken man, Andrus did not come in swinging a hammer and crowbar like David Knight. In fact, for months he did little besides study the situation. He finally concluded that the question was not *whether* to renovate the chapel, but *how* to renovate it. The parish had no need for separate churches, but it did need new religious education classrooms and an assembly center for parish activities. The best use of the money would be to convert the chapel to a multipurpose building to serve the whole community.

Knowing that he would need the support of the black parishioners in any such endeavor, Andrus proposed they undertake what in the church is known as a spiritual discernment, calling on the Holy Spirit to lead or give direction in a difficult matter. The parish would hold a series of meetings, discussions, and prayer sessions. Through this, God would show them the way. Darrell Burleigh worked closely with the priest in making it happen. "Father Dave did it right," Burleigh says. "We spent a lot of money, sent out a lot of letters informing everyone and giving everyone their opportunity to have input in the process." In early 2002, after months of prayer, deliberation, and debate, the discernment was concluded. The consensus was that a majority of the parish was in favor of remodeling the chapel into a multipurpose building. Andrus announced that the renovations would go forward. And this time it was the black congregation's turn to get pissed off about moving the furniture.

By now, Charles James was no longer parish council president, but he was still a board member as well as a singer in the chapel's choir. He made a point of standing out front at the seven-thirty chapel mass each Sunday to greet everyone and shake hands as people went in. But once James made his support for the chapel renovation publicly known, his fellow parishioners—lifelong friends, some of them—began freezing him out. "One morning I was out front before mass," James says, "and one of the parishioners walked right past me. I went to go shake his hand, and he wouldn't do it. We just looked at each other, and he said, 'You don't even have any business being here.'"

"This was a gentleman," James hedges, perhaps not wanting to name names, "whose father had had some problems back in the day."

He's talking, of course, about Wallace Belson. Under Belson, the same Knights of Peter Claver faction that had organized to protest the seasonal integration in 1994 was now holding meetings and organizing to stop it once again, which meant turning against one of their own. Charles James was a member of the Knights, had been for years. Not anymore. "When I was coming up," Belson says, "for me to go against my own color for a white man? Oh, no. I'd have got whipped. And that's how it was with Charles and us. You know what they did to us, so now why you want to side with them? We got rid of him." Belson says James was forced to leave; James says he quit. Either way, he was out.

After he left the Knights, James says, "the ugliness started getting interesting." The opposition went into high gear. Petitions circulated. Letters flooded the bishop's office. Calls were made to the local media, trying to gin up stories that painted the St. Charles Parish as antiblack. "They literally ostracized anyone who advocated the union," James says. "It got to the point where they were out in the community, finding people on the streets and saying, 'Don't talk to this one, don't talk to that one.'"

"It was a bad time," Darrell Burleigh says. "There were some pretty harsh words said. There were people that I had a lot of respect for in the black community, but I had to see another side to them; the things that they said to me and other staff members were very ugly. Anything you would say would be taken out of context. They'd just get angry and start swearing. You know, '*Y'all* the ones that's doing this.' And, '*Y'all* the ones that's causin' all this.' It would just get out of hand."

Few things will send white folks running for cover like a racial situation that's gotten out of hand. To look at the public record, one might think that the chapel issue was a matter fought over only by blacks among themselves with the Jesuits acting as referees. As Charles James had learned, the whites in Grand Coteau generally felt that whatever blacks did or didn't do with the chapel wasn't really their concern. As Darrell Burleigh had learned, to be white and take a public stance on unification was to invite some harsh words. It was the white man's catch-22: to oppose the unification of the churches was taboo, because it implied you didn't want blacks in the main church. Which meant that your motives were racist, or at the very least suspect. So you're supposed to support integration. But to endorse the unification of the churches was equally taboo, because it meant that you wanted to take the chapel away from the black community. Which meant you were trying to undermine it. Which meant that your motives were racist, or at the very least suspect. Which is why, any time a racial problem comes up, white people just throw money at it and run away.

Or they just keep being racist. Because there was plenty of that, too. Wallace Belson's faction was not the only antagonistic force at play, just the most visible one. Some whites strongly opposed the union. They had never wanted blacks at St. Charles in the first place, but modern racial etiquette prevented them from crowing about it too loudly. Their public silence makes it hard to gauge how pervasive the white opposition was, but from his central listening post in the rectory office, Darrell Burleigh saw and heard plenty of it. "A lot of people would come and say things to me they wouldn't say in public," he explains. "They'd say things under cover or 'around the back,' as I say. They'd go, 'Why don't y'all just leave 'em over there?' Or, 'We built them that church, and that's where they should stay.' I guess by telling me they figured I'd go and tell the priest."

Which he did. Directly or indirectly, every word from both camps eventually made it back to Father Andrus, and the mounting discord eventually took its toll on the mild-mannered pastor. To those around him, he appeared increasingly despondent, exasperated, and prone to very unpriestly outbursts. "Finally," Burleigh recalls, "Father Dave just threw up his hands and said, 'I give up! I'm not going to fight this anymore.'"

Andrus had reached his breaking point, was almost ready to pack his bags. But rather than scuttle the whole plan on his own, he decided to hold one last parish council meeting, an open town hall in which everyone could air his or her opinions and the council would vote the issue up or down.

On the night of the parish vote, the Knights of Peter Claver made one last, all-out push with a group demonstration in front of the church. "Wallace Belson had a whole bunch of people out there," Charles James says. "He had people I'd never even seen *at church*, let alone come to a meeting, all walking around with picket signs. Just silly crap."

But one man's silly crap is another man's lifelong cause. When I spoke with Belson, as he was telling me his side of this part of the story, he got up, went over to a closet, and pulled out an old dog-eared piece of posterboard. Then he brought it over. It was one of the signs from the rally. I WALK THE WALK FOR JUSTICE, it read.

"You see?" he said as he handed it to me. "My heart? How much it got hurt?"

In my conversations with Father Broussard, he tried to put his finger on Wallace Belson. "I had two relationships with Wallace," Broussard says. "When we'd meet one-on-one, we could talk. And I think we had respect for each other—certainly I did for him as someone who had been through a lot. I'd do home masses at his sister's house—she was very ill at the time—and he'd always be there. Our relationship was very friendly. But then at meetings it was this whole other experience with him. We were always on opposite sides. For me it was more about trying to represent the community, and for him it was more of a representation of his personal pain. There seemed to be a lot of anger toward what had happened when the churches moved together."

Talking with Belson one-on-one, you won't meet a nicer guy. He's generous with his time and his stories. He jokes with a sly grin that tells you he likes to cut up and have fun. But he's also candid about his resentments. "I didn't speak to Father Broussard for some time," Belson says. "If Father Broussard would have told me hello back then, he'd have to fight, you understand? Today I pass by him, and I'm polite but I go my distance and stay away from him." But that's not really the person Belson wants to be. "I was raised better than that," he insists. "I was raised Catholic."

As to why he's let anger dictate so much of his life, that much is obvious. So much as mention the incident, and his head cocks a few degrees down and the pain is suddenly right there at the surface. "It hurts me to this day even to talk about it," he says. "My daddy, after they beat him, he stopped going to church. He'd go every now and then, but before that he'd go every Sunday. That was done with. Then he started drinking even harder than he used to drink."

And that's all Wallace Belson says about his father.

Back in front of the church, as the final parish council hearing was about to begin, Belson and his fellow marchers folded up their picket signs and headed inside. The meeting was called to order. Then it descended quickly into chaos. Heated arguments and personal attacks flew from both sides. "For about forty-five minutes Father Dave and I were devils," Charles James says, "People said a whole bunch of stuff. I mean, I'm talkin' about lies. I'm talkin' about folks who stood up and just flat out told lies. And this is from people that I *knew*, you understand? People that I knew well. But as I sat there, God wouldn't let me say a word. Even with all the stuff people were yelling, I said nothing for that whole time until we were ready to vote."

Once everyone with a piece to speak had spoken, Father Andrus stepped forward to voice his opinion. He gave a lengthy speech, saying that he believed integration was the right thing to do, but in his heart he didn't think the parish was ready for it, spiritually. His recommendation was that they wait, but he would leave it to the parish council to decide. Then each member of the council stood in turn and cast his or her vote, giving the reasons behind it. "It was close," James says. "Some of those ladies on the council, they were tough. They weren't intimidated by all that mess."

In the end, the council was split, and the tie-breaking vote came down to Charles James. "When it got to me," he recalls, "there was this moment of silence. It was rather dramatic. But you see, now I had a conflict."

The day before, James had gone to Father Andrus personally. They talked, and James said he believed voting to unify the parish was absolutely the right thing to do. But he also believed if they forced people to go through with it, he didn't know if that would accomplish anything. The backlash might erase the progress they'd made, and any backlash that did come would fall squarely on the pastor. Given that, James told Andrus he would vote whichever way the priest decided. So when Charles James stood to vote, he said, "Listen, I told Father Dave that if it was his intent to move this thing forward or to stop it, that I would vote whichever way he felt was best. He doesn't think that we are ready, and I agree. We're not."

And then Charles James voted no.

The plan failed. Half the room sighed in disappointment. The other half rose up in cheers. "People were clapping," James says. "They took some vindication in it. But I told them, I said, 'Look, if you think you're fighting me, you're wrong. If you think you're fighting Father Dave, you're wrong. Understand that what we have done is that we've said no to God. God has allowed us the opportunity to live out our Christian values, but we, because of fear, have chosen not to. Now God is going to do it the way He wants it done.'"

The meeting adjourned, everyone went home, and Pastor No. 11 packed his bags.

....

Dave Andrus transferred out in August of that year, the earliest available opportunity. Today, he's settled at the Jesuit mission on Pohnpei, the main island of the Federated States of Micronesia, way out in the South Pacific, where, presumably, the political climate is easier on his nerves.

Reached by email, he was gracious but clearly reticent to revisit the subject. Not wanting to upset anyone further, he didn't offer much in the way of commentary.

One observation he did share is that he feels the discernment process, while torturous, brought a kind of catharsis to the town. "It allowed all the arguments," he said, "pro and con, to ferment in the minds and hearts of the parishioners, perhaps giving the Holy Spirit more opportunity to bring about enlightenment."

It did.

Charles James voted against integration in the parish council, but soon after he cast a different vote with his feet. The first Sunday following the parish council meeting, he went back to the seven-thirty mass at the chapel, only to let everyone know it would be his last. "I told them I have to do what I believe," James says, "and I didn't believe what we were doing was right. So I said, 'I'm done. I'm not coming to church here anymore.'

"At the end of that mass, I shook the dust off of my robe, and I didn't go back. I started going to nine-thirty mass over at the big church. And I was all right with that. I told God that, too. I said, 'I've done all I can do, God. I can't do any more.'

"A friend of mine, he would go to both churches. He was split in the middle. He'd bring me stuff, stories about what was going on over there, all the negative things people were saying. Finally I said, 'You know what, brother? I don't want to hear that. I have nothing, anymore, to do with that.' I felt good about it then, and I feel good about it now."

Charles James was not the only parishioner who came out of the experience a different man. Wallace Belson didn't leave the chapel, not until he had to. But he did fold up his protest signs and put them in the closet. And if he hasn't let go of his pain, he seems to have made peace with it. "My wife," Belson says, "three years she's dead. At one time she felt like I felt, but then she changed. She used to sit there and talk to me every week. 'Forget,' she'd say. 'Forget and forgive.'

"I'm not gonna lie to you. I had plenty of hatred in me from that time. I'm not perfect. I used to drink. I used to smoke cigars. I was Al Capone, did everything 'cept kill somebody. But a while back I was helping Father at the Peter Claver hall, and I had a fall from the ceiling, almost killed myself changing a filter in the air-conditioning. I said, Well, God didn't take me, so I made a promise to try and get along with everybody and just leave everything behind.

"So I did. I changed, completely, away from that. I respect anybody who respects me. With Charles James, he used to be in Knights of Peter Claver. We got rid of him then. But today I'm nice to him, and he's nice to me. The white guys in the fire department? My best friends. I get along good with them now. For New Year's we had a party together. Few years ago, something like that never would have happened."

"And the church?" I ask him. "Now that it's integrated?"

"It's not perfect," he says, "but it's better than it used to be. Got two good priests over there right now. Couldn't ask for better. My grandson, he's in the ninth grade. He don't know any different. Today or tomorrow, everybody have to realize we have to get along with one another.

"I don't have no regrets. I provided for my family. I'm not rich, but I don't have to worry about my medicines. If I want to go here or do this, I can do it. Most of my friends are dead or in the nursing home, and here I am, still makin' noise. So I'm happy with life 'cause I know God was good to me. But I also know God's gonna punish me. When I die, he's gonna punish me because of the hatred I had in me. So I forgive, but I don't forget."

$$\left[\ 5\ \right]$$

Milk and Honey

Even as America's racial landscape has undergone tectonic changes, the average churchgoer still worships in a world that looks remarkably like it did a century ago. America is Duson, Louisiana. St. Theresa's is still the white church, and St. Benedict's is still the black church. People can go back and forth if they want, but there's still a set of railroad tracks running right down the middle, symbolizing our inability to make contact with one another and to really be a part of each other's lives.

Some things are different, sure. Overtures have been made by white church leaders, here and there. In 1995, the Southern Baptist Convention issued a full-throated and unambiguous apology for its role in promoting slavery and Jim Crow, and some of its members have reached out and brought in black preachers to serve at white churches. The other mainline Protestant denominations have all made similar gestures. Evangelical Christianity, which rose to prominence after the end of Jim Crow, prides itself on having always preached and practiced a gospel that transcends race—and with megachurches the size of basketball arenas, they do draw congregations from a *slightly* broader spectrum. But nearly 90 percent of self-identified evangelicals are white. Demographically and culturally, the white church is still the white church. It has no reason to be anything else so long as the black church remains the black church.

If you're white and you go to a black church, you'll be immediately swept up in a warm, enthusiastic embrace. Lots of hearty handshakes. Lots of old black ladies in hats saying, "So *glad* you could join us today." The black church has always enjoyed the opportunity to show off its Sunday best to outside visitors. But that's exactly what you are when you're here: a visitor. As friendly as people are, the longer you sit in that pew—and at a black church you will sit there for a *long* time—the more you come to realize that this isn't meant for you. Because it isn't. It's the social, economic, political, and cultural hub of a separate black America. Its churchness cannot be divorced from its blackness.

As the black middle class spread out in search of suburbia, black churches followed the migration. Once established, they became centers of gravity, accelerating the move and concentrating it, eventually giving rise to the stupendously large black megachurch. From Dallas to Atlanta to Washington, D.C., black megachurches and their celebrity preachers are now the fastest growing segment of the faithful. They look like churches, these places, but they function more like independent city-states. With congregations that can range to upward of ten, fifteen, even thirty thousand members in size, they raise millions of dollars to build and maintain their own infrastructure, which can include everything from Bible schools to health clubs. Their extensive ministries offer the black community a full suite of social services, from ex-offender reentry programs to upper-tax-bracket financial planning. One black megachurch in Prince George's County, Maryland, the fifteen-thousand-member Jericho City of Praise, owns a 125-acre campus that includes its own office park and a $35 million retirement complex.

It would seem that just about everyone has settled quite contentedly on opposite sides of the spiritual tracks. By the most widely cited statistic, 93 percent of all churches in America are racially homogenous. And if you ever stop to suggest that maybe those churches should do something about it, people just look at you like you're crazy.

Down in Grand Coteau, Darrell Burleigh has been parish manager at St. Charles Borromeo for over thirty years now. Year after year, decade after decade, he's sat at his desk and watched integration not happen. Eventually, like most of the country, he figured it never would. "After the last fight with Dave Andrus," Burleigh says, "I said, 'That's it. It'll never happen.' People were talking so bad about the priests you would have thought they were criminals. I said, 'The only way we'll ever integrate is the blacks will have to come over and say they *want* to join the main church, and that's never gonna happen.'

"But Charles James, he would always say to me, he'd say, 'Darrell, you're gonna see. One of these days . . .'

"And I'd say, 'It'll never happen.'

"He'd say, 'Ah, you don't have no faith, you.'

"And I'd say, 'Maybe I don't. I might be in the wrong place, havin' no faith at church.'

"So ever since it happened, he still reminds me whenever I see him. 'What I told you?' he says. 'What I told you?'

"And I say, 'You know, I'm big enough I can admit when I was wrong.' So I said I was wrong. The only thing I've ever worked for was to see the church as one. It was what I'd always prayed for, but I never thought I would have seen it in my lifetime. And I tell you, it went off like a piece of cake."

....

In the fall of 2003, David Andrus's successor, Pastor No. 12, was transferred out, paving the way for Pastor No. 13, Tom Madden. Father Madden had been dispatched to St. Charles Borromeo as a temporary replacement from Grand Coteau's Jesuit Spirituality Center just across the way. His assignment was meant to last only a few months—he was technically retired—but all the area priests had been allocated to other parishes. A continuing shortage compelled him to stay on.

That problem was compounded when St. Charles's associate pastor took permanent leave due to illness, leaving Madden in charge of running the entire parish. It would have been a heavy workload for a young man in his prime; Madden was seventy-eight. Attempting to carry the whole mass schedule by himself, he suffered a fainting spell at the altar. Then he suffered another, landing him in the emergency room.

The cost of maintaining separate churches had been wearing on Grand Coteau for years, emotionally, financially, and in every other way. Now that burden had become manifest in the infirmities of its aging priest. "I got to talking with Father Madden about it," Darrell Burleigh says, "and he admitted he was just too old for it. So I said, 'You know what we need to do? What we've always needed to do: bring that chapel over here. Play the age card. You're too old, and you can't do it.'

"He was a little leery, given what the other pastors had gone through. But I told him, 'Tom, what can they do to you? You're already retired.'"

Madden eventually came around. "I had no intention of making any changes when I arrived," he explains. "It was never my goal to end the segregation, but I saw this as an opportunity to do so. So I solicited suggestions from the parishioners, black and white, and then proposed we move the seven-thirty chapel mass to the main church and cut the services down to two." Everyone agreed. Given the realities of the situation, there wasn't much choice. Besides, it was only temporary—or, at least, that's what everyone was led to believe. For several months, as Madden ran the parish without an associate, he quietly dragged his feet in searching for another. "Maybe it was somewhat duplicitous," he says, "but I felt if we got it in place, we might be able to continue with it, make it permanent. Then the whole problem of having a black church and a white church would be resolved."

Stalling tactics would last only so long. Another priest would show up eventually, and the chapel would reopen like always. Fortunately for Madden, as Charles James had predicted, the Lord had decided to do things His way. The integration of the church would be helped along by an act of God. On October 3, 2002, Louisiana had been hit by Hurricane Lili. The storm inflicted some $790 million in damage on the state. In Grand Coteau, the roof of the chapel took the worst of it. Water damage was seeping in. This was on top of the major electrical and heating repairs the building had needed since Father Andrus's time; they'd been put off by the leadership changes at the parish. If the chapel wasn't fixed soon, it would be in no shape to weather the next hurricane season.

Madden faced the same problem Andrus had: spend thousands restoring the chapel, or use that same money to build something the parish sorely lacked. "If we converted it into an all-purpose building," Madden says, "we could still use it as a chapel, but we could take out the pews and set up moveable walls for classrooms and such. Of course, the chapel had largely been built by the sweat equity of the black community; losing it was very painful for them. But I figured if I did it and moved on, then I could take the blame with me and it wouldn't be the problem of the successor. So that's what we did."

Madden went to the black parishioners to ask for their cooperation, but he also made it clear that, financially, there really wasn't an option. A few complaints were raised, but "not even very many," Madden says. The black congregation gave its blessing. On June 13, 2004, a brief announcement was placed in the church bulletin. The chapel would be closed and converted into classrooms, the seven-thirty mass would be held at the main church from now on, and . . . and that was it. Piece of cake. On the appointed day, the chapel renovations began. The black parishioners came to pack up the artwork and some keepsakes. They saved the woodwork, too. The handmade pews that their fathers and grandfathers had built were taken out, one by one, and carried off to find new purpose on patios and back porches.

Given the anger of the protest just two years before, it seems bizarre that the end would come so quietly. It's almost a nonstory, an anticlimax. But if you take the long view, it's easy to understand what happened here. David Knight and Charlie Thibodeaux took a sledgehammer to the problem for years and years and barely made a crack. But people kept after it, slowly chipping away. Warren Broussard sanded down the edges. Dave Andrus and Charles James took out a few chunks. Hurricane Lili gave it a good whack. And with decades of patience, diligence, dialogue, and compromise, the roots of Jim Crow had grown so weak that a seventy-eight-year-old man was able to knock the whole thing over with a feather. That is the Miracle of Grand Coteau.

....

Once the two congregations were joined, no one really knew what to expect. Among white parishioners, there remained a great deal of reluctance and indifference. In the black congregation, many of the age-old worries persisted. Not everyone felt as comfortable as Charles James, who'd been coming to the big church for some time. "There were still some people," he says, "every chance they got they would talk about 'our church' and what it was like in 'our church.' And it got on my nerves really bad. I recall this one lady said to me, 'Well, you know they're not going to let us do the things that we were doing in the chapel. They're not going to let us do this, and they're not going to let us do that ...'

"I said, 'What do you mean *let* you? This is your church, too. If you were doing them in the chapel, how can they not let you do them here? So those fears are your own. All we need to do is just keep doing what we were doing before.'"

The migration was not without compromise, but many of the chapel's traditions made the move intact. Indeed, much of the accommodation had to come from the white side of the aisle. Since the parish had no Knights of Columbus chapter, the Knights of Peter Claver migrated to become the church's principal service organization. Once the bastion of the anti-integration holdouts, the group has since taken on white members. In every pew, you'll also find copies of *Lead Me, Guide Me: The African-American Catholic Hymnal*. The songbook's Kente cloth cover sits right there beside Francesco Furini's *Annunciation*, the fifteenth-century Italian Baroque painting on the seasonal missalette.

Lead Me, Guide Me is there because the chapel's gospel choir came directly over to the new seven-thirty mass, which left one white parishioner, Andre Douget, without a choir. A divorce attorney from Lafayette, Douget has attended mass at St. Charles Borromeo since about 1995. He and his wife have a weekend home nearby. Rather than commute back to the city for church every Sunday, they come here. Douget used to sing in the Sunday choir at the nine-thirty service, but when the churches merged, that mass got pushed an hour back, to ten thirty—too late for Douget, who, like many Cajuns, prefers to spend his Sundays in the kitchen. So he started going to the seven-thirty mass. But the gospel choir, Douget felt, wasn't his to join. As a bespectacled, fortysomething white guy, he didn't imagine he'd be a particularly good fit. "I'd sit up front and sing," he says, "but only as part of the regular congregation."

Eventually, some members of the choir heard him singing every week and asked him to join. Not surprisingly, one of those who approached Douget was Charles James. "Andre told me he felt some people might not appreciate it," James says, "but I told him, 'Just get your ass over there.'"

Douget was right, however: not every black member of the choir was on board with the idea. "It wasn't tense," James admits, "but some people weren't so open to it. But Andre is the kind of person that brings an open spirit and an open heart to the situation, and he's educating *them*. He's educating those people who may not be able to understand that it just doesn't matter. It's all foolishness. Andre's a parishioner, period."

It's now been three years since Douget joined the choir. Whatever objections existed within the group have long disappeared. He's been known to take a solo every now and then, and he's even got a nickname. "They call me Creamy," he says. "We're way past the welcome stage. I'm just a member of the choir. We joke about it a lot.

"They laugh at me, too, for trying to get soul. I can read music, and so if it's a quarter note I want to sing a quarter note. I always try to sing the songs the way they're written in the book. They could throw the book away. They sing it the way they've been taught. Whenever a new song comes up in practice, if it's not in the hymnal, I'm like, 'Anybody got the words? Who has the words?' Because they don't pass along sheet music; it's traditional music that's been passed down generation to generation, and they all just know it.

"The best I can explain it is that they sing from the heart, and I sing from the book. That's the best I can describe it. And one of the first things you have to learn is to let go of that book."

James and Douget have since become close friends, dinner out with their wives, getting together for Sunday barbecue—which is a rare enough occurrence in these parts that it still gets noticed. "Some folks are a little critical of it," James says. "They'll use those age-old words on you—white-man lover, stuff like that. They never say that to me, but it's being said. But that's got nothing to offer. I don't pay it any attention. Andre's good people. It's getting to the point where, I guess, you have to be able to be free in your own skin. Andre is free in his own skin. He is who he is, and I've got no problems with who I am, either."

Prior to coming to St. Charles, though, Andre wasn't always so at ease with these things. "I grew up in a little town called Basile," Douget says, "which to this day is pretty segregated. My grandparents were—I'm not going to call them racist, but they were certainly prejudiced. And for me St. Charles is a constant reminder to banish how I grew up as a child. I can't let myself be that way, because there are faces associated with that now. You're not just talking about a black person, you're talking about my friend Charles, who sings next to me. Or Helen—Helen who gives me grief because I can never get the dress code right as to when we're supposed to wear the black shirts opposed to the white shirts.

"To this day I know prejudiced people, but now I find that I don't tolerate racial slurs being used around me, and I just choose not to be around people who harbor those views. And isn't that actually the call of the church? Not to just be this way on Sunday, but to incorporate that into my life the rest of the week?"

The changes in this town are indeed moving beyond the Sunday service and into people's weekly lives, albeit slowly. Perhaps the most noticeable differences have come through Grand Coteau's community outreach organization, the Thensted Center. Established in 1982, supported by the parish and staffed by the Sacred Heart sisters, the center is named for Father Cornelius Thensted, a beloved local priest who worked tirelessly among the poor in this area during the Great Depression. Julia Richard—the young black woman who marched up to the front pews of the white church back in 1970—now serves as the program's director.

Since the integration of the churches took place, the biggest change Richard has seen at the Thensted Center is that she's actually seen white people *at* the Thensted Center. "Ten years ago," she says, "there wasn't a white person who would come here for anything. People were still stuck on the fact that this center is for poor people and the only people who are poor are black. But people are starting to see past that now.

"One of the more integrated events we have is our seniors' day. They come in for lunch and activities every other Friday. When I was growing up here as a girl, we would walk up the street to school in the morning, and the whites who lived in the houses on that road would open their doors and sic their dogs on us, just to let them chase us up the street. Now we have the elderly whites coming here, and some of them are the same people who turned the dogs after you. They're sitting in here every other Friday enjoying a senior citizens' day, together. That's a big move. And they did it on their own. It wasn't like the chapel where they closed it and told everyone they had to be together. Here, they come, and they all sit and laugh and talk.

"They don't always sit together, at first," she adds. "I notice when the whites come in they all sit in the same little corner. But the blacks, the little old black ladies, they don't care. They'll just go over and sit right in the middle of the white folks' conversations. Just sit down and say, 'How you doin'?' And then they'll all talk together."

But if the Thensted community center is a sign of progress, it's also the place where the problems of an integrated church community cannot be swept under the rug. On the day I visited, a phone call came in from a white female parishioner: family counseling. The woman's daughter was dating a black man. The family didn't approve and was worried they'd get married. She was calling the nuns to ask what she should do. When the call came in, I turned to Julia and said, "So I guess integrating the churches hasn't fixed everything."

She shook her head. "Not by a long shot."

If you ever get a chance to stop by the Holy Land of South Louisiana, you won't find a land of milk and honey. What you'll find is that there are still black people here who insist things were better in "their" church. There are still white people here who'll be friendly enough to you on Sunday but pay you no mind when they see you at the Wal-Mart on Tuesday. There are still black people here who complain that whites won't let them do this or that. There are still white people here who gripe that the blacks "don't put nothin'" in the collection plate—even though the blacks always put in more than the whites. There are still a lot of people here who do a whole lot of things. But that's the point: they're all still here. Because the Promised Land isn't the place where our problems are solved. It's the place where we find the courage to solve them. And that's all it ever has been.

....

As I traveled around the country researching the stories in this book, wherever I was on Sunday I'd pull a church out of the phone book and check in to see what I'd find. In all of those Sundays, for the most part what I found was that 93 percent: people keeping with their own. It wasn't racially homogenous down the line. I saw black people at white churches, and I saw white people at black churches, but what I never saw, anywhere but here, was a black and white church. St. Charles Borromeo is a true hybrid, a staid and reserved Roman Catholic liturgy with an earthy, gospel feel woven in—subdued but soulful. Each side has given something up and each side has taken something of the other, and together they have built something new. Not surprisingly, Grand Coteau's seven-thirty gospel mass is the best-attended mass of the week, by blacks and whites alike, same as the Global Village Mass was in 1971.

"There is no other church in the Diocese of Lafayette," Charles James says, "and I dare say in the state of Louisiana or maybe even in the South, like this one. And I'm 100 percent confident in saying we were right in the way we've gotten to where we are. It came at a cost. Some people left. But those that wanted to stay, stayed. And it's gelled, I think, into a fine community. If you look around at other places, it's not happening. And they don't even try. The blacks prefer to be off to themselves and the whites prefer to be off to themselves—but that's not church."

James isn't alone in his feelings of pride about the parish. David Knight has no regrets. The anger and protest that boiled over in the 1990s opened a lot of wounds, but Warren Broussard and David Andrus both say it was what had to be done to come through stronger on the other side. And Tom Madden, retired from the politics of the church, has the luxury of being perfectly blunt: "We've done something here that the rest of the diocese should have done a long time ago, but they were too afraid."

But the person who looks upon Grand Coteau with the greatest joy would have to be Charlie Thibodeaux. The country boy from Carencro still treks home once or twice a year from his mission in Paraguay and sees, fully realized, the work that began so long ago. "It was agonizing," he says, "but to see it now, the tension gone, the people more at ease, I thank God they're finally united as brothers and sisters. Humanly speaking, it seemed like it was impossible. But with God there is always hope. It just takes time."

From the Sunday morning when Charlie Thibodeaux first denounced segregation from the pulpit in 1964 to the day when Tom Madden's bulletin announcement finally repealed it in 2004, the people of Grand Coteau wandered in the wilderness for a very long time indeed. Forty years, to be exact. For one parishioner at least, it was a longer, more painful journey than for most. He had a higher mountain to climb, but he made it to the mountaintop nonetheless. Now, every Sunday morning, the head of Grand Coteau's volunteer fire department wakes up, puts on his finest suit, leaves his house, and makes that same forty-year journey in just a few short minutes. Following in his father's footsteps, he heads down a long gravel drive to the end of a beautiful alley of live oaks and there, his head unbowed, Wallace Belson opens the door and walks into his church.

AUTHOR'S NOTE

Above my computer, I have posted a report card of mine from Lafayette's Episcopal School of Acadiana, dated 10/25/86. In the comment section my sixth-grade English teacher, Mark Crotty, has written, "Whenever Tanner turns in something, he says something like, 'This is great' or 'This is an A.' Well, he needs to do more than say it; he needs to do it. Tanner certainly has the ability and the desire. Now he needs the drive."

Grade for first quarter: C+.

I would first like to thank Mr. Crotty for my C+. Without him and a handful of other great teachers, I might still be an idiot. I might not have learned anything about race at Vestavia Hills High School, but thanks to Sue Lovoy, Marilee Dukes, and Beverly Brasell, I did learn how to think, a facility that came in handy once I started thinking about race. While I retain nothing from Cas McWaters's chemistry class, I learned a great deal from him during my trip to the principal's office, and owe many thanks to him and the entire VHHS administration and faculty: Charles Bruce, Daniel Steele, Pauline Parker, George Hatchett, Steve Williams, Lauren Dressback, Ben Osborne, and many others who opened their offices and classrooms to me.

Mostly, thanks are due to the many families and individuals who gave me, gratis, the personal stories and memories that make up the core of this book, as well as the authors of numerous other works of far more serious and rigorous scholarship whose research and information was of great help. In the past three years I've also read, consumed, highlighted, and dog-eared several hundred books, essays, and contemporary primary-source documents on the subject of racial integration—and

289

I'd be lying if I said I'd never checked Wikipedia—but major and specific works cited are acknowledged below.

In Vestavia, I owe thanks to the Williamses, Jerona, Tyrone, Tyrenda, Tyra, Tyrone, Jr., and my newly rediscovered and great friend Tycely, all of whom have adopted me as family. Alicia Thomas, who took me on the most interesting fifteen-minute bus trip of my life. U. W. Clemon, without whom my life would certainly be on a very different path. James Robinson and his sons, whom I'm told are now doing very well in their college years, Myles studying business and economics at UNC Chapel Hill and Malcolm majoring in psychology at Emory University in Atlanta. Also, Chad Jones, Janetta Howard, Sarah Wuska, William Clark, and Steve and Linda Erickson, who shared stories, a guest bedroom, and a mission-critical basement freezer. And last, thanks to all of my fellow Vestavians, too many to name here, who all joined me in person and on Facebook to share their thoughts and memories of that very strange time known as high school.

Any book on the strange story of integration has to start by consulting *The Strange Career of Jim Crow*, by C. Vann Woodward, which I did. The history of Birmingham and Vestavia Hills was drawn largely from *Carry Me Home: Birmingham, Alabama, the Climactic Battle of the Civil Rights Revolution*, by Diane McWhorter; "*Demagoguery in Birmingham and the Building of Vestavia*," by Glenn T. Eskew; and *Vestavia Hills: A Place Apart*, by Marvin Yeomans Whiting. Major source reference for the history of school desegregation include *Simple Justice: The History of* Brown v. Board of Education *and Black America's Struggle for Equality*, by Richard Kluger; *Bring Us Together: The Nixon Team and the Civil Rights Retreat*, by Leon E. Panetta and Peter Gall; *Acting White: The Ironic Legacy of Desegregation*, by Stuart Buck; and "*Brown v. Board of Education*, Fifty Years Later," a collection of essays edited by Kevin Gaines and published in the *Journal of American History*, June 2004. Statistics on racial makeup of schools were taken from reports compiled by the Civil Rights Project at Harvard University, the National Center for Education Statistics: Common Core of Data, and the Alabama State Department of Education.

I would not have found my way to Kansas City, Missouri, without the recommendation of Johnson County native Chris Suellentrop, who in-

troduced me to an author named Whitney Terrell—nephew by marriage
to one Miller Nichols, son of J. C. Nichols. Like me, Whitney woke up one
day and went digging into his own family history with race and real estate, and his novel, *The King of Kings County*, tells the story of Kansas
City's blockbusting and suburbanization in the way that only a novel
can: fictionalized, but brutally truthful. A generous KC tour guide, Whitney pointed me in the direction of 49/63 and all the thoughtful, helpful
people I met there: Ed and Mary Hood, Pat Jesaitis, Gene and Maureen
Hardy, Dave Bergman, Joe Beckerman, Father Jim Bluemeyer, Father
Luke Byrne, Father Norman Rotert, Albert Brooks, Helen Palmer, Jason
Peters, Josh Hamm and Dave Meingold, Calvin Williford, Ruth Austin,
Beth Brubaker, Renee Neades, Father Paisus Altschul. Special thanks are
also due to the Johnson County NAACP, Ruth Schecter, and the helpful
and patient staff of the Western Archives at UMKC. And, of course,
Krista and Brian Massilonis, for throwing a great Super Bowl party
where I got to meet lots of white people.

The history and mechanics of blockbusting were wonderfully laid out
for me in *Race, Real Estate, and Uneven Development: The Kansas City Experience, 1900–2000*, by Kevin Fox Gotham, and in *White Flight: Atlanta and
the Making of Modern Conservatism*, by Kevin M. Cruse. The racial geography of Kansas City, past and present, was drawn from *Take Up the Black
Man's Burden: Kansas City's African American Communities, 1865–1939*, by
Charles E. Coulter; *A City Divided: The Racial Landscape of Kansas City,
1900–1960*; and "Troost Avenue: A Study in Community Building," by
Father Paisus Altschul. The history of J. C. Nichols, suburbanization,
racial covenants, and real estate in general was informed by *Crabgrass
Frontier: The Suburbanization of the United States*, by Kenneth T. Jackson;
*J. C. Nichols and the Shaping of Kansas City: Innovation in Planned Residen-
tial Communities*, by William S. Worley; and *The J. C. Nichols Chronicle: The
Authorized Story of the Man, His Company, and His Legacy, 1880–1994*, by
Robert Pearson and Brad Pearson. All facts and information cited on the
history of 49/63 were drawn from the 49/63 Archives in the Western
Historical Manuscripts Collection housed at the University of Missouri–
Kansas City. *American Apartheid: Segregation and the Making of the Under-
class*, by Douglas S. Massey and Nancy A. Denton, was very helpful for

illustrating the bungled history of federal housing policy, as was *Sweet Land of Liberty: The Forgotten Struggle for Civil Rights in the North*, by Thomas Sugrue.

Richard Milhous Nixon was an asshole, but he was a complicated asshole, and I would not have fully understood his role in all this, particularly with regard to affirmative action and the workplace, without the thoughtful advice of Tim Naftali, Director of the Richard Nixon Presidential Library. I owe a great debt to my many colleagues from Ogilvy & Mather who, on the condition of remaining anonymous, agreed to share with me the secret inner workings of the old boys' network. Roy Eaton and Byron Lewis both deserve enormous gratitude for the trailblazing work that they've done and continue to do. I'd like to thank Vann Graves for becoming not only a great source but a great friend, and Geoffrey Taylor Edwards, for jumping in with both feet and trusting his story to a guy he'd only ever met on the telephone—advertising is making friends, after all. For giving me greater insight into Madison Avenue as a whole, I should mention the voluble Sanford Moore, Allen Rosenshine, Angela Ciccolo, Cyrus Mehri, Mark Bendick, Roger Clegg, Nancy Hill, Singleton Beato, Adrianne Smith, Carol Watson, Rebecca Williams, Rachel Donovan, Robert Shaffron, Angela Johnson Meadows, Orville Dale, Neal Arthur, Jimmy Smith, Keith Cartwright, Porsha Monroe, Kristen Clark, and the great Harry Webber, for telling me to piss off.

For the current state of race relations on Madison Avenue, one need look no further than the daily news digests of the industry trades, *Advertising Week* and *AdAge*, both of which contained volumes of wonderful, quotable information. Statistics on current minority employment in advertising were drawn from the study "Research Perspectives on Race and Employment in the Advertising Industry," by Mark Bendick, Jr., and Mary Lou Egan. Information on the history of advertising agencies, white and black, was drawn from *The Mirror Makers: A History of American Advertising and Its Creators*, by Stephen Fox, and *Madison Avenue and the Color Line: African Americans in the Advertising Industry*, by Jason Chambers. Additional information on black agencies came from the archives of *Black Enterprise* and *American Skin: Pop Culture, Big Business and the End of White America*, by Leon E. Wynter. The strange, sad, and cynical saga of Richard

Nixon, race, and affirmative action was drawn from *Nixonland: The Rise of a President and the Fracturing of America*, by Rick Perlstein; *Richard Nixon and the Rise of Affirmative Action: The Pursuit of Racial Equality in an Era of Limits*, by Kevin L. Yuill; *Nixon Reconsidered*, by Joan Hoff; "Black Power— Nixon Style: The Nixon Administration and Minority Business Enterprise," by Dean Kotlowski, published in *Business History Review*, 1998; and "The National Response to Richard M. Nixon's Black Capitalism Initiative: The Success of Domestic Detente," Robert E. Weems and Lewis A. Randolph, published in the *Journal of Black Studies*, 2001.

I would like to light a candle for Father Paul Patin, who served as pastor at Lafayette's St. Mary's Church in my youth, and who married my brother and his wife in 1999. But before all that, from 1977 to 1979, Father Patin was Pastor No. 5 in the integration saga of St. Charles Borromeo in Grand Coteau, and he helped me open the doors to a truly remarkable story without which this book would not be anything close to what it is. Thanks are due to everyone who made the Miracle of Grand Coteau possible: Father Charlie Thibodeaux, Father David Knight, Darrell Burleigh, Father Warren Broussard, Father Dave Andrus, Julia Richard, Sister Alice Mills, Sister Betty Renard, Charles James, Andre Douget, Father James Lambert, and, of course, Wallace Belson.

The story of Grand Coteau could not have been told without *Grand Coteau: The Holy Land of South Louisiana*, by Trent Angers; *For the Greater Honor and Glory of God: St. Charles Borromeo Catholic Church*, by Bonnie Taylor Barry; and the parish archives housed at the Diocese of Lafayette. The broader history of race and the church relied on a number of sources, mostly *The History of Black Catholics in the United States*, by Cyprian Davis, and *Black, White, and Catholic: New Orleans Interracialism, 1947–1956*, by R. Bentley Anderson. The bizarre facts of *Plessy v. Ferguson* were drawn from *We as Freemen: Plessy v. Ferguson*, by Keith Weldon Medley. "The Strange Career of Jesus Christ" was very well documented by the essays "Jim Crow Comes to Church," by Dolores Egger Labbe, published in the *American Catholic Tradition* in 1978; "A Canonical Investigation of Racial Parishes and Its Application to the Diocese of Lafayette, Louisiana, 1918–1978," by Herbert J. May; and "One Church or Two? Contemporary and Historical Views of Race Relations in One Catholic Diocese," by

Rhonda D. Evans, Craig J. Forsyth, and Stephanie Bernard. Additionally, much information and overall texture of the civil rights and post–civil rights eras can be gleaned from the archives of *Ebony* and *Time* magazines, both of which are online. No understanding of the integration dilemma can be complete without a thorough reading of *The Crisis of the Negro Intellectual*, by Harold Cruse. And, last, the book I kept handy and referenced most of all was *A Testament of Hope: The Essential Writings and Speeches of Martin Luther King, Jr.*, which ought to be required reading for all.

As always, I wouldn't be here without the agent of all agents, Peter McGuigan—who loans me his house at considerable risk to his own safety and welfare—and everyone else at Foundry Literary + Media: Yfat Riess Gendell, Stephanie Abou, Matt Wise, Hannah Gordon, among others. At Viking, I owe an eternal debt to Wendy Wolf and Kevin Doughten, who went to bat for this book when nobody wanted it, and whose Herculean patience allowed it to actually get finished and not be terrible. Additional thanks are due to Liz Parker, Maggie Riggs, Paul Buckley, Andrew Duncan, Andrew Luo, Sonya Cheuse, Carolyn Coleburn, and everyone else who made this possible.

I must give thanks for my old boys' network: Lane Greene, Brett McCallon, Jay Forman, Dan Hoffheins, and Brendan Greeley, who plowed through the early, overlong, often indecipherable drafts of this book and gave invaluable advice. I also owe many phone calls and visits to my family, Mom and Dad, Mason and Jenni, and Gus and Lena, for being too absent for too long.

And, finally, I give thanks and love to my beautiful wife, Danielle, who met me in the final stretches of this sprawling, unending endeavor and married me anyway, making me happier than I ever knew was possible.

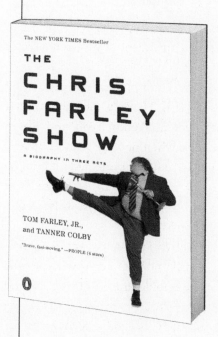